Torture as State Crime

Can we understand torture by focusing on the torture chamber or even on the states in which it is practiced, or do we have to consider the wider political context in which it is embedded? This is the central question of this book which explores concepts of state crime for understanding and responding to the indirect use of torture by external nation states.

Drawing on the cooperation between France and Argentina in Argentina's Dirty War, this book explores the utility of the concept of state crime for understanding and responding to the indirect use of torture by external nation states with a detailed examination of the exportation of torture techniques and training expertise as complicity in torture. Discussing the institutionalisation of torture in its international structural context, this book focuses on examining three alleged manifestations of the torturer: *direct* perpetrator, *institutional* perpetrator, and *transnational institutional* perpetrator.

Important reading for those in the fields of criminology, sociology, international relations and human rights law, this book will also be of key interest to scholars and students in the areas of state crime, human rights and imperialism.

Melanie Collard is a Senior Lecturer at the School of Law, University of Hertfordshire, UK.

Crimes of the Powerful

Crimes of the Powerful encompasses the harmful, injurious, and victimizing behaviors perpetrated by privately or publicly operated businesses, corporations, and organizations as well as the state mediated administrative, legalistic, and political responses to these crimes.

The series draws attention to the commonalities of the theories, practices, and controls of the crimes of the powerful. It focuses on the overlapping spheres and inter-related worlds of a wide array of existing and recently developing areas of social, historical, and behavioral inquiry into the wrongdoings of multinational organizations, nation-states, stateless regimes, illegal networks, financialization, globalization, and securitization.

These examinations of the crimes of the powerful straddle a variety of related disciplines and areas of academic interest, including studies in criminology and criminal justice; law and human rights; conflict, peace, and security; economic change, environmental decay, and global sustainability.

Gregg Barak, *Eastern Michigan University, USA*
Penny Green, *Queen Mary University of London, UK*
Tony Ward, *Northumbria University, UK*

Revisiting Crimes of the Powerful
Marxism, Crime and Deviance
Edited by Steven Bittle, Laureen Snider, Steve Tombs and David Whyte

Torture as State Crime
A Criminological Analysis of the Transnational Institutional Torturer
Melanie Collard

For more information about this series, please visit: www.routledge.com/Crimes-of-the-Powerful/book-series/COTP

Torture as State Crime

A Criminological Analysis of the Transnational Institutional Torturer

Melanie Collard

Routledge
Taylor & Francis Group

LONDON AND NEW YORK

First published 2019 by Routledge

2 Park Square, Milton Park, Abingdon, Oxon OX14 4RN
605 Third Avenue, New York, NY 10017

Routledge is an imprint of the Taylor & Francis Group, an informa business

First issued in paperback 2021

Publisher's Note

The publisher has gone to great lengths to ensure the quality of this reprint but points out that some imperfections in the original copies may be apparent.

British Library Cataloguing-in-Publication Data
A catalogue record for this book is available from the British Library

Library of Congress Cataloging-in-Publication Data
Names: Collard, Melanie, author.
Title: Torture as state crime : a criminological analysis of the transnational institutional torturer / Melanie Collard.
Description: Abingdon, Oxon ; New York, NY : Routledge, 2019.
| Series: Crimes of the powerful | Includes bibliographical references and index.
Identifiers: LCCN 2018014699| ISBN 9781138210059 (hardback) | ISBN 9781315456133 (ebook)
Subjects: LCSH: Torture. | State crimes. | Political crimes and offenses.
Classification: LCC HV8593 .C635 2019 | DDC 364.1/38–dc23
LC record available at https://lccn.loc.gov/2018014699

ISBN: 978-1-138-21005-9 (hbk)
ISBN: 978-0-367-48322-7 (pbk)

Typeset in Bembo
by Wearset Ltd, Boldon, Tyne and Wear

Contents

Acknowledgements

I would like to thank all those who have assisted, supported and inspired me during my research – a journey that has been both memorable and insightful.

I would like to express my gratitude to the Lacey French Travel Bursary and King's College London Centre of European Law Travel Grant for funding my various forays into France and Argentina, ventures that permitted me to undertake fieldwork, collect data and absorb something of French and Argentine cultures. Similar sincere gratitude is also due the Modern Law Review and King's College London Graduate School, for awarding me scholarships that afforded me the opportunity of undertaking doctoral research in a field of study in which I have a great interest.

I especially want to thank my supervisor, Prof. Penny Green, for her guidance during my research and study. Her perpetual enthusiasm for my project motivated this book throughout and I am deeply grateful to her for the invaluable and prompt comments on draft chapters. Thanks also to Prof. Mary Vogel and Prof. Ben Bowling for their useful comments on an earlier draft of the first two chapters of this book. All errors remaining are of course mine alone.

So many fellow critical thinkers have stimulated and supported me throughout my studies. Their names are too numerous to list here, although I must make mention of Dr Anastasia Chamberlen, Dr Henrique Carvalho, Dr Lisa Forsberg, and Dr Isra Black. They nurtured my academic development and they continue to keep me thinking.

I would also like to thank other friends who have brought a great deal of laughter and warmth into my life – especially Morgane, Jade, Frédérique, Daiana and Petra. This work could not have been completed without their encouragement and the much-appreciated diversions they gave me.

Finally, last but not least, I owe an incalculable debt to my incredibly patient family for their unflagging love and support. Special thanks to my amazingly amazing father, alias *Loup*, and my husband, Jody – this journey would have been simply impossible without them. I dedicate this book to my twins, Rose and Jack.

Abbreviations

AAA	*Alianza Anticomunista Argentina*; the 'Triple A'
ADF	*Archives Diplomatiques Francaises*; French Diplomatic Archives
AMA	*Archivos Militares Argentinos*; Argentine Military Archives
BDPA	*Bureau pour le Développement de la Production Agricole*; Office for the Development of the Agricultural Production
CADA	*Commission d'Accès aux Documents Administratif*; Commission for Access to Administrative Documents
CADHU	*Comisión Argentina de Derechos Humanos*; Argentine Human Rights Commission
CAQDAS	Computer-Assisted Qualitative Data Analysis Software
CONADEP	*Comisión Nacional sobre la Desaparición de Personas*; National Commission on the Disappearance of Persons
CONINTES	*Conmocion Interna del Estado*; Internal Upheaval of the State
DPU	*Dispositif de Protection Urbaine*; Urban Protection System
ESG Buenos Aires	*Escuela Superior de Guerra de Buenos Aires*; Buenos Aires Higher School of War
ESG Paris	*École Supérieure de Guerre de Paris*; Paris Higher School of War
ESMA	*Escuela Superior de Mecánica de la Armada*; Naval Higher School of Mechanics
FLN	*Front de Libération Nationale*; National Liberation Front
HIJOS	*Hijos e Hijas por la Identidad y la Justicia contra el Olvido y el Silencio*; Sons and Daughters for Identity and Justice Against Oblivion and Silence
OAS	*Organisation Armée Secrète*; Secret Armed Organisation

Introduction

Friday 13 November 2015. Again, horror in Paris. Bodies are counted, lying on streets. Friends and families make frantic calls, panic spreads. A nation is in trauma. A year that started with the Charlie Hebdo tragedy ends with a new, even more dramatic onslaught. As events continued to unfold, with dozens dead in shootings and explosions, it was already obvious that the fallout from these attacks would be momentous for the French republic, for its political developments and its social cohesion.

The same night President François Hollande announced a state of emergency. These words – 'state of emergency' – relate to, in French historical memory, the Algerian war (1954–1962) and France's general use of the practices of torture, summary execution and large-scale deportation. The 'ticking bomb' scenario argument opened Pandora's Box. It turned into a morally comfortable means of justifying various forms of excess. What was initially identified by the average French soldier freshly arrived in Algeria as an isolated act of cruelty – perhaps as something just about morally conceivable for the greater purpose of protecting his relatives from certain death – turned rapidly into the banal routine of everyday horror. Initial justifications of the exception ended up justifying the everyday.

Torture was not an epiphenomenon of the Algerian War: it was central to the army's defence of a colonial empire in its waning years (Branche 2001; Fanon 1963; Lazreg 2008; MacMaster 2004; Maran 1989; Paret 1964; Vidal-Naquet 1963, 2001). Its systematic use was the direct outcome of the French theory and doctrine of Revolutionary War – *Doctrine de Guerre Révolutionnaire* – that developed in the 1950s.[1] As Lazreg explains:

> Even though the theory did not initially advocate torture, it informed an anti-subversive war doctrine that could not be implemented successfully without its use. Without the theory, torture could not have been systematized. Similarly, without torture, the anti-subversive war doctrine could not have been implemented.
>
> (2008: 15)

Having set the theoretical and operational context, torture easily became institutionalised, in the sense that its use by the French military was not simply an instance of violence committed by a few isolated rogue individuals acting according to their personal whims (Fanon 1965).[2] The part played by torture throughout the Algerian War '[…] started as a police method of interrogation, developed into a military method of operation, and then ultimately turned into a clandestine state institution which struck at the very roots of the life of the nation' (Vidal-Naquet 1963: 15).

The French doctrine of Revolutionary War was intended to deal with both colonial and civil wars (Paret 1964: 9). It constructed 'a transnational conception of war that wove together a number of factors aimed at rallying a diverse audience comprised of recruits, politicians, and the public at large' (Lazreg 2008: 32). Furthermore, the ensuing doctrine did not distinguish 'insurgents' from 'population', and consequently merged civilians into a generic, dehumanized, 'satanic' enemy (Garrigou-Lagrange 1959: 515). The fact that France had lost its colonial wars in Indochina and Algeria apparently did not matter: the anti-subversive war doctrine 'provides a key for reading reality that makes intelligible a complex and changing reality and enables the armed forces, an institution that sinks its roots in medieval values, to cope with social complexity and change' (Perelli 1990: 101). It became very attractive to other governments and went far beyond the borders of Algeria. It is the transnational dimension of the doctrine that made possible the transfer of the French *savoir-faire* in torture practices from Algeria to Argentina.

Two events occurred in the summer of 2001 that triggered my investigation into the integral role played by France in educating Argentina's armed forces about the use of torture as part of waging its Dirty War and as part of its state strategy of insurgent warfare. The first was the case of Louisette Ighilahriz – a former Algerian revolutionary – who broke silence about the torture and rape she had endured in Algeria. She directly implicated French military figures General Massu and Colonel Bigeard (Ighilahriz 2001). Second, retired French General Paul Aussaresses provided an open and extraordinarily cynical acknowledgement of his personal involvement in the torture of many Algerians and described the methods he used. He wrote his memoirs on the use of torture in a detached manner, expressing no regrets and making no apology (Aussaresses 2001).

These revelations sparked interest in a chapter of French history in Algeria that government and public opinion 'had wished to bury in silence' (Lazreg 2008: 1). They provided important new evidence of the widespread use of torture and the assassination of political opponents during France's occupation of Algeria (1954–1962). At the same time, they raised important new questions relating to whether – and how – French military officers trained the Argentine military in both the psychological and physical torture of prisoners in Argentina. The origin of these new revelations was an investigation by the French weekly magazine *Le Point* into the role of the French military's

'Special Forces' during the Algerian War of Independence in the 1950s.[3] At the same time, French judge Roger LeLoire, who was investigating the disappearance of French citizens in Argentina during the last military regime between 1976 and 1983, interrogated General Paul Aussaresses about his knowledge of training in torture techniques given by his soldiers to the Argentine military. The former General's testimony helped to draw a complex picture of the French military's responsibility in transforming their Argentine colleagues into torturers in the state's employ, by introducing them to a new warfare ideology that refined their approach to the 'enemy'.

The justification by some French officials for this 'assistance' was that it had been requested by the Argentine military and government on a number of different occasions. As Pierre Messmer – French Prime Minister at the time – stated, 'Argentina wanted the advisers so we gave them what they wanted. Argentina is an independent country and there was no reason for us to deny their request' (Abramovici 2001; Chelala 2001). In doing so, he also revealed the existence of a permanent French military mission in Buenos Aires. In a later interview, he would explain this point even further:

> It was General de Gaulle himself who decided there would be a mission, on the proposal of the Minister of Foreign Affairs. [...] The United States had not yet, at that time, turned their hands to instruction and the supply of material to South American armies. But I think that in 1960 Argentina was particularly interested in France's experience in the field of Revolutionary War [...].
>
> (Pierre Messmer, as interviewed by Robin 2004: 175)

This indicated that the collaboration between France and Argentina was not the isolated decision of a few officials, but rather an actual agreement between the two states. Consequently, several intellectuals started their own investigation, in order to unearth new evidence concerning this deadly cooperation. For instance, French journalist Marie-Monique Robin made an independent film documentary (2003) – and subsequently wrote a book (2004) – entitled *Escadrons de la Mort, l'Ecole Française* ('The Death Squads, The French School'), which investigated ties between the French secret services and their Argentine and Chilean counterparts.

As a result of this exposure, society legitimately imagined that the French government was going to cast light on this untoward issue. And this is what seemed to happen at first: In 2003, three members of the Green Party, Noël Mamère, Martine Billard and Yves Cochet – followed by the Socialists – tabled a request for a French parliamentary commission of inquiry into the role played by France in support of Latin American military regimes between 1973 and 1984.[4] However, three months later, the parliamentary rapporteur – Deputy Laurent Bloom – rejected the request, arguing that no military cooperation agreement existed between France and either Chile, Brazil or

Argentina at that time.[5] And yet, a physical agreement between the French and the Argentinean governments did indeed exist in the form of a document located in the French diplomatic archives of La Courneuve, in Paris (see Appendix 1).[6]

My research provides new and systematic evidence relating to this deadly cooperation. It seeks to analyse this data within a transnational state crime framework. While Green and Ward (2004) provide the most coherent framework for understanding state crime, the transnational nature of state terror and torture is one of the few dimensions of their work that could be developed further. As Grewcock explains, 'State crime is often the by-product of complex political and socio-economic relationships and might be supported directly by other states' (2008: 155). If some states are to be routinely condemned and blamed for their use of torture on prisoners, the same condemnation should be extended to other states that not only use torture themselves but also export their techniques. The French-Argentine cooperation provides a case study of the institutionalisation and transnationalisation of torture. In the current literature on the subject, American influence is well documented, but only rarely is French participation mentioned (Aguila 2010; Chomsky 1991; Fagen 1992; Gareau 2004; Hey 1995; McClintock 1992; Schirmer 1998). Most commentators tend to agree on the existence of a French military presence in Argentine territory prior to 1976 but only in unspecified terms and always (comparatively) 'to a lesser extent'. Research conducted for this investigation suggests that it would be more appropriate for us to refer to the French influence as being 'to a greater extent'.

This book explains how the French ideological persuasion and technical training has contributed to the making of official torturer. Today more than ever, it becomes evident that the human rights tradition should not only condemn the most obvious torturing rogue states, but also the structures enabling torture – thereby promoting a deeper human right 'to live in a social and world structure that does not produce torture' (Galtung 1994: 134) … even when a 'state of emergency' is declared.

The case study of the cooperation between France and Argentina should highlight the role that criminologists could play in producing a better politics of crime (Loader and Sparks 2010; Bosworth and Hoyle 2011). If criminology has always, and often uncomfortably, found itself in close proximity to the state and its political needs, no discussion of its role is helpful that does not account for the historically specific conditions in which crime and crime policy operate today. From this perspective, the debate is not about whether criminologists should try to engage a broader non-academic audience, but whether and how criminological knowledge can make more 'effective' and 'intelligible' contributions in the public sphere in which it operates. By unearthing data that expose complicity in mass violence and murder and naming names of military attachés and politicians, I am hoping to be part of the globalised creation and transfer of knowledge that acts as some form of counterweight – alongside human right activists, forensic archaeologists, international criminal lawyers and others – to state crime.

Torture throughout history

Although some of its features have changed over time, torture is far from a new phenomenon. Torture was for centuries a legal, normal, and common-place institution throughout the world (Mellor 1961). In Ancient Greece, it was seen by the judiciary as the quickest way to gain proof of offences and was developed with clear rules and safeguards for its application (Lea 1878). Many writers on law have pointed out that it stemmed from the old provisions of Roman law against *crimen majestatis*, or crimes against that state, to which were later added crimes against the Church, and that its practice was reintroduced into the West at the end of the eleventh century (Vidal-Naquet 1963: 18). From the twelfth century, the safeguards held within these ancient societies came to be disregarded, and torture was often recklessly applied and associated with overt spectacles of state power (Evans and Morgan 1998; Peters 1985; Stanley 2008). The public was encouraged to witness the punishment of the criminal's body (Foucault 1977; Rejali 1994). In this way, 'the victim was an integral part of the ritual performance of [state] power through their confession, bodily destruction and public agony' (Humphrey 2002: 30). But these forms of public displays gradually faced opposition and became regarded as 'the pinnacle of unjust violent state power' (Stanley 2008: 159). They also prompted imitative violence (Archer and Gartner 1984). From the eighteenth century, torture – hitherto considered a legitimate means of investigation and punishment – came to be perceived as an unacceptable attack on the individual. This was due to the influence of the European Enlightenment and the subsequent shift to humanitarian practices (Evans and Morgan 1998; Sottas 1998). The best-known exposition of this new way of thinking is the Italian Beccaria's (1963) *On Crimes and Punishments*.[7] The arguments used by the abolitionists of that time were identical with those which have reappeared today, but in those days they were new arguments and played an essential part in the growth of modern liberalism: Torture, it was said, was inhuman, inefficient, frequently used against innocent people and the confessions extracted by it have no validity (Vidal-Naquet 1963: 19). On this point, it is important to note that rationalist critiques of the ineffectiveness of torture as a truth-finding device long predated the abolition of torture, but only became effective because of a change in sensibilities (Spierenburg 1984: 188–189). Beccaria summed up the problem with sarcasm: 'The strength of the muscles and the sensitivity of the nerves of an innocent person being known factors, the problem is to find the level of suffering necessary to make him confess to any given crime' (1963: 25).

The 'birth of the prison' represented a significant change in the administration of brutality since 'punishment no longer addressed itself to the body of the criminal, but to the soul' (Foucault 1977: 16). Yet this body–soul shift was quite hypocritical, as sentences continued to be harsh for those brought before the courts and states continued to vigorously engage in torture abroad (Evans and Morgan 1998).[8] Indeed, in colonial settlements torture presented a means by which economic and ideological control could be established, as it was used to 'encourage' productive bodies for labour (Fanon 1963; Taussig 2002).

Yet, following discovery of the horrors that took place during the Third Reich, torture was designated as a crime in a range of widely framed and largely unenforceable international documents.[9] More specifically, the abolitionist view seemed finally to have gained a world-wide victory in 1948, when the General Assembly of the United Nations adopted a 'universal declaration on the rights of man'. Article 5 of this declaration lays down that 'no man will be subjected to torture or to cruel, inhuman, or degrading punishment or treatment'. Moreover, the preamble to this declaration recalls that 'disregard or contempt for the rights of man has resulted in acts of barbarism which revolt the conscience of humanity'. Clearly, nearly two centuries after Beccaria (1963) had written *On Crimes and Punishments*, the problem of torture was still present (Vidal-Naquet 1963: 20).

As states came to the conclusion that torture was forbidden on pragmatic as well as moral grounds, one might have presumed that torture would have little contemporary use or value. However, as Peters argues,

> Torture was a first-order word and a first-order fact to the framers of human rights legislation after the Second World War. Its semantic history since then indicates that it became a second-order word and fact in many parts of the world
>
> (1985: 155)

– especially the late colonial world.[10] This exercise of colonial power is important in explaining the role of modern democratic states in the practice of torture. As Green and Ward put it, 'After all, states which elevated the civil rights of the individual citizen such as France and England have both been responsible for torture in the name of the "métropole", specifically in colonial formations' (2004: 128). This point is agreed with by Peters, who also acknowledges the contribution of colonialism in his theory:

> The colonial experience indeed seems to have contributed to the reappearance of torture, but not because colonial administrators and police learned such practices from the populations they governed; rather, the very circumstances in which they governed populations, which became increasingly restive during the 20th century, led to the abuse of authority that included torture and later became routine in places like Algeria.
>
> (Peters 1985: 138)

In France, the general feeling immediately before the outbreak of the war in Algeria was that torture was a characteristically foreign institution – there had been no case of torture since the 1789 French Revolution and there would be none after 1945 (Vidal-Naquet 1963: 21). Both suppositions were wrong. This does not, of course, mean that torture had become a common feature of life in France. But both in France, and still more in the French colonies, the practice of torture continued, the existence of such practices being taken seriously by very few Frenchmen (Vidal-Naquet 1963: 21).

What happened in Algeria completed a lesson that finally had to be learned by the late twentieth-century world: 'Torture had not died with the Enlightenment legislative and judicial reforms, and their optimistic view of human nature. Nor was it exclusively the eccentric practice of deranged and psychotic governments' (Peters 1985: 140). The endurance – and not the *resurgence* – of torture in the twentieth century is directly related to the nature of the modern State (Kelman 2005; Stanley 2008). Paradoxically, 'in an age of vast state strength, ability to mobilise resources, and possession of virtually infinite means of coercion' (Peters 1985: 7), the idea that the state remains insecure has persisted. This refers to Elias's (2000) 'paradox of state violence', which has been explained by Green and Ward as follows: 'If states depend on a monopoly of organized violence [...] but cultivate an abhorrence of violence, why does this not lead to abhorrence, or at least deep unease, at the state's own practices?' (2009b: 163). This is the issue that the next section attempts to address.

Torture and criminology

Despite the fact that torture is a crime under international frameworks and in most domestic jurisdictions, it has remained on the periphery of criminology when, arguably, it should – because of its violence, criminality and popularity – be an essential part of it (Grewcock 2008; Stanley 2008). 'Criminology's traditional and persistent bias' (Fattah 1997: 67) is related to the more general problematic that it has never regarded state crime 'as an integral part of its subject-matter' (Green and Ward 2004: 1). Indeed, in two separate studies, both Michalowski and Kramer (2006) and Tombs and Whyte (2003a) found that research articles focusing on state crimes 'typically constituted less than 3 per cent of all articles in the major U.S. and British journals of criminology and criminal justice' (Kramer 2009: x–xi). This is probably due to the fact that it might seem challenging to explain how the state could be a criminal actor, when legally it is the state itself that defines criminal behaviour by making and enforcing the law (Grewcock 2008: 146; Rothe 2009: 5; Shute 2012: 46). Furthermore, Kramer (2009: x) argues that the 'normalisation of deviance' that developed during the Second World War within state organisations and national political cultures (Vaughan 1996, 2007; Kramer 2009), and the fact that orthodox criminology generally tends to operate in the service of power (Michalowski and Kramer 2006; Michalowski 2009), might constitute two more reasons for this lack of consideration.

Yet, thanks to a few notable commentators who argue that the focus of criminology should also be firmly on state criminality – such as Barak (1991); Cohen (2001, 2003); Green and Ward (2004); Kauzlarich and Kramer (1998); Pickering (2005); Ross (1995); Rothe and Friedrichs (2006); Schwendinger and Schwendinger (1975); and Tombs and Whyte (2003) – criminology has built a body of theory and data focused on understanding state crimes. According to these scholars, if criminology is to develop as a discipline that studies and analyses criminal, violent, abusive and deviant behaviours, then it is necessary to include state criminality in its field, on the grounds that the consequences of state crimes are more widespread and destructive than those of conventional crimes. This acceptance has been exemplified by the fact that both the *British Journal of Criminology* (45: 4, 2005) and the *Journal of Critical Criminology* (17: 1, 2009) have recently published special issues dedicated to state crime (Cameron 2009: 6). Furthermore, there is now a dedicated international and interdisciplinary journal on the subject, *State Crime*.

If the establishment of state criminality in the criminological field seems now to be undisputed, there is still continued disagreement over definitional issues. As Barak points out, 'the study of state criminality is problematic because the concept itself is controversial' (1991: 8). Long-standing debate within criminology about the scope and subject matter of state crime is reflected in the 'polarity of definitions of the concept, which locate breaches of the law by states at one end of the spectrum, and definitions based on non-statutory breaches of human rights at the other' (Cameron 2009: 6). While 1970s radical criminologists presented a definition of state crime wherein any institution in society that tolerates and/or promotes violations of human rights is criminal – irrespective of whether it is an individual, a corporation, or the state that does the depriving (Schwendinger and Schwendinger 1975: 133–134) – legalistic criminologists have limited conceptions of 'state organised crime' to 'acts defined by law as criminal, and committed by state officials in the pursuit of their job as representative of the state' (Chambliss 1989: 184). The first perception is problematic because it seeks to include too broad a spectrum of rights within the realm of criminology by ignoring significant distinctions between social harms and more serious human rights abuses (Cohen 2001: 542; Green and Ward 2000b: 104). This 'moral crusade' (Cohen 1993: 98) by a state 'doing nasty things' (Sharkansky 1995) provides no basis for coherent criminological perspectives (Grewcock 2008: 149). As for the second legalistic perception, although international law undoubtedly constitutes a substantial footing for defining state criminality, a definition of state crime that is based on a highly legalistic use of law lacks legitimacy (Green and Ward 2000b). Indeed, 'if states define what is criminal, a state can only be criminal on those rare occasions when it denounces itself for breaking its own laws'

(Green and Ward 2004: 1). The problem of self-incrimination would render such a definition meaningless.

This book, however, does not aim to resolve such debates but argues for the further development of a paradigm of state crime based on the concepts of human rights and deviance (Grewcock 2008: 146). Therefore, Green and Ward's (2004) conception of state crime – that draws upon the work of labelling theorists such as Becker (1963) – will be used here. According to them, state crime is 'state organisational deviance involving the violation of human rights' (Green and Ward 2004: 2). As they explain,

> Relying solely on a human rights discourse leaves us with the borderless condition of 'social harm' – politically valid, but criminologically less satisfactory. However, when a human rights analysis is used within a framework of deviance and legitimacy and the audience for whom state norms are breached is extended beyond that of the powerful to those from 'below', then we have a conceptually coherent definition of state organized crime.
>
> (Green and Ward 2000b: 111)[11]

In this manner, human rights will provide the conceptual basis for identifying and challenging state crime, especially when their violations are committed by states that proclaim to uphold them (Grewcock 2008: 152–153). By utilising a framework of state crime – which consists in examining torture as a behaviour which is perceived as deviant by the international community and by certain domestic audiences – this book aims to produce a more complex and layered understanding of a specific universal human right violation: torture. Indeed, examining torture with criminological eyes offers the opportunity to make connections between the structural, institutional, social and personal frames through which such a form of violence is undertaken and experienced. Before progressing to these debates in Chapter II, however, this chapter proceeds with a brief examination of the history of torture.

Methodology and the investigation of a sombre collaboration

Since the aim of my book is to bring forward new and consistent evidence concerning France's involvement in the transformation of Argentine military officers into torturers, shortly after the tragedy of its own Algerian War in the 1950s, it was apparent that its methodological framework would have to be both flexible and sensitive to the social context in which the relevant data was produced. Indeed, the methods of data analysis and generation had to enable me to understand how the regime of torture came about in Argentina, and the extent to which France played a role in its institutionalisation.

There were two analytical and methodological lenses through which France's implication in the Argentine regime of torture had to be analysed.

From a criminological perspective, the issues at stake were *why* and *how* states and individual officials come to export, order, condone or engage in torture (Blaikie 2000, 2004). Following Green and Ward (2004), my study of this 'transnational institutionalisation of torture' draws on the concept of state crime using psychological approaches (Haney *et al.* 1973; Huggins and Haritos-Fatouros 1998; Milgram 1974; Sottas 1998; Zimbardo 2007), through socio-cultural/humanist analyses (Arendt 1965; Staub 1989), to political economy and structural explanations (Chomsky and Herman 1979; Peters 1985; Rejali 1994; Tomasevski 1998).

It also employs Foucauldian historiography (Foucault 1969, 1977, 1983, 2002).[12] Kendall and Wickham have explained that, to some extent, the Foucauldian historiography requires the researcher to write a detective story:

> We start with a known outcome, but what we need to do is find the precursors that lead to this outcome. The work is about putting together the various pieces of the puzzle so we can see sufficient conditions for the emergence of the problem or issue under investigation.
>
> (2007: 133)

Thus, through genealogical and archaeological study, I attempted to simultaneously unravel the received explanations for an existing phenomenon – the institutionalisation of torture in Argentina – and build up new grids of analysis 'which could enable [its] intelligibility to be appreciated differently' (Barron 2002: 959). This revealed the involvement of another actor in the genesis of that phenomenon.

This project dealt with the specific state crime of torture and was, therefore, an investigation of a politically 'sensitive topic' (Lee 1993; 1995). The issue of concern in this book – that is, the transformation of Argentine military officers into torturers by the French – covered a particular facet of the social world and how it was interpreted, understood, and experienced (Mason 2002). For example, those who research the crimes of the powerful have to understand accurately the networks of power that operate in a given society (Hillyard 2003). Politically sensitive topics often involve incidents that are less common in other areas of research, and which can consequently pose difficult methodological problems (Lee 2004b). On the one hand, they can render laborious the collection, holding, and/or dissemination of research data. On the other hand, they can sometimes raise difficult issues related to the ethics,[13] politics, and legal aspects of research. Indeed, if it is true that each academic investigation has its own obstacles, it must also be acknowledged that 'some settings or aspects of social life are easier to research than others' (Lofland and Lofland 1984: 17).

Researching the field of criminology is perhaps even more problematic than many other academic areas, because it touches the state at a raw nerve: 'almost automatically, if we are studying crime, we are messing around with some of the most powerful constructs the State has at its disposal' (Carson, cited in Presdee and Walters 1998: 158).[14] As Tombs and Whyte noted, this claim is even more pertinent with respect to '*critical* criminology, especially work that focuses critically upon the illegalities of states and corporations, the most powerful institutions within capitalist social orders' (Tombs and Whyte 2002: 218). In comparison with perpetrators in the context of state crime, conventional crime researchers are dealing with the relatively powerless, which renders such work immediately more feasible than seeking to focus upon the relatively powerful (Hughes 1996: 77). One reason for this is that the 'inner sanctums' of the corridors of governments 'are likely to be even more tightly sealed from outside scrutiny when the aim is to investigate actual or possible illegality' (Tombs and Whyte 2002: 219). As one of my interviewees rightly pointed out, concerning the topic of my research:

> I personally know it is not easy to address the issue of the French training of the Argentine military [...]. In 1987, that is, four years after the end of the Argentinian dictatorship, I interviewed François Mitterrand at the Elysée Palace, just before he flew off to Buenos Aires where he had been invited by President Raúl Alfonsín. I put the following question to him: A quarter of a century ago, France emerged from a colonial war and started the conversion of military officers who had taken part in human rights violations, to reintegrate them into a republican model. Some of these officers also became instructors to the Argentinian military. Are there any elements of this process of rehabilitation that could be used in the Argentina of today? He answered that there was no need to exaggerate, as France had not suffered a military regime! That there had been a rebellion in a small part of the territory that at that time formed part of the French Republic. He insisted that it was not possible to make a strict comparison.... He purely and simply made me leave when I brought up the presence of the French military advisers in Argentina.
>
> (Horacio Verbitsky, Interview #3 – see Appendix 3)

However, researchers should not assume that 'empirically investigating' crimes committed by powerful perpetrators is intrinsically impossible or dangerous (Green and Ward 2012: 734). During my research, access to former members of the Argentine military and to archives evidencing their criminogenic processes was not systematically denied and ended up being – with tenacity and persistence – less difficult to secure than I had first imagined. As Tombs and Whyte explain, 'the internal contradictions and conflicts that exist within and between various state agencies and departments, and between individual state representatives, creates opportunities for engaging in critical research' (Tombs and Whyte 2002: 224). Furthermore, the 'risks' involved can sometimes be exaggerated, and fieldwork 'dangers' can be negotiated (Lee 2004a: 234). For my part, I never felt in danger while gathering my data and was *gently* threatened or made to feel uncomfortable only twice in the course of my fieldwork in Buenos Aires: both examples involved pressure from former members of the Argentine military. Once, I was having an informal conversation with a former military officer who suddenly brought the discussion to an end (General Matias, Interview #6 – see Appendix 3). He told me, 'I think you should leave now', to which I replied that I had no further questions anyway. He then added, 'No, I mean I think it is time for you to leave Argentina.' I faked a smile, thanked him for his time and left. Another time, I 'coincidentally' spent a 14-hour-flight from Buenos Aires to London sitting next to a former Argentinian Lieutenant-Colonel (Lieutenant-Colonel Juan, Interview #8 – see Appendix 3). It took me a couple of hours to realise that he had often been present in the room where I was working when looking for archival documents in the military school of Buenos Aires. By the end of this long flight, I had been given a significant lecture as to the role of the military in protecting Argentine citizens back in the late 1970s, and how I should keep that in mind at all times while proceeding with my research. Both perseverance and imagination were required to cope success-fully with the problems and issues raised by the politically sensitive topic I chose to research.

There may be inevitable ethical costs in the conduct of potentially bene-ficial state crime research. I am referring here to issues of value judgement and the use of deception (Bryman 2001, Hammersley 2000, Miller 2004, Wilson 1993). My research was concerned with the export of torture exper-tise that helped generate massive abuses. I could not claim to be objective or detached from the subject matter of my research, as my activist and academic endeavours are inextricably linked with the importance of respecting human rights.

Also, my fieldwork was carried out in Argentina at the moment when the atrocities of the Dirty War were coming to light. Indeed, from 1985 onwards, members of the military began to be brought to trial and sentenced to impris-onment. However, the need for accountability was frustrated when the government of Raúl Alfonsín – under threat of a new military *coup d'état* – enacted the 1986 *Ley de Punto Final*[15] and the 1987 *Ley de Obediencia Debida*,[16] both of which afforded immunity to members of the former regime. Further-more, two years later, President Carlos Menem, who felt that the support of the military would benefit his party as well as the country, granted a pardon to already convicted or still indicted members of the junta. But Argentine civil society refused to turn its back on the search for truth and justice. The *Madres y Abuelas de la Plaza de Mayo* continued, and still continue, to seek clarification of the fate and whereabouts of the disappeared, whereas other organisations like *H.I.J.O.S.* have denounced former military officers by exposing them as torturers and killers to neighbours and community, using slogans such as 'If there is no Justice, there is Outing' – *Si no hay Justicia, hay Escraches*.

In these circumstances, it would have been inappropriate, offensive and generally counter-productive to claim that I was neutral. In any case, had I tried to proclaim my neutrality, I would in fact have concealed my own sympathies and, by doing so, deceived at least some of the people involved in the research settings (Lee 1995: 23). While it can thus be said that I adopted a partisan approach, the testimonies of the torture victims and their perceptions of the human rights abuses that took place in Argentina between 1976 and 1983 were situated within their historical, political and economic contexts. Furthermore, those testimonies and perceptions were always contrasted with the views of the French and Argentine generals on the way ideological training justifies the use of torture, and this remained the focus of the study. Overall, I would assess my influence on the nature and type of response given as minimal: The evident desire of generals to tell their story demonstrated the force of those experiences and the opinions they held.

Although clearly identifying with the victims of the Dirty War, the most profitable approach in all interactions was to present myself as being 'on their side' (Cameron 2009: 35). Indeed, it seemed more appropriate to pretend to be 'fascinated' by the techniques of counter-insurgency used against 'subversives' at the time to ensure the 'security' of Argentinians, when interviewing (former) military officers. If it is established that some interviewees have very strong views, 'it may be essential to show a basic sympathy with them to get started at all' (Green 1993: 107). Expressing repugnance for interviewees' opinions or actions would hardly have helped to secure their cooperation in data gathering. Lee argues that deception of this kind is 'permissible, indeed laudable, in highly stratified, repressive, or unequal contexts' (Lee 1995: 23).

Furthermore, my research – by necessity of securing evidence – involved some degree of concealment, which was also based on deception (Lee 1995). In the French diplomatic archives, for example, my 'reader card' was coloured yellow, indicating that I had to sit in front of the curator of the reading room and that I was not allowed to take photographs of the different memoranda. Depending on the curator, security was more or less tight and, accordingly, I decided to sit far from their view and take photos of the documents with the camera on my cell phone hidden in the inside pocket of my jacket. Adopting such an attitude is sometimes necessary for securing both access and information. As Green explains, 'it does not implicate the researcher in the activities of the regime nor does it represent complicity or sympathy with those being interviewed. It is merely a strategy to secure information' (Green 2003: 170).

The use of deception was thus deemed occasionally necessary. In so doing, I was adopting Scheper-Hughes's notion of 'ethical orientation', in which the personal accountability of the researcher is answerable to the 'other' (Scheper-Hughes 1992: 24). As Green and Ward explained,

> this ethical orientation speaks to a commitment to justice and moral alignment with the victims of state violence and corruption, in the

pursuit of truth and change. When overt routes to knowledge are denied and secrecy characterises the practices to be studied, clandestine methods may offer the only route to enlightenment.

(Green and Ward 2012: 735)

Becker (1967) suggested that it is not possible to objectively investigate society from within one particular value-framework. Objectivity, however, needs to be rescued from value-neutrality (Hobsbawm 1998, Pearce 2003), which is 'a dangerous illusion' (Tombs and Whyte 2002: 230). Researching state crime in an *ethical manner* is possible, and it seems to require the adoption of a partisan objectivity that allows the researcher to justify and qualify his or her work with regard to the possibility of bias and distortion (Green 1993; Tombs and Whyte 2002). As Green explains, 'no research is free from bias. The important question in controlling for it is the researcher's recognition of her own position and opinions, and how they might influence the research situation' (Green 1993: 111). Thus, I could still pretend to the 'value objectivity' of my critical research but only after recognising that much of it was highly partisan in the first place, in the sense that it was linked to 'counter-hegemonic struggles' (Tombs and Whyte 2002: 229) that were committed to denouncing and labelling France as a 'transnational institutional torturer' that played a significant role in the architecture of Argentine state terror.

In order to establish the role played by the French government in the Argentine Dirty War, my analysis was based on two sets of empirical data collected in France and Argentina between 2011 and 2013. The primary set consists of an extensive examination of official and unofficial documentation concerning diplomatic relations between the two countries. The second consists of both semi-structured interviews and less formal conversations with human rights activists (such as the mothers and children of the 'disappeared'), former military members, journalists, politicians, and victims of state terror.

The rationale of this mixed-method research is underpinned by the principle of triangulation, which implies that 'researchers should seek to ensure that they are not over-reliant on a single research method and should instead employ more than one measurement procedure when investigating a research problem' (Bryman 2004: 677). Thus, the argument for using both sources is that it enhanced confidence in my findings. Indeed, the data had to be trustworthy: '[a]uditability, credibility and fittingness' had to be meticulously validated in oscillating between documents and interview transcripts (Guba and Lincoln 1981, cited in Rudestam and Newton 2001: 98). I believed that triangulating the data would prevent my findings from being – as much as possible – susceptible to unacknowledged, alternative interpretations (Cameron 2009: 40; Jupp 1996: 298–299).

Most of the archival documentation I found, and many of the interviews I conducted were either in French – my mother tongue – or in Spanish, which

I had to learn for the purposes of this project. Having talked to colleagues who researched the same kind of topics and who later regretted having employed interpreters, I thought it would – at least in the end – be more beneficial and rewarding to spend some time learning 'Argentine-Spanish', as my Argentinian friends often call it. Moreover, I feared that appealing to third parties to cope with language differences would have had a significant impact on my book: an interpreter could have affected the interviewees, the communicative process as a whole, or the translation itself. Having said that, learning a new language for the purpose of research should not be underestimated, as it is an exhausting process that can often cause additional anxiety.

As a foreign researcher, I was also acutely aware of the possibility of 'cultural oversights and obfuscations that might influence the course of the research, of nuances misunderstood or overlooked that might be significant to the outcome of the inquiry' (Green 2003: 173). In order to control this, I decided to live in student accommodation in the heart of Buenos Aires, where I was surrounded by local people. This cultural immersion also enabled me to present 'a multidimensional perspective' on the issue (Mason 2002: 103). It was surprising how little the new generation knew (or was willing to learn) about the Dirty War, despite the continuous efforts of Argentine civil society to preserve memories. The monument to the victims of state terrorism and the sculptures installed in the *Parque de la Memoria* in Buenos Aires, such as Claudia Fontes' *Reconstrucción del Retrato de Pablo Míguez*, Nicolás Guagnini's *30,000*, Marie Orensanz's *Pensar es un Hecho Revolucionario*, the *Nosotros No Sabíamos* collages by León Ferrari, the *Buena Memoria* by Marcelo Brodsky, Gustavo Germano's set of photographs *Ausencias* and the *Manos Anónimas* series by Carlos Alons are just a few examples of the way in which artistic work engages in the construction of collective memory (Foucault 1969).

Because the previous qualitative inquiries related to my topic – and referred to in the literature review of this book – often involved intensive data collection using methods such as semi-structured interviews, ethnographies and analyses of official documents, they created data sets that contain a wealth of information beyond that which was included in these primary research reports (Thorne 2004: 1006). Qualitative secondary analysis was therefore seen as an efficient and effective way to pose questions that extended beyond the source of grounded knowledge, as it allowed the exploration of themes where the entire theoretical potential can emerge only when a researcher from another field re-examines the original findings (Thorne 2004: 1006).[17] Referring on a few occasions to previously published NGOs and journalistic or academic materials from other authors – who had the opportunity to interview people who were either deceased or otherwise inaccessible at the time this research took place – was a priceless source of evidence for my own criminological investigation. For example, Amnesty International occasionally interviews individuals who have been involved in torture and publishes these interviews as appendices to specific reports (see Amnesty International 2001a). Reputable journalists have also spoken to perpetrators or victims and published their interviews in various media (see Robin 2003, 2004; Verbitsky 1995). Investigative journalists have often played a more important role than academics in exposing corporate and state illegality and immorality (Hillyard 2003; Tweedale 2000), even though their methods and sources are sometimes ill-defined and problematic, and control over representation and content is never guaranteed (Tombs and Whyte 2002: 228). Doctoral students who have interviewed protagonists relevant to the inquiry at hand have also published their testimonies in their theses (see Périès 1999). My secondary analysis inherently involved distinct approaches to conceptualising sampling, data collection procedures and interaction between data collection and analysis (Heaton 1998; Hinds *et al.* 1997; Thorne 1994).

Thus, while going into the field and generating primary data were the main methods used for information gathering, I employed a flexible approach throughout the book – that is, one that attaches more importance to primary sources but still recognises the value of secondary sources.

Overview of chapters

The present introduction provides an overview of the literature pertaining to the issue of torture. It presents the methodology by which the empirical study was approached. It also offers a chapter outline.

Chapter 1 is an exposition of the themes and definitions of the key concepts of the research. It provides an introduction to the problem being explored, situates it globally, and discusses the relationship between torture and state terror.

Chapter 2 examines the existing analytical literature on torture and the factors and conditions by which it is generated. It explores the individual torturer, before proceeding to a socio-historical discussion of the factors that lead a state to use torture. It also examines the evidence for a third category of perpetrator involved in the institutionalisation of torture: the state that exports torture techniques and training expertise.

Chapter 3 begins by briefly restating the extent to which the Argentinians were taught by the French military a methodology of warfare that justifies the systematic use of torture. The skills of the latter were based on the experience they had acquired in the wars in Indochina and Algeria. The chapter then engages in an 'archaeological' reconstruction of the formation of the torture regime in Argentina, detailing the military relationship that France nurtured in Argentina and exploring especially the role of French military advisers, and transnational dynamics of politics and economy. Primary data from my own fieldwork in France and Argentina, and secondary data drawn from various sources, were used to develop the analysis.

Chapter 4 challenges the idea that the intensification of French influence and the beginnings of state terrorism in Argentina should be taken as a mere spatio-temporal coincidence. Rather, it argues for a causal relationship, by drawing on the previous chapter in an attempt to develop an original argument about the nature of the 'transnational institutional torturer'. More specifically, this chapter aspires to demonstrate that the French contribution was crucial to the development of the legitimising narrative used by the dictatorship to justify, both within the Armed Forces and to society, the repressive actions deployed. It also raises the question of international legitimacy and the coexistence of two processes: the duality of denial and exposure.

The final chapter provides a comprehensive and integrated overview of the research objective fulfilled, the expectations that were met and those that were changed. It discusses strengths within the research, including the importance and implication of this book in the field of state crime, the aspects of the research which may be considered original and novel, and opportunities for future research.

Notes

1 The conceptual groundwork for the theory was laid out by Colonel Lionel-Max Chassin and Colonel Charles Lacheroy, after both had completed a tour of duty in Indochina and written about the manner in which Mao Tse Tung led the revolution in China and assumed power (Ambler 1966: 308; Lacheroy 2003: 19, 68–69).
2 In *Algeria Unveiled* (1965), Fanon takes the veil as a starting point for an exploration of the new Algeria that was being created through the revolution. According to him, the veil stood as confirmation of Algeria's backwards patriarchy, of its primitive insularity and of the passivity of Algerian women. However, Fanon also inverts the veil and shows how by fighting the French, women also asserted their place in Algerian society. Behind the veil, their thoughts were unknowable: they could be observing the colonial administration with contempt, calmly plotting its downfall or carrying grenades rather than pliantly accepting its reign. The veil also stirred less pragmatic concerns: it spoke to a highly sexualized realm of 'exotic themes deeply rooted in the unconscious' (Fanon 1965: 173). The Algerian women's privacy, in which their thoughts and feelings were hidden from the coloniser, invoked a frantic response. Occupation became a conduit for the most basic and vicious of human impulses: torture, dehumanisation, and sexual assaults. It shifted the rules of the game and empowered the allegedly placid: Algeria became a playground for phobias and sadism. This was also witnessed during the Abu Ghraib scandal.
3 *Le Point*, n°1500, 15 June 2001.
4 Assemblée Nationale, Constitution du 4 Octobre 1958, Douzième Législature, Proposition de Résolution n° 1060, *Tendant à la Création d'une Commission d'Enquête sur le Rôle de la France dans le Soutien aux Régimes Militaires d'Amérique Latine entre 1973 et 1984*, Enregistré à la Présidence de l'Assemblée Nationale le 10 Septembre 2003.
5 Assemblée Nationale, Constitution du 4 Octobre 1958, Douzième Législature, Rapport n° 1295, Fait au Nom de la Commission des Affaires Etrangères sur la Proposition de Résolution n° 1060, *Tendant à la Création d'une Commission d'Enquête sur le Rôle de la France dans le Soutien aux Régimes Militaires d'Amérique*

Latine entre 1973 et 1984, Enregistré à la Présidence de l'Assemblée nationale le 16 décembre 2003.

6 It has to be noted that the diplomatic archives of Quai d'Orsay have moved to Courneuve since September 2009.

7 This book was published in 1764 and was immediately translated into 22 European languages. In France, Voltaire wrote the preface to the translation. In England, Jeremy Bentham became the apostle of the views of the Italian philosopher.

8 Lazreg explained that Foucault's view that the modern state found better methods of disciplining its citizens than torture, which he defines as a 'technique of pain', 'is singularly shortsighted' (2008: 7). According to her, 'it assumes that these new methods have a self-sustaining socializing function but fails to consider that the modern state can purposely sponsor torture and use it as an instrument of behavior modification' (Lazreg 2008: 7).

9 These include Article 55 of the 1945 UN Charter; the 1948 Universal Declaration of Human Rights; the 1975 UN General Assembly Resolution 3452 (XXX) – 'Declaration of the Protection of All Persons from being subjected to Torture and other Cruel, Inhuman or Degrading Treatment or Punishment'; the 1976 UN General Assembly Resolution 2200 A (XXI) – The International Covenant on Civil and Political Rights; and the 1975 Helsinki Agreement, to cite but a few.

10 Indeed, Amnesty International (2000b) found that between 1997 and 2000, torture was inflicted in 70 countries by three quarters of the world's government.

11 Although this approach has been judged by Rothe to be 'far too vague concerning what constitutes a social audience and which audiences may legitimately label behavior a crime' (2009: 5), it is generally admitted that Green and Ward (2004) have provided one of the most coherent and considered criminological frameworks for understanding state crime.

12 The French philosopher Michel Foucault (1926–1984) produced a body of work that is difficult to fit within a singular discipline. As Kendall and Wickham explain, Foucault's 'own sense of what he was – a philosopher who used fragments of history to examine and disturb the self-evidence of the human sciences – is a clue to the diagnosis of his work as multidisciplinary' (2007: 129). Having said that, the aim of this book is not to rely on Foucault's substantive work, but rather on his own particular methodology: what we are interested in here is the relation between his early historiography – namely, the 'archaeology' – and his later historiographical approach – the 'genealogy' (see Gutting 2011; Kendall and Wickham 1999).

13 It is interesting to note that the Milgram experiments on obedience to authority have had a profound impact on considerations of ethical issues in research. Indeed, the routine use of institutional review boards to assess ethical aspects of research prior to the conduct of such inquiry can be viewed as a highly significant legacy of the ethical criticisms of his experiments (Baumrind 1964; Miller 1986, 1995). Having said that, although the use of deception and the lack of a truthful informed consent were important features of these experiments, these factors, in themselves, are not a crucial feature of the relevance of the Milgram experiments (Miller 2004: 644–645), and a significant proportion of contemporary psychological research endorses a judicious use of deception (Epley and Huff 1998).

14 A point made in a discussion of an attempt by the Australian Attorney General to censor two papers presented at the 1996 Australian and New Zealand Society of Criminology Conference.

15 The Full Stop Law No 23,492 of December 12, 1986 stopped prosecution of such cases.

16 The Due Obedience Law No 23,521 of June 4, 1987 granted immunity in such cases to all members of the military except those in positions of command.

17 It might be argued that the aim of the empirical investigator is to create or consult original sources through interviewing subjects and searching archival documents. This is in preference to referencing other authors' works based on such sources (Webb and Webb 1932: 100) because there can be no substitute for the primary data itself. Yet it has been emphasised that 'gaining access to information while conducting criminological research is an ongoing process of negotiating and renegotiating' (Walters 2003: 103, referring to Hughes 1996). Therefore, a purist argument for the necessity of primary sources *only* is problematic; a more appropriate approach to them is the adoption of a flexible view of the value and merit of secondary analysis of qualitative data (Lichtman and French 1978: 18; Scott 1990: 12) – that is 'the re-examination of one or more existing qualitatively derived data sets, in order to pursue research questions that are distinct from those of the original inquiries' (Thorne 2004: 1006).

Chapter 1

From Algeria to Argentina

The transfer of French *savoir-faire* in
the making of official torturers

> There is not a single country, not even the most liberal in the world,
> which is safe from the infection whose symptoms I'm about to describe, or
> which can be certain of being able to disentangle itself from a chain of
> events similar to that with which I shall be dealing.
>
> (Vidal-Naquet 1963: 18)

Setting the scene

Many books have been written concerning state terror in Algeria in the
1950s.[1] The renewed winds of democracy which blew in France after its liberation very quickly came into conflict with the colonial inheritance, out-
dated imperialism, conflict which first broke out in Indochina (1946–1954),
and in Algeria (1954–1962) shortly afterwards. It is now common knowledge
that, throughout most of the Algerian War, France made general use of the
practices of torture, summary execution and large-scale deportation. The
current debates focus more on the scale of the methods and on the French
senior officials' degree of involvement. Both alleged extensions – horizontally
as well as vertically – reveal the vicious circle that led an increasing number
of officers to commit illegal acts, while most of the political leaders, in Algiers
as well as in Paris, hypocritically gave the military a free hand while abdicating their own responsibility. Vidal-Naquet summarised the part played by
torture throughout the Algerian War in these few words: 'it started as a police
method of interrogation, developed into a military method of operation, and
then ultimately turned into a clandestine state institution which struck at the
very roots of the life of the nation' (1963: 15). Torture became institutionalised in Algeria, in the sense that it was exercised by the state through its
repressive apparatus. The torturers had good reasons to feel that they were
acting within legal bounds (Droz and Lever 1982: 139; Vidal-Naquet 1963:
60–75). By 1962, over 25,000 French soldiers had been killed and 60,000
wounded in Algeria, while on the Algerian side, over a million died,[2] many
of whom were also tortured (Lazreg 2008: 9–10). Despite these enormous

numbers, for a long time no one was officially allowed to use the word 'war': one spoke only of the 'events in Algeria'. Only in October 1999 did the French National Assembly (parliament) decide to officially permit the term 'Algerian War'.[3]

An increasing amount of academic work has been undertaken concerning Argentina and its Dirty War.[4] On 24 March 1976, the powerful Argentine armed forces installed their dictatorship, launched the 'National Reorganisation Process' – *Proceso de Reorganización Nacional* – and initiated a phase of anti-insurgent warfare known as the 'Dirty War' – *Guerra Sucia* – that would last until 1983. Although Argentina had long been marked by the presence of armed forces in political life, through *coups d'état*, dictatorships and exceptional regimes, the military government that settled itself between 1976 and 1983 exhibited new features that were distinct from those of earlier authoritarian regimes. During this period Argentine soldiers kidnapped, tortured and murdered between 15,000 and 30,000 people, according to human rights organisations (Abramovici 2001; Chelala 2001; MacMaster 2004: 8). It is also well known that the Argentine military intentionally employed the same methods of torture as the French army (Aguila 2010; Carlson 2000; Chomsky 1991; Fagen 1992; Gareau 2004; Hey 1995; McClintock 1992; Schirmer 1998). This is consistent with the argument that states learn techniques of repression from their own experience, but also from other states (Gurr 1986: 55).

What is less familiar, however, is the suggestion that France was directly implicated in transforming the Argentinian war and security professionals into official torturers. It was the clash between Argentine willingness to confront its past and French willingness to bury and deny its involvement in the Dirty War immediately following the Algerian conflict that made this particular case study so compelling. This book argues that France continued to be centrally involved in international human rights abuses and actions considered deviant by civil society, shortly after the tragedy of its own Algerian War. This is a bitter irony for a state that considers itself the '*Pays des Droits de L'Homme*'.

Explanation of key concepts

The making of official torturers

Before going any further, it is important to explain the choice of words used in the title of the present chapter. For the purposes of this study, a *torturer* should be understood as an agent of the state or as an extra-state functionary, acting as a direct perpetrator, rather than as a private individual committing domestic acts of torture or acting as a bystander (Cameron 2009: 107; Cohen 2001: 140). Indeed, this book is not concerned with acts of torture as 'ordinary' crimes – that is, acts committed in violation of the expectations and instructions of authority or carried out by individual officials at their own initiative and in disregard of the policies and orders under which they function – but as state crimes. These are acts of torture that are explicitly prescribed, implicitly expected or at least tolerated by the authorities (Kelman 2005: 125–126). This is an important distinction because, as Green and Ward noted, it is the 'public/state element of torture which allows for its capacity as "world destroying". If the state perpetrates or tacitly condones the terror there can be no escape, no other world' (2004: 127). In this context, the world itself is the torturer and 'extreme forms of abuse follow predictably' (Huggins et al. 2002: 235). Indeed, once you have what De Swaan (2001) calls the 'enclaves of barbarism' – which depend on states for their production – then torture has no limits and will never stop.

Torture refers here to the definition adopted by the United Nations General Assembly in 1984, and contained in the UN Convention Against Torture and Other Cruel, Inhuman or Degrading Treatment or Punishment, which stipulates that torture consists of:

> [...] any act by which severe pain or suffering, whether physical or mental, is intentionally inflicted on a person for such purposes as obtaining from him or a third person information or a confession, punishing him for an act he or a third person has committed or is suspected of having committed, or intimidating or coercing him or a third person, or for any reason based on discrimination of any kind, when such pain or suffering is inflicted by or at the instigation of, or with the consent or acquiescence of a public or other person acting in an official capacity. It does not include pain or suffering arising only from, inherent in or incidental to lawful sanctions.[5,6]

Many academics have examined whether torturers, acting as agents of the state, were initially different from the normal population. In their study of the violence workers employed during the repressive military regime in Brazil (1964–1985), Huggins et al. (2002) related that they had neither heard nor seen evidence that any of the torturers had sadistic predispositions prior to their immersion in an atrocity unit. These people 'were quite ordinary, showing no evidence of premorbid personalities that would have predisposed them to such careers' (Huggins et al. 2002: 240). On the contrary, where torture was concerned, authorities looked for cool-headed men with no hostile impulses, who could 'predictably and dispassionately follow orders' and who presented the 'detachment necessary for carrying out prolonged torture sessions' (Huggins et al. 2002: 240). Indeed, Brazilian officials did not want to train people who were initially psychologically 'uncontrollable' or could not be shaped into 'predictable performers of designated atrocity tasks' (Huggins et al. 2002: 241).

Another example of these findings emerged more recently from Iraq, where members of the U.S. military tortured detainees in the Abu Ghraib prison. Lankford has demonstrated that, even though these acts of torture have been characterised as isolated incidents and blamed on a few rogue soldiers, the evidence indicates that most of these people 'were relatively normal when they entered the military, and did not have psychological disorders, pathologies, or early life traumas which provide an explanation for their cruel behavior' (2009: 388). As in the two previous cases, a screening process was specifically designed to keep those with sadistic predispositions from joining the service, since unreliable employees are difficult to control and less likely to conform to institutional norms. Indeed, 'for the U.S. military, criminal record checks, psychological evaluation, and basic educational requirements help ensure that the new recruits are relatively normal and that they can be successfully trained to serve the system' (Lankford 2009: 388).

These cases seem to demonstrate that 'the willingness or, better, the ability to torture and to commit atrocity is not confined to a limited number of sadistic, mentally deranged individuals' (Green and Ward 2004: 140). There are many other studies to indicate that 'normality' in terms of personal and social background characterises the vast majority of those who carry out violence to serve a system. Examples include Arendt's 1963 study of Nazi slaughterers, Browning's 1998 research on members of the Reserve Police Battalion 101, Lifton (1986) in his study of Nazi doctors, Staub (1989) in his examination of SS paramilitary death squads, and Haritos-Fatouros's 1988 work on Greek torturers.[7]

Following most evidence it can be inferred, as Gibson did in her study of factors contributing to the creation of torturers, that 'individual personality and background information about individuals, by themselves, cannot distinguish individuals who will commit torture or other cruel acts from those who will not' (1990: 79). Since there is no evidence to suggest that men or women, in order to torture, have to be sadistic or mentally unbalanced from the start, it can be inferred that normality and ordinariness characterise perpetrators of torture. Given that it has been established that torturers are not born, it follows that they must be *made*.

From Algeria ...

In Algeria, torture was intimately linked to the nature of the colonial state. Indeed, its use had begun in the aftermath of the French invasion in 1830 (Le Cour Grandmaison 2005: 152–156). However, torture had not initially been institutionalised in the way that it was after 1954 (Le Cour Grandmaison 2005: 154). The war of decolonisation (1954–1962) was the culmination of 'a long process of economic immiseration, political disenfranchisement, and colonial intolerance of Algerians' attempts to agitate for change within the system' (Lazreg 2008: 4). At the time, the population of Algeria was mainly made up of two different cultural groups: on the one hand, there were the *Pieds-Noirs* – that is, nearly one million French nationals born on Algerian soil

– and, on the other hand, the Muslim community. The Algerian War saw the rise of a generation of young nationalists, many of whom joined the *Front de Libération Nationale* (FLN). These young people rejected their status as 'protected subjects' or 'French-Muslims', which they were accorded under a special legal system called the *Code de l'Indigenat* (Vaujour 1985: 48). Algerian nationalism was subjected to fierce repression in which members of the *Pieds-Noirs* civilian population took part at times, further exacerbating the ethnic nature of the conflict. With international decolonisation processes under way in other latitudes, tensions also took on an ideological perspective. As I shall explain in Chapter 3, the Battle of Algiers was a focal point of the war, in which torture became systematic (Lazreg 2008: 5), and it was conducted in an identical way to what French journalist Pierre Abramovici calls the 'Battle of Buenos Aires' (Abramovici, as interviewed by Llumá 2002b: 20).

Torture was everything but an epiphenomenon of the Algerian War: it was central to the army's defence of a colonial empire in its waning years (Branche 2001; Fanon 1963; Lazreg 2008; MacMaster 2004; Maran 1989; Paret 1964; Vidal-Naquet 1963, 2001). Its systematic use was the direct outcome of the French theory and doctrine of Revolutionary War – *Doctrine de Guerre Révolutionnaire* – that developed in the 1950s.[8] Six torture techniques in particular were regularly employed 'gradually, concomitantly, or alternately': kickings, hangings, forced submersion of the victim into water, electro-shocks, cigarette burnings and rapes (Branche 2001: 326). As Lazreg explained:

> Even though the theory did not initially advocate torture, it informed an anti-subversive war doctrine that could not be implemented successfully without its use. Without the theory, torture could not have been systematized. Similarly, without torture, the anti-subversive war doctrine could not have been implemented.
>
> (2008: 15)

Having set the theoretical and operational context, torture easily became institutionalised. Therefore, its use by the French military was not just an instance of violence committed by a few rogue individuals.

The Revolutionary War theory and doctrine were elaborated by a number of soldiers who were veterans of the Second World War and subsequent colonial wars, especially in Indochina. These men – such as Colonel Charles Lacheroy (2003) and Colonel Roger Trinquier (1964) – saw in the Algerian War an opportunity for overcoming the humiliation of the loss of Indochina in May 1954 (Lazreg 2008: 3, 18). The French experience in Algeria in the 1950s also revealed that even people who had recently experienced torture could in turn become torturers and justify their practices (Clarke 2008: 17). Notwithstanding that it had a legal tradition aligned closely and explicitly with the doctrines of human dignity and civil protection, France turned to torture soon after its own late colonial political agony. It consequently betrayed the very values that had served the French Resistance so well in its combat against Nazi occupation (Le Sueur 2006: xv; Peters 1985: 133–134). As McCoy pointed out:

> Despite the Third Reich's defeat in 1945, its legacy persisted in the former occupied territories, particularly among French officers in colonial Algeria. As partisans who fought the German occupation during the Second World War, some of these officers had suffered Nazi torture and now, ironically, used the experience to inflict this cruelty on others.
>
> (2006: 18–19)

This was ironic, indeed, given that France had so often, verbally at least, championed universal moral values and human rights (Alleg 2006a: 98).

The centrality of torture to the debate on the Algerian War resided not only in the horrors of the practices that took place, 'but rather in the extent to which it served as a symbol of a deeper corruption, both of the state and of the structures of military, administrative and judicial power that had made it possible' (MacMaster 2004: 9). Some suggest that torture – and more generally state terror – became established in Algeria at the behest of the government in France, which saw torture as necessary for the achievement of its war objectives. Its anti-torture rhetoric was really just a way of keeping up democratic appearances (Carlson 2000: 80; Maran 1989: 57). Although torture does not appear to have been as systematised in France as it was in Algeria, Algerian political prisoners and some of their French supporters were either jailed or tortured in Paris police stations; some of them were subsequently thrown into the Seine on October 17, 1961, by orders of the police prefect of Paris, Maurice Papon (Einaudi 1991). After 1957 news of the French government's use of torture in Algeria turned from a trickle into a flood. As we shall see in more depth in Chapter 3, the use of torture eventually contributed to the demise of the Fourth Republic, the re-entry of Charles de Gaulle into politics, the creation of the Fifth Republic, the recognition of Algerians' unconditional citizenship in 1958, the short-lived putsch by the disappointed *Organisation Armée Secrète* (*OAS*) in 1961, and finally the signing of the Evian Accords in 1962, which led to the declaration of Algerian independence later in the year (Lazreg 2008: 5; Peters 1985: 133).

The French government's virtual inability to engage with the subject of colonial violence started with Charles de Gaulle's 1960s political manoeuvering and grants of amnesty (Le Sueur 2006: xiii). Despite several assassination attempts on de Gaulle by the torture expert members of the *OAS*, his government reached an agreement with the majority of them: Those who agreed to abandon all conspiratorial activity against de Gaulle were amnestied and shortly after allowed to return to France; those who did not accept the agreement were immediately expelled from Spain to Venezuela, Paraguay,

Uruguay, Argentina and Portugal (Blanquer 1992: 87; Kauffer 2002: 388–389; Segura Valero 2004). Furthermore, as recently as February 2005, the French National Assembly – responding to the political pressures applied by veterans, ex-colonials, and the *harkis*[9] – passed a hypocritical law designed to rehabilitate French colonialism. Amongst other things, it called for teaching the 'positive role' of colonialism, especially in North Africa, in French schools (Liauzu 2005).[10] Following high profile protests by leading French historians and intellectuals, as well as diplomatic pressure exerted by the Algerian government and demonstrations in the overseas territories of Guadeloupe and Martinique, however, this controversial legislation rehabilitating French colonialism was ultimately repealed on February 2006 (Lazreg 2008: 2; Le Sueur 2006: xiv).[11] Although the French government made enormous efforts to bury past abuses of the Algerian War by denying the use of torture and refusing to call it an actual 'war' for a long time (Maran 1989: 5; Paret 1964: 12; Vidal-Naquet 1963: 21),[12] paradoxically it appears to have continued becoming involved in situations systematically contrary to human rights abroad, as research conducted for this book suggests.

The transfer of French savoir-faire

The *savoir-faire* in this book refers to the French theory and doctrine of Revolutionary War which, as I shall explain in detail in Chapter 3, suggested that to combat and triumph over a revolutionary war, armies must adjust their conventional methods to their adversaries' subversive strategies (Branche 2001: 326; Lazreg 2008: 15). The direct outcome of the Revolutionary War doctrine is the systematic use of torture techniques. These include: amputation; asphyxiation; attacks by animals; beatings; breaking bones; burnings, including roasting on a red hot grill; cuttings; deprivation of food, water, sleep or sanitary conditions; electro-shocks; *falacca* or *falanga*, blunt trauma to the soles of the feet with rods; genital mutilation, rape and other forms of sexual assault; the use of chemical substances to cause, for example, blindness; kickings; sensory deprivation or overload; stretchings; *submarino*, forced submersion of the victim into water, urine, vomit, blood, faeces or other matter until the point of suffocation is almost reached; suspension, including hangings and crucifixions; teeth or fingernail extraction; *teléfono*, boxed ears rupturing the tympanic membrane in the process; whippings; and psychological pressures such as forced nakedness, brain-washing, infected surroundings, confined isolation, mock executions, death threats or forced witnessing of others being tortured (Arcel 2002; Peters 1985: 169–171; Rasmussen *et al.* 2005; Rejali 2003).

The French doctrine of Revolutionary War was intended to deal with both colonial and civil wars (Paret 1964: 9). It constructed 'a transnational conception of war that wove together a number of factors aimed at rallying a diverse audience comprised of recruits, politicians, and the public at large'

(Lazreg 2008: 32). Furthermore, the ensuing doctrine did not distinguish 'insurgents' from 'population', and consequently merged civilians into a generic, dehumanised, 'satanic' enemy (Garrigou-Lagrange 1959: 515). The fact that France had lost its colonial wars in Indochina and Algeria apparently did not matter: The anti-subversive war 'theory-doctrine package' 'provides a key for reading reality that makes intelligible a complex and changing reality and enables the armed forces, an institution that sinks its roots in medieval values, to cope with social complexity and change' (Perelli 1990: 101). It became very attractive to other governments and went far beyond the borders of Algeria. On the one hand, it was taught at the *École Supérieure de Guerre* (ESG) in Paris to an impressive body of international students, a quarter of whom came from Latin America, including 22 per cent from Argentina; and on the other, French assessors who honed their torture skills in Indochina during the early 1950s and in Algeria were invited to the United States and Latin America a few years later (Dhombres 2003; Le Sueur 2006: xxiii; McClintock 1992; Périès 1999: 709; Ray 2006: ix–x; Robin 2004: 168–169). As Périès explained, this French doctrine of Revolutionary War also possessed a 'transnational dimension' (1999: 697). It is this transnational dimension that made possible the transfer of the French *savoir-faire* in torture practices.

In this way, French specialists in torture were able – 'with the authorisation of their superiors in the cabinet ministries and the military general staff' (Alleg 2006a: 101) – to pursue new careers well beyond the borders of Algeria as soon as the conflict there ended in July 1962. They contributed to the 'culture of fear' (Corradi *et al.* 1992: 1) that developed between the 1960s and the 1980s in the Southern Cone of Latin America – namely, Argentina, Chile, Brazil, and Uruguay.[13] Among those four countries there was no historical precedent for the regimes of terror that would threaten and ultimately transform political, social, and cultural life.

... to Argentina

In the context of Latin American politics, the Argentine democratic transition has been exceptional for two reasons (Acuña and Smulovitz 1997: 93–94). The first sign of Argentina's peculiarity was the trial and conviction – although it was followed by a pardon and an amnesty – of those individuals most responsible for torture and other human rights violations during the Dirty War (Acuña and Smulovitz 1997: 93). The second is that it remains the only Latin American state whose military leadership – although with varying degrees of clarity – issued public statements admitting to their own complicity in carrying out systematic human rights violations during the years of dictatorship (Acuña and Smulovitz 1997: 94).[14] It is the clash between Argentine willingness to confront its past and French willingness to bury and deny its involvement in the Dirty War immediately after the Algerian conflict that made this particular case study so compelling.

Following the line of inquiry of Robin's (2003) independent film documentary *Escadrons de la Mort: l'Ecole Française* ('The Death Squads, The French School'),[15] research conducted for this book suggests that the French government actively sent some of its best-qualified torture experts to Argentina as official military advisers. In order to avoid oversimplification, however, it is necessary to remind ourselves that both the use of torture in Argentina and military intervention in Argentinian politics existed long before the French entered the fray, dating back to the nineteenth century (Feitlowitz 1998: 12; Molas 1984). Military involvement was relatively sporadic until the 1930 coup that deposed President Yrigoyen and installed General Uriburu – an officer very partial to the new totalitarian doctrines contained in Mussolini's principles (Périès 1999: 743). On June 4, 1943 a new military regime was established under Colonel Juan Domingo Perón. The era of Peronism – which, according to its creator, was a 'third position' between capitalism and communism – lasted until 1955, when the Colonel was overthrown in another military coup (Feierstein 2010: 44; Périès 1999: 744).

Perón was forced to leave Argentina and two generals, General Lonardi followed by General Aramburu, replaced him until the elections of 1958. From that moment on, the Argentine military continued to exercise power – at least de facto – including during the civilian presidencies of Arturo Frondizi, José Maria Guido and Arturo Illia (Feierstein 2010: 44; Périès 1999: 744). On June 28, 1966 the military opened the period of the 'Argentinian Revolution' and a new president, General Ongana, was installed. After four years, he was replaced by General Levingston, who was in turn supplanted by General Lanusse in March 1970. The latter was worried about Argentine political instability: following the success of the Cuban revolution of 1959, several armed left-wing groups had emerged in Argentina during the 1960s (Périès 1999: 745). The perception of the military was that social and political movements would bring with them Marxist and Communist influences threatening to take over the country and lead to 'a second Cuba' (Heinz 1995: 66).

Lanusse wanted Perón to return to the public arena in order to create a new radical social movement and thus tarnish the former dictator's own reputation: in other words, Peronism would be removed thanks to Perón himself (Périès 1999: 746). In 1973, elections were organised and Hector Campora – a Peronist candidate whose only programme was to resign in favour of Perón, who was still in exile in Franco's Spain – was easily and unsurprisingly elected. Consequently, on 23 September 1973, Perón was re-elected with his third wife, Isabel, as Vice-President. But even he was unable to reunite the Peronist movement: Only a few days after the elections, José Ignacio Rucci, the secretary general of Argentina's largest labour union – *Confederacion General del Trabajo* (CGT) – was murdered, allegedly by members of a left-wing Peronist guerrilla group. Following this event, Perón ordered his social welfare minister, José Lòpez Rega, to eliminate left-wing militants. Rega transformed the 'Triple A' – *Alianza Anticomunista Argentina* (AAA) – into a death squad and enlisted members of the security forces to maintain order (Feierstein 2010: 45; Périès 1999: 746). But when Perón died suddenly in July 1974 and his wife Isabel assumed power, with Lòpez Rega as her de facto prime minister, the atmosphere of violence and uncertainty increased. To restore the country to order, Junta commander General Videla overthrew the failing Peronist government. On 24 March 1976, the armed forces installed its dictatorship, launched the 'National Reorganisation Process' – *Proceso de Reorganización Nacional* – and initiated a phase of anti-insurgent warfare known as the 'Dirty War', that would last until 1983 (Carlson 2000: 71).

Although Argentina had been marked by the constant presence of armed forces in political life, be it through *coups d'état*, dictatorships or exceptional regimes, the military government that settled itself between 1976 and 1983 exhibited new features which were distinct from those of prior authoritarian regimes in that country, in terms of both strategies and practices (Aguila 2010: 137). During this period, Argentinian soldiers kidnapped, tortured, and murdered thousands of people, most of them non-combatants (Carlson 2000: 71). Human rights organisations calculated the number of 'disappeared' victims throughout this long reign of terror at between 15,000 and 30,000 (Abramovici 2001; Chelala 2001; MacMaster 2004: 8). Most of them were killed before the Inter-American Commission on Human Rights visited Argentina in 1979 (Feierstein 2010: 46).

Torture and state violence

All societies and political systems consciously manufacture and then wrestle with fear (Garreton 1992: 13). As such, fear is a central dynamic in the civilising process: 'that against which human beings seek to protect themselves must be used to keep them together' (Corradi 1992: 269). A number of scholars, such as Moore (1966), Tilly (1985), and Keane (1996), have focused attention on the violence and consequent fear intrinsically involved in the construction of the modern world. Weber's famous analysis that the state is the entity that 'claims the monopoly of the legitimate use of physical force within a given territory' presupposes that the very existence of the state is determined by the right to use violence (1948: 78). Indeed, by stating that 'the pursuit of war and military capacity, after having created national states as a sort of by-product, led to a civilianization of government and domestic politics', Tilly makes it clear that state formation is driven by war and preparation for war (1992: 206). On the back of this argument, it has been emphasised that war-making remains central to defining states and fostering their capacity for violence (Green and Ward 2009a: 117). The circle is generally not a vicious one, but the civilising process may become self-defeating (Elias 1982/1983; Freud 1961). Although it has always been assumed that the business of the state was to use, or threaten, violence – imprisonment, execution, or acts of war – in order to protect its own people from internal and external disruption (Claridge 1996: 48), sometimes the civilising process – which was understood to diminish state violence – does not accord all citizens equality (Elias 2000). Indeed, certain groups within society – because of their status or identity – can be excluded 'from the protection generally afforded by the state's monopoly of violence' (Green and Ward 2009b: 171). Yet, it is obviously not the case that all use of force by states is legitimate.

At the outset, it is important to distinguish between the concept of legality and that of legitimacy. Legality denotes the constitutional lawfulness of a particular regime, constitutional or legal system or legal rule; legitimacy characterises a state acting in accordance with the rules that it sets for itself and its citizenry. Those rules are seen to be justified by shared beliefs, a concept that belongs to the domain of legal ethics (Green and Ward 2004: 3; Habermas 1976; Van Der Vyver 1988: 62), which produce a sense of duty to obey. What is legal is not necessarily legitimate, and vice versa. Former U.S. president George W. Bush illustrated this point while 'justifying/denying' the use of torture:

> And whatever we have done is legal. That's what I'm saying. It's in the law. We had lawyers look at it and say, 'Mr. President, this is lawful.' That's all I can tell you.
> (Clarke 2008: 2, quoting George W. Bush during an interview)

Thus, while it may be questionable whether the violent actions taken by states are 'technically' legal, they can nonetheless appear as illegitimate. Without lingering on Walter's (1969) differentiation between 'force', 'coercion', 'violence' and 'power', we need to make it clear that this book is focused on the state's illegitimate use of violence – meaning state terror. This is an important point to keep in mind since, according to the report *Nunca Más* ('Never Again') by the Argentine National Commission on the Disappearance of Persons (*Comisión Nacional sobre la Desaparición de Personas*) that was set up to 'clarify the tragic events in which thousands of people disappeared' (CONADEP 2006: 8), the human rights violations perpetrated by the military government were the result of 'state terrorism' (CONADEP 2006: 479). The next section attempts to explain this concept and its relation to torture.

Torture and state terror

As the Algerian and the Argentinian cases showed, torture cannot be understood in isolation, but only as one key component in a wider, integrated system of repression. Indeed, as MacMaster explains,

> the army and police could only carry out brutal interrogations in a situation in which victims could be arbitrarily arrested and held in secret for long

periods of time, without the normal protections of due process, habeas corpus, access to lawyers and the courts, proper indictment and fair trial.

(2004: 6)

Once a state has committed torture it can hardly just free its victims (Clarke 2008): 'As we slide down the slippery slope to torture in general, we should realize that there is a chasm at the bottom called extrajudicial execution' (McCoy 2006: 194–195). For example, the French in Algeria and the Americans in Vietnam could not release torture victims without risking their stories becoming known (Rejali 2007b: 255–259; McCoy 2006: 119). Thus, one cannot examine torture without also examining the features of state terror because torture is made possible by, and feeds into, terror (Heinz 1995: 74). Torture may take place without terror, but terror seldom applies without torture, as it would lose its capacity to sustain fear and silence in its victims. As Lazreg put it, 'Terror and torture worked together like Jekyll and Hyde, feeding on each other, supporting each other, filling in for each other' (2008: 7). Thus, it is necessary to understand the system of repression and its implications.

State terror is terrorism in the service of the established order. It is a technique of governance which consists of acts of terror perpetrated by a government against its own citizens (Green and Ward 2004: 122; Van Der Vyver 1988: 60–61). It commonly involves 'the threat and often the use of violence for what would be described as terroristic purposes were it not great powers who were pursuing the very same tactics' (Chomsky 1991: 12). Academics have used different terms, such as 'official terrorism' (Falk 1981: 162), 'enforcement terror' (Thornton 1964: 72), 'regime of terror' (May 1974: 277), 'repressive terrorism' (Wilkinson 1974: 40) or 'authorised terror' (Bell 1975: 14), to refer to this same concept.

When a state perpetrates or tacitly condones torture, there is a characteristic sense amongst inhabitants that there is no escape, no other world (Feitlowitz 1998: 82; Green and Ward 2004: 127; Scarry 1985: 27). Scraton explains that

> terror is a strategy which ostentatiously denies the conventions of 'acceptable' conflict. Its purpose is to demonstrate as widely as possible a disregard for the boundaries or limits to formal combat. To strike terror into the heart of an identifiable community is to frighten people so deeply that they lose trust and confidence in all aspects of routine daily life.
>
> (2002: 2–3)

The following testimony is quite illustrative of this feeling:

> I have to confess that I have no idea what human dignity is […]. But what I am sure of is that with the first beating one receives, he/she is dispossessed from what we will temporarily call *faith in the world*.
>
> (Amery 1995: 60, emphasis added)

While centres devoted to the study of terrorism – such as the St. Andrews Centre for Studies in Terrorism and Political Violence – almost exclusively cover political violence directed *against* states, rather than *by* states (Burnett and Whyte 2005: 9), it is our opinion that, if we are going to apply the language of 'terrorism' at all to non-state actors, then the label must be applicable to states as well. If violence has all the appropriate characteristics of terrorism, it must be included in the analytical category of terrorism, regardless of which actor perpetrates it (Green and Ward 2004: 105; Jackson *et al.* 2010: 3). This is even more pertinent when we realise that 'wholesale' terrorism is terror in a form that 'retail' terrorists cannot duplicate,[16] since only governments have the necessary resources to enable systematic terror of this kind (Green and Ward 2004: 132; Herman 1982). As Jackson *et al.* explain, 'In comparison to the terrorism perpetrated by non-state insurgent groups, the few thousand deaths and injuries caused by 'terrorism from below' every year is quite insignificant besides the hundreds of thousands of people killed, kidnapped, 'disappeared', injured, tortured, raped, abused, intimidated and threatened by state agents and their proxies in dozens of countries across the globe' (2010: 1). For instance, the truth commission established by the United Nations to investigate and report on human rights abuses during the civil war in El Salvador (1980–1992) found that those giving testimony attributed almost 85 per cent of extra-judicial executions, disappearances and torture to agents of the state, paramilitary groups allied to them and death squads, whereas only 5 per cent of complaints were registered against the guerrilla organisation, the *Frente Farabundo Martí para la Liberación Nacional* (Gareau 2004: 35). Furthermore, abuses committed by the '*FLN* grocerie' during the Algerian War are nothing compared to the colonialist violence of the 'French army hypermarket' (Jauffret 2005: 13). While in Algeria and Argentina national movements of liberation – such as the *FLN* and the Tupamaros – also used torture, they did not attain the sophistication of the means and functions of torture employed by the French and Argentine governments, which induced fear in a population they commanded. Although their use of torture cannot be justified – and the pain endured by victims is no less real – such movements cannot be equated with the states against which they fought, as the latter have *both* the obligations to preserve the law *and* the monopoly on the use of force (Lazreg 2008: 8). They also tended to engage in torture on an industrial scale. Regardless of significant distinctions observed between Algeria and Argentina, the development of a common culture of fear was the consequence of this combination of elements (Aguila 2006: 169; Alves 1992: 191; Koonings and Kruijt 1999: 10; Stepan 2001: 75).

The use of an inclusive definition of subversive

Although the first to suffer repression in Algeria and Argentina were sectors that had mobilised during the period preceding the war or dictatorship, state terror spread over the whole society (Alleg 1958; Feierstein 2010). Subversion was specified as 'inclusive'. Leaders in the traditional political parties, trade unions and student organisations, as well as prominent figures in artistic, cultural and media circles, were confronted, as their words or actions were perceived as defending and extending legitimacy to the armed left (Fagen 1992: 41; Koonings and Kruijt 1999: 10). The following statements harshly illustrate the magnitude of the repressive project:

> First we will kill all the subversive criminals, then we will kill their collaborators, then their supporters, then those who remain indifferent, and then we will kill those who are undecided.
>
> (Aguila 2006: 169, quoting General Saint Jean in 1977, as regards the Argentine dictatorship)

> A terrorist is not just someone with a gun or a bomb, but also someone who spreads ideas that are contrary to Western and Christian civilization.
>
> (Navarro 2001: 244, quoting the Argentine President, General Jorge Rafael Videla in 1978)

> Any individual who, in any fashion whatsoever, favours the objectives of the enemy will be considered a traitor and treated as such.
>
> (French Colonel Roger Trinquier 1964: 27)

In keeping with these sentiments, the French and Argentine armies tortured 'anthropologists, literacy advocates, priests, psychologists, labour leaders, and high school children' (Carlson 2000: 79). The breadth of state terror in these two countries owed much to this inclusive definition of the 'subversive' because it encompassed so many (Fagen 1992: 43; Navarro 2001: 244). Indeed, in the terror process, the categories of transgression are abolished and anyone may be a victim, no matter what action he engages in. 'Innocence is irrelevant' (Walter 1969: 25–26).

The proliferation of arbitrariness

During the Algerian War (1954–1962) and the Argentinian Dirty War (1976–1983), the French army and the Argentine military government were also respectively characterised by the general proliferation of arbitrariness, a key element of state terror (Koonings and Kruijt 1999: 10).

Most constitutions provide for possible 'states of exception' – also called states of emergency, states of siege, or security measures – during which some otherwise protected rights may be temporarily abridged. The 'civilising mission', the defence of 'National Security' and the fight against 'international communism' were typically the main legal grounds for justification (Maran 1989; Marchak 1999; Schirmer 1998). In Argentina, however, immediately upon seizing power, the military government declared states of exception and permanently invoked security measures to bypass legal limits on their power without ever technically departing from formal constitutional rules (Fagen 1992: 48–49). Judicial protection, due process, and executive accountability were consequently undermined through the utilisation of special military tribunals to judge crimes against national security, while the rights to habeas corpus and other individual guarantees were withdrawn for many years, and limitations were imposed on civilian judges to control their actions (Alves 1992: 190).

Trying to justify comparable excess during the Algerian War, French Colonel Roger Trinquier explained that:

> [T]he peacetime laws gave our enemies maximum opportunities for evading pursuit; it was vital to them that legality be strictly applied.
>
> (Trinquier 1964: 47–48)

In Algeria and later in Argentina, the weakening, indeed the suppression, of constitutional and juridical mechanisms of protection cast shadows over democracy and civic life; the de facto autonomy of the security forces offered few channels for popular protest and contributed to the perpetuity of violence and fear (Fagen 1992: 42; Koonings and Kruijt 1999: 16).

The two-sided terror: individual but general, secret but public

To be effective, state terror must subjectively and symbolically affect a broad population, beyond the particular persons targeted (Fagen 1992: 62–63; Salimovich et al. 1992: 75–76). Furthermore, while for political reasons and to preserve international legitimacy, the use of terror is largely denied by state officials, it would lose its intended impact if it were to be executed without publicity (Fagen 1992; Graziano 1992; Salimovich et al. 1992; Van Der Vyver 1988). In Argentina, as Aguila put it, the 'ostentatious repression was an integral part of the atmosphere of terror implemented by the dictatorship' (2010: 144).

The violent tactics employed by France and Argentina were extremely well suited to instilling terror: kidnappings, bombings, public executions, show trials, extra-judicial assassinations, or arbitrary arrests, to cite a few. The most efficient methods adopted by these two states to achieve the desired combination of publicity and concealment were the use of torture, death squads,[17] and disappearances[18] (Claridge 1996: 51; Green and Ward 2004: 116). All these tactics have the effect of breaking specific targets, warning the public at large and augmenting fear.

The decision to specifically focus on torture in this study is open to question by readers. Indeed, as has already been indicated, the French have exported an entire new theory of counter-insurgency warfare that developed in the 1950s: the doctrine of Revolutionary War, *Doctrine de Guerre Révolutionnaire*. This French doctrine advocates the use of several efficient tactics and methods to install terror. However, it was decided that this research would focus only on torture because it is the main aspect of the doctrine of Revolutionary War, without which it could not be implemented successfully (Branche 2001: 326; Lazreg 2008: 15). Indeed, as we shall see in Chapter 3, in the counter-revolutionary struggle, the key problem is that of obtaining information – or *renseignement* – enabling one to know the enemy's organisational structure. According to the drafters of the Revolutionary War doctrine, interrogation is the main tool for obtaining information, and recourse should be made to any means to get it, including the torture of those who are merely suspects (Mazzei 2002: 125; Vidal-Naquet 1963: 41).

Having said that, torture during the Algerian and Argentinian wars was closely linked to other repressive techniques, such as *disappearances*. As Llumá explains, 'the institution of the *disappeared* as an instrument of terror [...] is also a French creation applied in Argentina' (2002a: 15). Indeed, French Colonel Roger Trinquier, a veteran of the Indochina War (1946–1954) and Algerian War (1954–1962), had already started to theorise on the disappearance of individuals in Algeria (Trinquier 1964).[19]

According to French journalist and Dirty War expert Pierre Abramovici, in order to terrorise the Argentine population, it was necessary to make at least a part of it *disappear*:

> Competent professionals were needed for this, not angry types who might get up to anything. It was necessary to act consistently. The goal was to obtain information. For this it was fundamental that the population should collaborate, and it did collaborate because it was afraid, and to achieve this it was necessary to direct arrests. And that is why there were disappearances. It was so that the population knew that anyone passing through the army's hands ceased to exist. Trinquier wrote this.
> (French journalist Pierre Abramovici, as interviewed by Llumá 2002b: 22–23)

Yet, as pointed out by an Argentine General:

> The 'disappeared' were probably a mistake [in Argentina], because if you make a comparison with the disappeared of Algeria it is very different: they were the disappeared from another nation; the French went home and moved on to something else!
> (General Matias, Interview #6 – see Appendix 3)

In Algeria and Argentina, many concentration/torture camps were located within the urban perimeter or in nearby towns, surrounded by private homes, in places where thousands of citizens passed by every day; some were even rented out by their owners to the security organisations. Thus, the invisibility of torture was not meant to be total; torture emerged through local gossip, by strange sounds behind walls, through photographs and films, in unusual arrests on the street and on the blank faces that came out from detention centres (Humphrey 2002; Kappeler 1986; Stanley 2008). However, the absence of real evidence of such processes was so important – as reflected in the common refrain *el silencio es salud*, 'Silence is health' (Feitlowitz 1998: 34) – that the rare guard, nurse, or officer in detention centres who broke discipline and gave information to families was certain to become the next victim (Fagen 1992: 64). This was the case with two Argentinian women – a midwife and a nurse – who disappeared because they contacted the relatives of a *desaparecida* who had given birth to a baby girl in the hospital where they worked (CONADEP 1985: 281). Likewise, newspaper editor Jacobo Timerman[20] was faced with a dilemma when a desperate mother whose two children had disappeared asked him to publicise their stories:

> How can I tell this woman that if I published the story about her children, it would most likely amount to a death sentence? How can I tell her that the government will never tolerate the assumption that a newspaper article can save a life? To permit this would mean losing the power of repression, the utilisation of Fear and Silence.
>
> (Timerman 1981: 43)

Navarro (2001: 248) explains that denial even affected the military at times, as the following case illustrates: immediately after his daughter was abducted, Brigadier Major Jorge Landaburu had an interview with General Videla, who assured him that the navy had nothing to do with her disappearance. In fact, she had been imprisoned in the infamous detention centre of the Navy Mechanics School and was later dumped into the sea (CONADEP 1985: 250–251). This is an example of 'death flight', another French method used in Algeria. Indeed, during the Battle of Algiers, tortured victims who were dumped at sea – a practice generally attributed to General Bigeard – were given the derisive name of *Crevettes Bigeard*, or 'Bigeard shrimps' (Vidal-Naquet 2001: 72).[21]

The outward show: denial and techniques of neutralisation

As previously stated, it is the clash between Argentine willingness to confront its past and French willingness to bury and deny its involvement in the Dirty War right after the Algerian conflict that made this particular case study so compelling. However, even though France and Argentina decided to deal with the legacy of their terrorist past in different ways, in an earlier stage both states denied the use of torture and for a long time used techniques of neutralisation in their official reports and speeches. As Shute explains, 'Most authors accept that there are a limited number of *techniques* of moral neutralisation with perhaps *denial of responsibility* being the master category' (2012: 51–52).

Indeed, for the sake of appearances, the communication of terror to the audience at large must be coupled with a certain level of denial by the state. If, in the past, public spectacles of death and torture were accepted means of inspiring obedience and impressing outsiders (Walter 1969; O'Kane 1996: 195), terror is an illegitimate and largely clandestine activity in modern states (Green and Ward 2004: 106). This makes the desire for motivational accounts a feature of almost all terrorist states (Van Der Vyver 1988: 68), and this was no exception in Algeria nor in Argentina. As Sykes and Matza (1957) first noted, situationally-specific temporary removals of moral constraint, better known as 'techniques of neutralisation,' imply an awareness of infringing a rule that the delinquent, at some level, accepts as legitimate. They further argue that these neutralisations are available not just to delinquents but can be found throughout society. Indeed, Cohen (1993) explained that exactly the same techniques appear in the manifestly political discourse of human rights violations. He describes the stages involved in the 'complex discourse of denial', in which states engage in order to deny or justify their involvement in violations of human rights. These range from outright denial to reclassification of what has taken place, to admission coupled with claims of complete justification. Remembering Sykes and Matza's original list, Cohen noted that each technique of neutralisation is a way of denying the moral binding of the law and the blame attached to the offence: denial of injury ('they are used to violence'); denial of victim ('they are the terrorists'); denial of responsibility ('I was only doing my duty'); condemnation of the condemners ('the whole world is picking upon us'); and appeal to higher loyalties ('the defence of state security').

During the Algerian War, a number of rationalising 'theories' also appeared: that torture was an aberration carried out by the Foreign Legion and not by Frenchmen; that the alleged torture was exaggerated; and that, according to the notorious Wuillaume Report of 1955, duress was indeed used, but it was 'not quite torture' (Peters 1985: 133). The testimony of Louisette Ighilahriz – who had been tortured by French officers in Algeria – is particularly illustrative of how differently officers responded to the same event: General Massu apologised and admitted the excesses, General Bigeard called her a liar, and General Aussaresses seized the moment to reveal his own secrets (Le Sueur 2006: xxii).

Likewise, the Argentine military government generated a richly verbal and sophisticated version of the 'double discourse' in responding to allegations of torture: the tactic of making state terror known, yet hiding or denying its details. As Cohen explains, 'the regime would deny (by definition) the existence of disappearances, and simultaneously proclaim that victims got what they deserved. Everything is normal – yet at the same time opponents are demonised, repression justified, and terror heightened by uncertainty' (2001: 153). Feitlowitz explains that it was a common occurrence for Argentinian officials to 'use language to disguise its true intentions, say the opposite of what it meant, inspire trust, instil guilt in parents to seal their complicity and spread a paralysing terror' (1998: 20).

The following speeches are acutely illustrative of the phenomenon of state denial:

> Systematic subversion and terrorism have cost the lives of many police and military and have compromised the security of the Argentine people [...]. If anybody violates human rights in Argentina, murdering, torturing and bombing, it is undoubtedly the terrorists. These people use violence for its own sake or to create chaos and destruction. We understand that the state has the right to defend itself, using whatever force is necessary.
> (Amnesty International 1977: 49, quoting an Argentine government official's explanation during a mission in November 1976)

> We must accept that there are missing persons in Argentina. The problem is not in ratifying or denying this reality, but in knowing the reasons why these persons have disappeared [...] I accept that some of them might have disappeared owing to excess committed by the repression. That is our responsibility and we have taken steps to ensure that it will not be repeated; the other factors are beyond control. On more than one occasion, persons who were thought to be missing later appeared before the microphones on television in some European country, speaking ill of Argentina.
> (Feitlowitz 1998: 28, quoting General Jorge Rafael Videla on December 18, 1977)

> The armed security and police forces acted in defense of the national community whose essential rights were not secure, and contrary to subversive actions, the armed forces did not use their power directly against innocent third parties, even though these might have suffered consequences indirectly. The actions undertaken were the result of assessments of what had to be done in an all-out war, with a measure of passion which both combat and defense of one's own life generate, within an ambience stained daily by innocent blood, and by destruction, and before a society in which panic reigned. Within this almost apocalyptic framework, errors were committed which, as always happens in every military conflict, could have passed, at times, the limits of respect for fundamental human rights. These errors are subject to God's judgement, to each person's conscience, and to the comprehension of man.
> (The Argentine Junta on their methods in 1983, in Loveman and Davies 1989: 207)

Conclusion

As we shall see, this book examines the argument that anyone could become a torturer under certain conditions (Crelinsten 2007b; Gibson 1990; Haritos-Fatouros 2003; Huggins *et al.* 2002; Kelman 2005; Lifton 1986). This is not to say that everyone can be turned into a torturer, and certainly not that everyone can be induced to become a torturer with the same degree of ease or to engage in torture with the same degree of enthusiasm (Kelman 1995: 24). As Zimbardo (2007) has emphasised, there are some cases of 'celebrated heroism' – a point widely demonstrated by Jauffret (2005) in his study on the French officers who refused to torture during the Algerian War. However, it does appear that one does not have to be a sadist or a psychopath in order to become a torturer (Milgram 1963, 1974; Haney *et al.* 1973).

The above acknowledgment means that, in order to fully understand torture in a given context – in our case, the Argentinian Dirty War – one has to look at the complete process through which an ordinary soldier becomes an official torturer. Kelman has noted that,

> for every subordinate who performs acts of torture under official orders or with the encouragement or toleration of the authorities, there is a superior – or typically an entire hierarchy of superiors – who issue the orders and who formulate the policies that require or permit these acts of torture.
>
> (2005: 126)

This book explores that argument. It also considers whether, for most of the states that issued the orders and formulated the policies that required or permitted these acts of torture, there was an external imperialist state that taught them the methods of torture. Central to the main argument of this book is the view that an adequate explanation of the perpetration of torture requires us to look beyond the confines of the torture chamber, or even of the states in which torture is institutionalised. We need, in addition, to focus attention on the larger policy context in which torture is embedded, and that necessarily demands an analysis of imperialist powers and their role in the manufacture of global terror practices.

Notes

1 See, for example, Alleg 1958; Aussaresses 2001; Boniface 2001; Branche 2001; Fanon 1963; Horne 2006; Ighilahriz 2001; Jauffret 2005; Lazreg 2008; Le Cour Grandmaison 2005; Lefebvre 2001; MacMaster 2004; Maillard de la Morandais 1990; Maran 1989; Paret 1964; Tallandier 1972; Thénault 2001; Vaujour 1985; Vidal-Naquet 1963, 2001; Vittori 2000; Wall 2001.

2 More recently, some references (in Algeria) estimated that the figure is probably nearer two million (Horne 2006: 538). This is an example of 're-writing history'.

3 See Loi n° 99–882 du 18 octobre 1999, relative à la substitution, à l'expression 'aux opérations effectuées en Afrique du Nord', de l'expression 'à la guerre d'Algérie ou aux combats en Tunisie et au Maroc'.

4 See, for example, Acuña and Smulovitz 1997; Aguila 2006, 2010; Corradi *et al.* 1992; Fagen 1992; Feierstein 2010; Feitlowitz 1998; Garreton 1992; Heinz 1995; Koonings and Kruijt 1999; Marchak 1999; Navarro 2001; Osiel 2004; Perelli 1990, Pion-Berlin 1989, 1997; Potash 1980; Rock 1993; Rouquier 1978; Salimovich *et al.* 1992; Seri 2010.

5 Resolution 39/46, Article 1 (Burgers and Danelius 1988: 177–178). The document then proceeds, in Article 2, to spell out three implications of the Convention: that each state should take all the necessary measures to prevent acts of torture in any territory under its jurisdiction; that no exceptional circumstances whatsoever may be invoked as a justification of torture; and that an order from a superior officer or public authority may not be invoked as a justification of torture. Article 4 goes on and requires that the states declare all acts of torture offences under their criminal law. Torture is also subject to the principle of universalism under humanitarian law 'in order to protect against the emergence of "safe-havens" for torturers' (Green and Ward 2004: 146).

6 It has to be noted that the 1998 *Rome Statute of the International Criminal Court* presents a wider definition of torture as a crime against humanity (Art. 7.2.e). Also, the International Criminal Court foregoes the public status of the torturer. This allows a consideration of torture by other actors such as militia members, paramilitaries, private contractors or resistance groups but, as a crime against humanity, the torture would need to be part of a widespread or systematic attack against a civilian population (Stanley 2008: 158).

7 On the other hand, it should be noted that Goldhagen (1997) argues that perpetrators of the Holocaust were not ordinary people but rather *ordinary Germans*, that is, true believers motivated by an historical and virulent anti-Semitism, which logically encouraged an exterminationist ideology (Cohen 2001: 77). Bauman sums up Goldhagen's approach as follows: 'Nazism was cruel because Nazis were cruel; and Nazis were cruel because cruel people tended to become Nazis' (1989: 153). This extreme opinion, however, does not explain the violence or indifference to suffering in other cases characterised by atrocities similar to the Holocaust (Green and Ward 2004: 177).

8 The conceptual groundwork for the theory was laid out by Colonel Lionel-Max Chassin and Colonel Charles Lacheroy, after having both completed a tour of duty in Indochina and written about the manner in which Mao Tse Tung led the revolution in China and assumed power (Ambler 1966: 308; Lacheroy 2003: 19, 68–69).

9 The *harkis* are Algerians who fought for France against their own compatriots.

10 Law No. 2005–158 of February 23, 2005. Article 4, paragraph 2: 'Les programmes scolaires reconnaissent en particulier le rôle positif de la présence française outremer, notamment en Afrique du Nord, et accordent à l'histoire et aux sacrifices des combattants de l'armée française issus de ces territoires la place éminente à laquelle ils ont droit.'

11 Decree No. 2006–160 of February 15, 2006.

12 See Loi n° 99–882 du 18 octobre 1999, relative à la substitution, à l'expression 'aux opérations effectuées en Afrique du Nord', de l'expression 'à la guerre d'Algérie ou aux combats en Tunisie et au Maroc'.

13 Although in Brazil the *coup d'état* took place in 1964, military dictatorships of a new type became consolidated in the area during the 1970s. These included Chile (1973), Uruguay (1973) and Argentina (1976).

14 On 25 April 1995, the Argentine army Chief of Staff, General Martín Balza, admitted in a speech broadcast on a television news programme that the military

persecuted and killed political opponents during the Dirty War against 'subversives' – that is, leftists and dissidents – from 1976 to 1983. According to him, the Argentine army 'employed illegitimate methods, including the suppression of life, to obtain information'. It was the first time a high-ranking military official had acknowledged that the army tortured and killed political opponents during the Dirty War (General Martín Antonio Balza, as interviewed by Robin 2004: 200–202).

15 TV documentary broadcast in September 2003 on *Canal Plus*.

16 According to Herman and Peterson (2002), 'wholesale' terrorrism refers to terrorism as implemented by state actors, while 'retail' terrorism is terrorism as implemented by non-state terrorists.

17 Campbell describes 'death squads' as clandestine and irregular organisations, often paramilitary in nature, which carry out extrajudicial execution and other violent acts against clearly defined individuals or groups of people (2000: 1–2). Even though death squads involve private interest and operate with a degree of autonomy, they are generally related to the state. Thus, it appears that the death squad phenomenon 'lies on the borders between state and non-state violence [...] and between terrorist and non-terrorist murder' (Green and Ward 2004: 117). Death squads primarily target specific undesirable individuals but they also aim to terrorise the population at large. For instance, Chomsky notes that killing is not enough for death squads: 'rather, bodies must be left dismembered by the roadside, and women must be found hanging from trees by their hair with their faces painted red and their breasts cut off' (1991: 21).

18 According to the International Criminal Court Statute, 'enforced disappearance' refers to acts of arrest, detention or abduction conducted directly or indirectly by a state, which are 'followed by a refusal to acknowledge that deprivation of freedom or to give information about the fate or whereabouts' of the victim (Art. 7(2)(i)). It is generally accepted that the use of disappearances removes opponents and sends a clear message to others (Claridge 1996: 51). As Graziano writes, 'the eerie, overwhelming silence of the victims – tortured but absent – was paralleled by that of the audience, terrorized by having witnessed the abstract spectacle that the Junta at once staged and forbade' (1992: 73).

19 An officer in the colonial infantry, Roger Trinquier led counterguerrilla units against the Viet Minh, including thousands of montagnard tribesmen in the climactic battle of Dien Bien Phu during the Indochina War (1946–1954). Narrowly escaping being purged as a Vichy sympathizer, he rotated between training assignments in France and duty as a paratrooper during the Algerian War (1954–1962), including with the 10th Parachute Division under General Jacques Massu during the Battle of Algiers in 1957 (Trinquier 1964: xi–xviii).

20 Timerman edited and published the Argentine left-leaning daily *La Opinión* from 1971 to 1977.

21 In the French army, they insist that it was Aussaresses who developed the *'crevettes Bigeard'* ('Bigeard shrimps') technique in Indochina, which consisted of throwing people out of helicopters. Its historical paternity, however, is Bigeard's because it was he who practised it in Algeria; his speciality was throwing people into the sea, mirroring what occurred in Argentina with the death flights (see French journalist Pierre Abramovici, as interviewed by Llumá 2002b: 23).

Chapter 2

Torture perpetrators' levels of complicity

An analytical review of the literature

This chapter focuses on the perpetration of torture and addresses the issue from a different angle, by exploring the notion of torture as a process involving several sets of actors. It contains three substantive sections. Section 1, 'The individual torturer', examines existing research that questions whether ordinary people become torturers, and the process by which this occurs. Section 2, 'The institutional torturer', considers the structural conditions that may give rise to state torture. Finally, Section 3, 'A transnational dimension?', investigates the involvement of a third level of perpetration in the process of torture – the state that exports its *savoir-faire* in torture techniques. This raises the question of imperialism and the export of violence through counter-insurgency strategies. The chapter explores both empirical and theoretical evidence, as a basis for formulating competing hypotheses to test against data gathered from both field-work and existing literature.

The individual torturer

This section will discuss the extent to which torture can be explained in terms of the characteristics, training or circumstances of an individual torturer.

The Milgram and Stanford Prison experiments[1]

Modern psychology and behavioural sciences demonstrate that ordinary people are capable of great kindness, just as they are also capable of great cruelty (Clarke 2008; Milgram 1963, 1974; Zimbardo 2007). This may cast doubt on the 'few bad apples' theory. A great deal depends on the facts of a given situation, which can bring out the best – or worst – in everyone. Those who emphasise the relative or absolute importance of social and environmental factors over individual psychological characteristics invariably point to the studies by Stanley Milgram (1963, 1974) of obedience to authority, and those by Phillip Zimbardo (2007) of the structure of bureaucracy. Both their experiments provide empirical evidence that, even when they have been socialised for many years against the infliction of cruelty, ordinary people regularly and reliably carry out violence when ordered or authorised to do so.

In a series of now famous experiments, Milgram (1963, 1974) sought to test the individual's ability to resist the authority vested in scientific expertise in 1960s America.[2] The experimenter selected people with varying backgrounds, screening out individuals predisposed to cruelty and sadism. They were asked to come to a Yale laboratory to participate in a learning test. Upon arrival they were given the role of 'teacher' and instructed to administer an escalating series of (fake) electric shocks to a 'learner' (actually an actor), seated in the next room, every time he got a test question wrong. Under orders from a white-coated 'scientific authority', the subjects delivered shocks they believed to be between 15 and 450 volts, despite the hidden actor's screams and pleas.

When the supposed shock level exceeded a certain point, most of the 'teachers' became concerned about the pain they were inflicting, expressed dismay and considered that the experiment should stop. However, the 'scientific authority' insisted that they continue with the assigned task, otherwise the experiment would fail. Once the 'scientific authority' assumed full responsibility in the event of serious harm befalling the 'learner', most 'teachers' felt reassured and continued with the experiment, sometimes even when the actor feigned unconsciousness.

In this basic experiment, Milgram found that two-thirds of his subjects were fully obedient to authority, to the point of inflicting extreme pain on a person they could not see but who they could hear suffering (1974: 13–26). Several variations on the experiment produced significantly different results: people were less compliant when the victim was physically close to them, or when they were part of a peer group (other actors) that refused to follow the directions of the authority figure; they were not compliant when a non-authority figure gave the orders; and they were almost totally compliant when they performed subsidiary or accessory tasks, but did not personally inflict the electric shocks (Milgram 1974: 32–43, 55–72, 93–97, 113–122).

Milgram professed surprise at the outcome of his disturbing experiments: 'This is perhaps the most fundamental lesson of our study: ordinary people simply doing their jobs, without any particular hostility on their part, can become agents in a terrible destructive process' (Milgram 1974: 6). As Luban puts it, 'Milgram demonstrate[d] that each of us ought to believe three things about ourselves: that we disapprove of destructive obedience; that we think we would never engage in it; and, more likely than not, that we are wrong [about that]' (2000: 97). It seems that Jean-Paul Sartre agreed with this point when he analysed Henri Alleg's torture by the French military in Algeria: 'Anybody, at any time, may equally find himself victim or executioner' (Sartre 2006: xxvii). According to Mann, trying to keep good and evil separate from each other and away from real life is pointless: '[As for] the rest of us [we] can breathe a sigh of relief that we ourselves have not been forced into such choices, for many of us would also fail them' (2005: ix).

In the Stanford Prison experiment of Haney, Banks and Zimbardo (1973), 24 'normal' individuals were selected from a pool of male college student volunteers.[3] Those who had criminal records or scored outside the normal range in medical and psychological tests were excluded. They were then randomly divided into 'prisoners' and 'prison guards' and placed in a simulated prison, situated in the basement of the building housing Stanford University's psychology department. The 'prisoners' lived in their cells and performed non-stop duties in the prison, whereas the 'guards' operated on eight-hour shifts and then went home. The aim was to determine what kind of interaction (positive or negative, supportive or disproving, etc.) would result from the confrontation between the two complementary institutional roles of the participants.

In order to optimise the extent to which their behaviours would reflect their reactions in this environment, the two groups were given only minimal guidelines on how to behave. Even though the experimenters explicitly and categorically prohibited the use of physical aggression or punishment, most of the ordinary young men who had been assigned to the role of guards participated in aggressive behaviour and psychological abuse. The 'prisoners' experienced a weakening of personal identity, which resulted partially in passivity and helplessness, whereas the 'guards' found their roles psychologically rewarding.

Given the rapidly escalating brutality, humiliation and dehumanisation, the experiment, which was designed to run for two weeks, had to be stopped after six days (Haney *et al.* 1973: 88). The conclusion drawn was that the prison situation alone was sufficient to produce cruel behaviour (Haney *et al.* 1973: 88–91), despite the fact that, at the start of the experiment, nothing differentiated the 'prisoners' from the 'guards', and none of the volunteers were said to be sadistic or mentally disturbed.

The Stanford team were no less shocked by their findings: 'Most dramatic and distressing to us was the observation of the ease with which sadistic behavior could be elicited in individuals who were not sadistic types' (Zimbardo, as interviewed by Browning 1998: 168). As Clarke explains,

> Zimbardo's experiment adds to Milgram's results by demonstrating the group dynamic that can help to create the situation where abuse can occur. It adds a larger social dimension to our understanding of why abuses happen and helps to explain why insular organizations, such as the police, corrections, and military, may be vulnerable to such.
>
> (2008: 14)

These two studies were prompted by claims in the aftermath of WWII that those working in the death camps and perpetrating genocide were simply following orders. Scholars set out to test whether ordinary people could be induced to engage in torture by means of authoritative commands. The combined results of both experiments suggest that situational power can induce the vast majority of 'normal' people to engage in what can only be described as the mistreatment or even torture of other human beings (Huggins *et al.* 2002: 263; Clarke 2008: 12; Osiel 2004: 135).

It seems that institutionalised torture may be carried out by otherwise ordinary people, who, when caught up in certain situations − or in the absence of enforced prevention − abuse their fellow humans (Clarke 2008: 12). As Bourke notes, 'it is not necessary to look for extraordinary personality traits or even extraordinary times to explain human viciousness. Numerous studies of cruelty show how men and women 'like us' are capable of grotesque acts of violence against fellow human beings' (1999: 5). On the back of these findings, Green and Ward pushed the analysis one step further by concluding that

> if such dramatic effects could be achieved by a relatively informal and non-coercive exercise of authority in an ostensibly democratic culture, it is little wonder that widespread obedience is accorded to formal authorities, in authoritarian cultures, backed by formidable coercive power and locked in a state of war
>
> (2004: 178)

The making of a torturer

With those laboratory experiments in mind, we can examine some arguments as to how a person presumed to be 'normal' might become a torturer in a real-life situation. Indeed, adopting torture as part of one's way of life in a generally peaceful modern society is not quite the same as the institutionalisation of torture within a state (Green and Ward 2009: 125). However, even Zimbardo − the 'superintendent' of the simulated prison − recently noted the parallels with events at Abu Ghraib (2007: 352–355). Thus, it can be said that 'Although controlled social-psychological laboratory experiments can never fully portray the realities of real-world violence settings, they can offer parallels that highlight the operation of relevant dynamic process' (Huggins *et al.* 2002: 141). These experiments, if anything, probably understate the potential complicity of most individuals.

It has been highlighted that, in the two celebrated experiments described above, Milgram (1963, 1974) and Haney *et al.* (1973) 'very specifically screened out individuals predisposed to cruelty and sadism' (Green and Ward 2004: 140). If neither personality nor abnormal psychology turns ordinary people into torturers, what else might do so? What are the factors that may help to turn people into torturers? As Crelinsten explains, 'Torturers are not born; nor are they very easily made' (2007b: 214). As I shall demonstrate in this, French military advisers contributed to the transformation of their Argentine peers into torturers. The main argument of my research is that this conversion was made possible through the exportation and teaching of the so-called French doctrine of Revolutionary War – *doctrine de Guerre Révolutionnaire* – whose direct outcome was the systematic use of torture (Branche 2001: 326; Lazreg 2008: 15). Indeed, this doctrine was based on a furious anti-communist ideology that helped justify the practice of torture and led to its institutionalisation in Argentina during the Dirty War (1976–1983).

Thus, it is important to understand the process by which ordinary people come to behave in ways that contravene essential internalised social norms, even though those norms sometimes shift to condone deviance in the context of state-sanctioned violence (Green and Ward 2009: 117–120), and how complicity in such acts is cultivated. Having assumed that these people were not predisposed to violence and cruelty, it now makes sense to explore how complicity in such acts is cultivated.

Obedience to authority/ideological persuasion

One argument suggests that ordinary people torture other human beings because they are told to do so by a relevant authority figure. Osiel argues that it is essentially inconceivable that torturers think that they are simply obeying legitimate orders and that nothing more needs to be said (2004: 129): he suggests that the process is far more complex. Kelman and Hamilton (1989) have identified three specific conditions for crimes of obedience in state-sanctioned massacres that make it easier for individuals to commit acts such as torture: authorisation, dehumanisation and routinisation.

Authorisation refers to explicit orders (as in the Milgram experiment), implicit encouragement or tacit approval (as in the Stanford Prison experiment) given by those in authority to commit torture. It therefore includes the processes by which regime leaders and officials justify the use of torture and, in a wider sense, reflects social relations within society. As Maran explained,

> Ideology tends to be politically and culturally rather than objectively defined. It can be used to justify means to attain goals, be they noble or repressive. In this sense, ideology is a propagandistic weapon. Ideology represents concepts, notions, or doctrines that form people's motivations for action; it can be used as an organising system for values, and as an aid in understanding the world
>
> (1989: 11)

Indeed, ideology and propaganda play a central role in cementing the idea that certain people deserve to be victimised. Torturers come to share the view of the authorities that 'the task they are engaged in serves a high purpose that transcends any moral scruples they might bring to the situation' (Kelman 2005: 131).

Kelman and Hamilton argue that willingness to commit unspeakable acts is enhanced when authorised by a higher official (1989: 16). 'The fact that torture is authorised eliminates the necessity of making personal judgments or choices, since their very authorisation is interpreted as an automatic justification for them' (Crelinsten 2003: 301). The perpetrators have to be assured that they are not and will not be held responsible, just as in Milgram's experiment. 'Insofar as they see themselves as having had no choice in their actions, they do not feel personally responsible for them. Thus, when their actions cause harm to others, they can feel relatively free of guilt' (Kelman and Hamilton 1989: 16). At this stage, torturers are not required to deny moral values, but only their application to this particular situation; their own morality is irrelevant since a superior authority makes the moral decisions (Cohen 2001: 89).

Dehumanisation is the gradual and progressive exclusion of members of certain groups, achieved by depriving them of their humanity and redefining them as enemies. Indeed, the creation of an out-group maintains the cohesion of the in-group. It is a prime way of legitimising, in the eyes of the torturers, the moral transgressions against the people who have been scapegoated (Crelinsten 2003: 301; Fein 1990; Lankford 2009; Zimbardo 2007): 'The main thing is to make the prisoner feel that he does not belong to the same species' (Sartre 2006: xxxii). Consequently, 'The idea that human beings are sacred rights-bearing creatures would be true only for their own' (Ignatieff 1988: 24). States have always played an important role in dehumanisation. Indeed, in the Roman legal system, torture – as a means of obtaining confessions – was originally applied only to slaves and foreigners, and not to citizens (Peters 1985). In colonial settings, racist ideologies were similarly used to cast the colonised person as 'other' (Fanon 1963; MacMaster 2004; Vidal-Naquet 1963). Contemporary victims of torture are presented as so-called enemies of the state – terrorists, insurgents or dissidents who want to endanger it. They are consequently treated as guilty non-citizens who are not entitled to government protection, and as people 'who have placed themselves outside the moral community shared by the rest of the population' (Kelman 2005: 133). This 'xeno-racism' (Sivananda 2001: 2) seems to be 'more about status than skin colour' (Stanley 2008: 164). Practically speaking, as Kelman explains, the victims' ethnic or religious identity is itself often the primary reason for their exposure to torture, as these criteria are seen as factors in dissent or insurgency. This has been the case with Kurds in Iraq, Bahais in Iran, Palestinians in Kuwait and in the Israeli-occupied territories, Irish Catholics in Northern Ireland and Bosnian Muslims in the former Yugoslavia, to cite but a few (2005: 133). Whatever the alleged criteria may be, the essential feature of torture practices is that 'one class of society claims absolute power' over another (Vidal-Naquet 1963: 167).

According to DuBois, 'The incredible violence of the late 1970s [in Argentina] can be partially understood in terms of the *creation* of an "enemy" in fulfilment of the military's ideology' (1990: 317). Once the enemies are placed outside the perpetrators' moral universe, there is no normal human obligation towards them (Fein 1990). One way to achieve this is the use of certain terms to refer to the victims. Nazis depicted the Jews as 'vermin', characterised by 'vanity', 'soullessness', 'stupidity', 'malice', etc. (Browning 1998); in Latin America, victims of the state were named as 'subversives', 'terrorists', 'dangerous prisoners' and 'communist guerrillas' (Huggins et al. 2002: 255; Heinz 1995; Stanley 2004); the U.S. military encouraged soldiers to call Iraqi prisoners 'dogs' (Lankford 2009); in Rwanda, the enemy were seen as 'cockroaches' (Kassimeris 2006: 9); and in Algeria, tortured victims who were dumped at sea were, as we have seen, given the derisive name of *'crevettes Bigeard'*. (Vidal-Naquet 2001: 72). Other methods of dehumanising the victim include forced nudity and hooding, as witnessed in the scandalous photographs taken in Abu Ghraib. As Crelinsten explains,

> The dehumanization of the torture victim, the euphemistic language to describe the torture techniques and the mocking, ridicule and laughter at the victim as s/he reacts to the torture all function to counter the natural inhibition to directly inflict pain and suffering on another human being.
> (2007a: 146–147)

The testimony of an Argentinian victim of torture made it clear that this dehumanisation was sometimes only partial, due to a 'web-like range of ambiguities' (Feitlowitz 1998: 71):

> I would say that they saw us, no matter our origins – guerrilla, student, labour activist, intellectual – as other beings. We were [M]artians as far as they were concerned. For a guy to torment someone with 220 volts of electricity or with a rubber truncheon he first has to consider his victim a nonperson. And he has to believe that he is right to be doing what he's doing. Afterward, the *desaparecido* can go back to being a person, of sorts, a being not exactly of the human type. But someone the repressor could play cars with.
> (Mario Cesar Villani on his detention in a torture camp in Argentina during the Dirty War, cited in Feitlowitz 1998: 80)

While the torturers have to forget that their victims are fellow human beings, the victims have to remember that they are. Indeed, Feitlowitz was told by survivors of an Argentine camp that the most difficult thing was to remember that they were human:

> The physical evidence goes against you, you're so weak, so sick and so tormented, you think, if you *can* think: I *am* my shit; I *am* these stinking wounds, I *am* this festering sore. That is what you have to fight. And it's

goddamn difficult; because whenever they feel like it, they replenish the physical evidence that goes against you.

(A survivor of a concentration camp during the Dirty War in Argentina, cited in Feitlowitz 1998: 66)

Routinisation involves the professionalisation of those who commit torture by the supplanting of conventional moral values with those of obedience to authority and unquestioning acceptance of the regime's ideology. This is done in order to normalise and ennoble their work (Crelinsten 2003: 301; Kelman 2005: 132). Once the torturer overcomes initial moral restraints – the first beating, the first use of electric shock, the first rape – then each subsequent step becomes a mechanical action and they come to see themselves as performing a job, as doing their duty. This makes it all the more difficult to refuse to continue, because it would question the earlier steps (Cohen 2001: 90). The first time a soldier engages in torture 'unlocks the door to its routinisation' (Lazreg 2008: 122), even though the first prisoner will be looked at 'almost timidly' (Vittori 2000: 45).

The perversion of language can also play an important role here; it helps to make this daily routine easier for the torturer. Indeed, the different torture techniques and chambers are usually designated by special names, 'often with a euphemistic or ironic quality' (Kelman 2005: 132). As Feitlowitz emphasised, 'Constant talk of omnipotence led mortals to believe they could torment others with a godlike impunity. Euphemisms created psychological distance between the doer and his act' (1998: 50). Indeed, in Abu Ghraib, those authorising torture used terms such as '*tea party, dance, birthday party, the telephone, the submarine, the swallow* and *the airplane*' to describe torture techniques (Lankford 2009: 392). As fictional Colonel Mathieu explains to his subordinates in Pontecorvo's famous 1965 film, *The Battle of Algiers*,[4] the term 'police method' became a euphemism for torture and, eventually, the elimination of internal enemies (Seri 2010: 186). The use of such vocabulary enables torturers to 'construct a social reality that distorts facts and events, reallocating the infliction of pain in a different cognitive world' (Cohen 2001: 83). This socially constructed reality – the routine of torture – supplants conventional morality, substituting in its place the ideological dictates of the authority structure within which torture occurs (Crelinsten 2007a: 148). Yet, Kelman explains that these names are not so much designed

> to hide the reality of what is actually taking place as […] to give the work an aura of professionalism, which allows the torturer to perceive it not as an act of cruelty against another human being, but as the routine application of specialized knowledge and skills
>
> (Kelman 2005: 132)

As Scarry noted, 'There are words, random words, names for torture, names for the prisoner's body, and this idiom continually moves out to the realm of the man-made, the world of technology and artifice' (1985: 43).

During the Algerian War, such euphemistic grammatical codes were not only used by the practitioners of torture, but also by officials and the Church. They referred to the techniques employed in terms of 'alleged atrocities', 'pressures and brutality', 'cleansing', 'vigorous interrogation', 'muscular interrogation', 'tight questioning', 'extreme questioning', 'interrogation under constraint', 'coercive methods', 'professional errors', 'certain methods peculiar to Intelligence services', 'methods that do not respect the other', and 'intrinsically bad methods' (Alleg 2006a: 101; Branche 2001: 60–61; Lazreg 2008: 114; Lefebvre 2001: 84; Vaujour 1985: 356; Vidal-Naquet 2001: 167).

As Crelinsten put it, 'What is being done *to* someone transforms into what is being done: information gathering' (2007a: 146, emphasis as in original). The following testimony is quite explicit with regard to habituation:

> I can only say that when you first start doing this job, it is hard ... you hide yourself and cry, so nobody can see you. Later on you don't cry, you only feel sad. You feel a knot in your throat but you can hold back the tears. And after ... not wanting to ... but wanting to, you start getting used to it. Yes, definitely, there comes a moment when you feel nothing about what you are doing.
>
> (Chilean ex-torturer who defected from his job with Air Force Intelligence, cited in Crelinsten 2007a: 146)

Training/desensitisation

The three conditions for crimes of ideological persuasion may already exist in the perpetrator's organisation or political culture (Cohen 2001: 90). If not, training becomes necessary for creating torturers. As I shall evidence in this book, the French contribution was crucial to the development of the legitimising narrative used by the Argentine dictatorship to justify, both within the armed forces and to society, the repressive actions it deployed. French training awoke great interest on the part of the Argentine military and Catholic traditionalism: any social protest would conceal, behind its social, financial or political demands, action aimed at weakening the 'Catholic West' – the goal was to subvert the established order and put an end to Western Christian civilisation. This, in turn, made it possible to put any manner of actions into practice – no matter how cruel and inhuman – to defend a civilisation threatened with death.

As Haritos-Fatouros argues, 'Milgram's model [...] does not explain obedient torturing or killing over a long period in the absence of authority' (2003: 160). It seems psychologically implausible that the attitude of the ideal torturer – which needs to be thoroughly detached, able to apply pain without emotional satisfaction or distress – could be sustained for long (Wolfendale 2006: 273). That is why some torturing regimes decide to initiate future torturers into a parallel world in which the norms of ordinary life do not apply (Huggins *et al.* 2002; Haritos-Fatouros 2003).

States continue to produce torturers, and there appear to be consistent elements engineering the transformation of the initiate from ordinary person to violent torturer (Golston 2007: 125). In such cases, training gradually desensitises normal people to the idea of torture by raising their own threshold for cruelty, forcing them to dehumanise the 'enemies of the state' and encouraging them to consider themselves as superior elite members of a military group (Green and Ward 2004: 141). The process relies heavily on the creation and exploitation of dissociative responses in the trainee and is promoted by two training phases: the first aims at making recruits less sensitive to the pain they experience, and the second intends to make them less sensitive to the pain they inflict on others (Crelinsten 2007a: 144; Golston 2007: 125; Haritos-Fatouros 1988: 1116; Huggins *et al.* 2002: 248; Sironi and Branche 2002: 544).

During the first phase of training, the recruits endure intensive initiation rites that push them to the limits of their physical and psychological endurance, as well as desensitising them to their own pain. For example, Greek military recruits were humiliated and brutalised for weeks on end (Huggins *et al.* 2002: 237), being forced to run to exhaustion, fully equipped, while also being beaten. Haritos-Fatouros wrote that the Greek recruits she interviewed described this procedure as aiming to 'make them love the pain' (1988: 1116). Similarly, Lankford explained how U.S. military recruits were systematically desensitised to their own pain during basic training (Lankford 2009: 390). Huggins at al. pointed out that this instilled a 'personal reality to the kind of violence that would be acceptable in the recruit's later career' (2002: 237).

The second phase consists of a systematic desensitisation to the act of torture itself. For example, the Greek recruits learned about torture strategies, tactics and technologies before inflicting these cruel treatments themselves (Haritos-Fatouros 1988: 1116; Huggins *et al.* 2002: 239). As Huggins *et al.* explained,

> To start, a recruit would simply watch a torture session. Soon, he would join a small group of torturers, where he would at first be just one of a pair of interrogators at a *tea party*. Finally, the recruit – whether at the centre of the torture group or alone – was charged with obtaining a confession.
>
> (2002: 239)

In this context, Gibson suggested that

> the formal lessons are designed to make the act of torture efficient by utilising new scientific information about the body and its nervous system, but also to reduce the strain of committing torture by providing prospective torturers with social modelling and systematic desensitisation to acts of violence.
>
> (1990: 85)

The Milgram experiments showed that obedience reduced when the victim was physically close to them (1974: 32–43). However, by first desensitising the recruits to their own pain, suffering and humiliation, their obedience was almost guaranteed when they proceeded to a face-to-face torture session (Crelinsten 2007a: 146).

Such a systematic process of brutalisation serves to

> break down the recruit's personality, desensitize him or her to pain (and so to the pain of others), induce a state of unquestioning dependence on and obedience to his superiors, and produce a sense of pride in the recruit's hard-won new identity as a tough, disciplined servant of the state.
>
> (Green and Ward 2009a: 124)

The end result, therefore, as Golston explains, is not mere accommodation, but the emergence of a new identity, enabling the future official torturer to fulfil his duty: 'From then on, the trainee is operating from a post-traumatic personality, which lays a foundation for his accommodation to abusive authority and for his susceptibility to further personality change' (2007: 125).

The training process particularly highlights what is meant by the phrase *making of an official torturer*. As we shall see, training plays a crucial role in the transnational institutionalisation of torture.

Bureaucratisation/institutional barbarism

Another way to create a torturer may be by his or her exposure to bureaucratisation, meaning the phenomenon of diffusion of responsibility: individuals engaged in torture are just one part of a complex bureaucracy, all elements of which contribute to the overall process of repression. As Lifton argued, some institutions are 'atrocity-producing [...] so structured [...] that the average person entering [...] will commit or become associated with atrocities' (1986: 425). Indeed army personnel, police officers, doctors, nurses, psychologists, judges and magistrates, amongst others, are all involved in the implementation and maintenance of state torture (Cohen 2001):

> Interrogators may torture, but doctors monitor the condition of the victim and advise the interrogators on how far they can go; guards watch the cells and torture chambers, ignoring the screams and broken bodies … and the list goes on.
>
> (Crelinsten 2003: 307)[5]

For example, at the height of the Argentine 'Dirty War' (1976–1979) there was 'a huge torture complex [...] which require[d] an increasing number of staff-jailers, drivers, executioners, typists, public relations officers, doctors and others' (Feitlowitz 1998: 8).

Each protagonist has a distinct role, but all of them are linked and depend on each other to act; this is often illustrated by the use of the pronoun 'we' in the testimonies of former torturers (Branche 2001: 323). In such a system, it is easy for the perpetrator to claim that he was just following orders, while his superiors can just as easily claim that they never directed the perpetrator to commit torture. This institutional barbarism diffuses responsibility for torture by separating decision from action (Bauman 1989).

Indeed, Huggins *et al.* illustrated how institutional segmentation and the organisational division of labour in Brazil fostered moral disengagement: 'Central to their not recognising personal responsibilities was that such conduct was supported, assisted, and bolstered by an array of legitimate facilitators' (2002: 183). Osiel also emphasised how facilitators were necessary during the Dirty War in Argentina, pointing out that several priests in the military chaplaincy were present during torture sessions, 'encouraging victims to confess and collaborate for the good of their souls' (2004: 133). As it will be showed later, years earlier in Algeria, the French military also drew on the unconditional support of organised religion, in particular *La Cité Catholique*, which could provide it with justifications for its un-orthodox methods of fighting the war (Boniface 2001: 408; Garrigou-Lagrange 1959: 521, 536; La Cité Catholique 1959: 697, 700; Paret 1964: 109; Robin 2004: 160–161). As Lazreg put it, 'In Algeria *La Cité Catholique* could fight a "just crusade" against Islam' (Lazreg 2008: 207).[6]

Similarly, Lankford noted that military bureaucracy played an important role in creating torturers at Abu Ghraib: 'Because the guards were just tiny parts of the enormous system ... they may have thought that decisions about the morality or legality of abusive techniques were simply above their pay grade' (2009: 393). The key feature of the 'bureaucratisation of barbarism' is the 'compartmentalisation' of the victims, the perpetrators and facilitators (De Swaan 2001: 269).

The result of such compartmentalisation may create a sense of what Lifton (1986) calls 'doubling', whereby torturers split themselves into the amoral perpetrator of atrocities and the moral citizen. Staub argues that this 'differentiated self' is capable of excluding targeted groups from his 'moral universe' and of inflicting extreme and inhumane violence (1989: 64). In these ways, torturers can continue with their actions without facing the consequences of their own psychological and moral integrity (Crelinsten 2003: 308). The following account highlights this 'doubling' effect and how the face of the torturer changes when his private world intrudes into his working world:

'You are the son of a whore!' a man would shout, while his face clenched with hatred. Then someone would call, 'Dr. Paulo, telephone!'. As he crossed the room and picked up the receiver, his face would open up again, and he would be smiling and smoothing his hair and murmuring endearments.

(Brazilian victim talking about his torturer, cited in Crelinsten 2007a: 149)

Being exposed to such a bureaucratisation, where responsibility is diffused, might ease individuals' participation in the torture process and eventually make them turn into official torturers.

Conformity to a violent group/membership of an elite group

Browning's 1998 research demonstrated that neither bureaucratisation nor obedience to authority could adequately explain how ordinary men, members of Reserve Police Battalion 101 in Poland, became mass killers.[7] Even though the facilitating psychological effect of division of labour for the killing process was not negligible, these men did not have the luxury of the physical distancing and depersonalising aspects of bureaucratisation (1998: 162–163). Nor was obedience to authority relevant in the case of Reserve Police Battalion 101, since the commander even offered to excuse and protect those 'not up to it' (Browning 1998: 170–171). Yet 80 to 90 per cent of the men proceeded to kill (Browning 1998: 184). As Browning explains, 'To break the ranks and step out, to adopt overtly nonconformist behavior, was simply beyond most of the men. It was easier for them to shoot' (Browning 1998: 184). Why? It seems that conformity to the group assumed a more central role within the battalion. Indeed, those who refused to get involved in the killing risked rejection by their comrades, because they were seen as either disapproving of the actions of those who did join in, or as 'too weak' to kill (Browning 1998: 185). The lack of 'toughness' of most dissenters reaffirmed, in turn, the masculinity of the majority (Browning 1998: 185).

Even though torturers and killers are quite different as individuals, their violence is very likely to have many taught, organisational and situational factors in common (Huggins et al. 2002). Therefore, it is worth analysing whether group dynamics could also explain the behaviour of torturers. Torturers tend to operate within policing or military bodies that promote a hierarchical culture marked by male domination and are encouraged to see themselves as superior and elite members of a state which at all costs must be protected (Branche 2001; Green and Ward 2004; Huggins et al. 2002; Gibson 1990). 'To himself, [the torturer] is a hero, defending the motherland, ridding the world of subversives' (Hochschild 2007: 136). They usually come to see themselves as performing a job that often involves hard work which, above all, they can be proud of because it provides a significant service to the state and often carries with it membership of an elite corps (Kelman 2005: 132, 2006: 20). General Trinquier, who epitomised the French practice of Revolutionary War in Indochina and Algeria, described in his book *Modern Warfare: A French View of Counterinsurgency*, the dirty but honourable job of a soldier: 'the risks he runs on the battlefield and the suffering he endures are the price of the glory he receives' (1964: 21). Indeed, many of the units where torture is carried out are elite corps with exalted reputations within the state command structure; they are often highly respected and/or highly feared (Crelinsten 2007a: 143).

The membership of such a unit, which benefits from an insular culture that depicts those who belongs on the basis of 'bonds of solidarity, the sense of common purpose and mutual understanding' (Chan *et al.* 2003: 256) can, in turn, produce violent outcomes. For example, Lankford explained that U.S. soldiers in Abu Ghraib experienced a kind of peer pressure: 'Since most of their colleagues were not resisting orders, they did not dare to do so either' (2009: 393). While they did not refer to the concept of conformity as such, Huggins *et al.* pointed out that a combination of work socialisation (2002: 172), insularity (Huggins *et al.* 2002: 248) and group masculinity (Huggins *et al.* 2002: 249) contributed to the maintenance of the structures within which torturers could be created. As the authors said, 'Group dynamics are more than the sum of their individual parts; there are also emergent phenomena' (Huggins *et al.* 2002: 241).

The unit is the permanent protective environment in which torturers evolve: to refuse to engage in torture is to risk being excluded from the group, and this is dangerous (Branche 2001: 95). As Staub explains,

> If your primary identification comes to be based on membership in a group, as you oppose this group what happens to your identification? If you deviate from it, who are you then? It can become threatening to even internally separate yourself. If you begin to think that something your group does is a problem or is wrong, that may demand of you to publicly separate yourself by speaking out or taking action. But this endangers you, not only in terms of what those in power will do to you, but in terms of who you are, and how your friends and colleagues look at you. In contrast, alignment with the group strengthens your bond to others and affirms your identity.
>
> (1995: 104)

Although Milgram's experiments found that commitment to obedience reduced when his subjects performed in groups (1974: 55–72), in real-life situations this response is almost reversed. The pressure is usually to commit torture, and the temptation that must be resisted is that of following one's own humane sensibilities:[8] 'Alone, there is a possibility that disobedience will occur, while in the group, we saw that obedience was more than exemplary' (Crelinsten 2007a: 152). According to Crelinsten, cruelty is facilitated in social groups and, consequently, torture is more usefully understood as a group phenomenon (2007a: 150, 151). Green and Ward agree with this point when they emphasise that 'Obedience to *authority* as a psychological trait is to be distinguished from obedience to *violent authority*' (2009b: 166, referring to Haritos-Fatouros 2003). It follows that torturers are usually asked to work in units to avoid the 'momentary exercise of self-doubt':

Even the worst torturer showed some human instincts when he was alone. [...] It was when he was with others that he became like a wild beast.

(Greek prisoner arrested and tortured by ESA – the Greek military police, as cited in Crelinsten 2007a: 151)

In becoming a member of the unit, through shared experience, the torturers come to identify themselves with the group:

Their individual self-concept, the 'I', will be embedded in and defined by their group concept, the 'We', to a substantial degree. [...] The power of the group to define the 'correct' or morally acceptable reality becomes great and deviation from the group unlikely.

(Staub 2007: 207)

However, the members' perception of reality will still be shaped by the state and by the support they receive from each other in interpreting what it prescribes.

The institutional torturer

Having reviewed the literature explaining why individuals come to engage in the torture process, it appeared necessary to understand why states such as Argentina embark on this practice. As the Argentine Dirty War illustrated, torture cannot be understood in isolation, but only as one key component in a wider system of repression. Thus, one cannot look at torture without looking at other features of state terror simultaneously because – here – torture is made possible by terror (Heinz 1995: 74). 'Terror and torture worked together like Jekyll and Hyde, feeding on each other, supporting each other, filling in for each other' (Lazreg 2008: 7).

Building on Merton's (1961) theory of anomie as extended to organisational crime by Passas (1990), and on earlier work by Kramer and Michalowski (1990), Kauzlarich and Kramer (1998) established an integrated analytical framework designed to indicate the key factors that contribute to, or restrain, various forms of state crime, one of which is state terror. Taking into consideration the fact that states to some extent behave as rational actors, the authors argue that criminal behaviours by states result from the coincidence of pressure for goal attainment (*motivation*), availability and perceived attractiveness of illegitimate means (*opportunity*), and an absence or weakness of social control mechanisms (*social control*) (1998: 148). Since for a subject as complex as state criminality 'something does not cause every single thing' (Enloe 2004: 22), these three interdependent concepts, which integrate 'structural, organisational and social psychological factors', constitute the starting point of this investigation into the role of the state (Green and Ward 2000b: 107, 2004: 6).

It has been noted that there are other important features of state terror that the rational theories do not seem to explain (Arendt 1985: 190; Katz 1988: 7; Mahmood 2000; O'Kane 1996; Pion-Berlin 1989; Taussig 2002: 167). However, even when states appear to act irrationally, there is always some room for rational explanation – as illustrated by the paradoxes of irrationality (Muir 1977: 43) and paranoia (Green and Ward 2004: 114). State violence – such as torture or terror – seems, indeed, to be both rational and irrational. This is explained by the fact that, in hierarchical organisations, 'Those who calculate whether violence is necessary are [often] not those who carry it out' (Green and Ward 2009b: 166). The apparent irrationality embodied in the degree of violence used by the official torturer is, from the perspective of a torturing state, brutally rational: although torturers might seem out of control, the decision to torture remains a product of measured decision-making to facilitate state domination (Crelinsten 2003; Stanley 2008).

Motivation

States have used violence with varying degrees of commitment to achieve multiple, overlapping and sometimes contradictory goals. A sample of the most common uses of violence includes the following: terror, intimidation, demoralisation, polarisation and radicalisation of the public, building of group morale, enforcement or disruption of control, mobilisation of forces and resources, elimination of opposing forces, punishment for cooperation with the enemy, provocation of countermeasures and repression, and advertisement of the movement (Kalyvas 2004: 98). Some theorists have argued that the greater the emphasis on goal attainment, the more likely that behaviour will be criminal (Kauzlarich and Kramer 1998: 150).

Drawing on Habermas's (1976) work, Rejali identifies three different kinds of instrumentalist rationality with regard to torture, which might either stand alone or be combined: confessions, deterrence, and strategy to defeat opposition (1994: 163). It is often argued that the purpose of torture is to force the 'tortured' to reveal critical information and that, consequently, it is a justifiable practice employed only to protect the lives and integrity of the threatened state's citizens (Green and Ward 2004: 130–131). As such, the use of torture has been 'regarded by many practitioners to be a practical necessity' (Morgan 2000: 182). Legitimising state violence in the case of torture surely requires the deployment of effective public justifications that have consistently been rejected by the judiciary (Green and Ward 2009b: 166–167; Rodley 1999: 80–84). This is exemplified by Dershowitz (2002) and Ignatieff's (2004) 'ticking bomb' pleas for the US use of torture in the 'War on Terror' – an argument that had been used by General Massu's paratroopers during the Battle of Algiers (MacMaster 2004: 3).

Scarry (2004: 281, 284) points out just how fallacious their reasoning has proven to be, since torture seldom leads to revelation of secrets. This was an experience encountered, among others, by the French in the Algerian War, who tortured thousands yet gained relatively little in the way of useful information (Branche 2001; Lazreg 2008; Rejali 2007b; Thénault 2001; Wall 2001). Indeed, General Massu admitted that the use of torture had served no useful or necessary function in combatting terrorism. Instead, the deployment of inhumane violence merely served to deepen resistance and drive most civilians into the arms of the *FLN* (MacMaster 2004: 9). Even in ancient Rome, the use of torture as a reliable way of extracting evidence was debated. The Romans concluded that any extracted evidence was weak, and acknowledged that those who were subjected to torture would lie rather than endure pain (Lea 1878). As Marton noted: 'The victim's confession is useless. The torturer knows that the victim's words are worthless. For a tormented person will tell the torturers what they want to hear, empty mute speech' (1995: 4) – a key point also made by Cesare Beccaria in his classic treatise *On Crimes and Punishments* (1763: 30–36). Moreover, it has been demonstrated that information can be secured without torturing (Maillard de la Morandais 1990: 336–337). Finally, the use of torture poisons and brutalises the society which allows it to happen (Kassimeris 2006: 14). It is in this sense that the use of torture in Algeria became for France a 'growing cancer' (Bernard 2000; Horne 2006; Vidal-Naquet 1963). The cancer was not the torture itself, but 'the public indifference to it that eroded and rendered meaningless even the most explicit protections afforded by civil rights and public law' (Peters 1985: 140). This inexorably led to the degeneration of the liberal democratic state, its institutions, and its supposedly fundamental respect for human rights and dignity (MacMaster 2004: 9). Today, in the United States, the public has similarly become 'anaesthetised' to what is happening in the 'War on Terror' (Ray 2006: xi). MacMaster noted in his article that '*torture advocates* reinvented the wheel as it were', without any reference to the huge field of knowledge that exists in relation to the practice of torture (2004: 2). In particular, he argued, it was well known that: 'Historically, whenever states started on the slippery slope of enabling a restricted or *controlled* use of duress, this inevitably deteriorated into a monstrous system of brutality' (MacMaster 2004: 12).

It would seem that in Algeria – and probably elsewhere – torture was not primarily about gaining intelligence (Scarry 1985: 28–29): 'torture is effective, not in extracting confessions so much as in silencing opposition' – in this case the *FLN* and its sympathisers (Green and Ward 2004: 131). Torture can thus be seen as a process – 'a limited dialectic between torturer and prisoner and an expressive dialectic between a torturing regime and its internal enemies' (Green and Ward 2004: 125) – that embodies 'the conversion of absolute pain into the fiction of absolute power' (Scarry 1985: 27). This led Stover and Nightingale to conclude that: 'The purpose of torture is to break the will of the victim and ultimately to destroy his or her humanity' (1985: 5). Sartre also forces us to confront this counterintuitive reality:

It is sometimes said that it is right to torture a man if his confession can save a hundred lives. This is a nice hypocrisy. [...]. Was it to save lives that they scorched his nipples and pubic hair? [...] Torture is senseless violence, born in fear. The purpose of it is to force from *one* tongue, amid its screams and its vomiting up of blood, the secret of *everything*. Senseless violence: whether the victim talks or whether he dies under his agony, the secret that he cannot tell is always somewhere else and out of reach.

(2006: xxxvii, xxxix; emphases as original)

The real purpose of torture is both to silence and to politically paralyse opposition through fear and terror, terrifying and disbanding perceived opponents and demonstrating to the general populace the risks of acting against powerful interests (Stanley 2008: 161). In this sense, torture is the 'actualisation of a victory on the individual, a metaphor of a desired victory on the group' (Branche 2001: 325). Indeed, torture is a process characterised by 'standard operating procedures in multiple detention centres, applicable to hundreds of detainees and used with the approval and intent of the highest authorities' (Herman 1982: 113–114). It can thus be seen as a mode of governance, a process of control through terror (Chomsky and Herman 1979). As mentioned earlier, the invisibility of torture is not meant to be total (Humphrey 2002; Kappeler 1986; Stanley 2008). Indeed, in Algeria and Argentina, most of the concentration camps were located within the urban perimeter or in nearby towns, surrounded by private homes, in places where thousands of citizens passed by every day.

The motivation of a state is essential in explaining its behaviour. It should be noted that a strong commitment to ideological goals (particularly anticommunism) is another important motivational factor (Green and Ward 2004: 108). As I shall explain in this monograph, thanks to the counterinsurgent commitment of France, an entire generation of Argentine military officers were armed, trained and 'professionalised' (Chomsky 1991; Fagen 1992; Gareau 2004; McClintock 1992; Schirmer 1998). The French military advisers exported and taught them the doctrine of Revolutionary War, whose direct outcome was the systematic use of torture (Branche 2001: 326; Lazreg 2008: 15). This counter-insurgency doctrine was based on a furious anticommunist ideology that helped justify the practice of torture and led to its institutionalisation in Argentina during the Dirty War (1976–1983). Thus, Latin Argentina became a perpetrator of torture acts drawing on assistance from the Elysée.

Opportunity

The motivation to act in a particular way means little if the opportunity to carry out that action is not available. It is generally assumed that states will turn to illegitimate means if legitimate ones are unavailable or less efficient (Kauzlarich and Kramer 1998: 150). According to Brockett (1991a), the use of repression by states is determined notably by the resources available for repression and those available to resolve conflict by other means. Many authors have studied the conditions under which states will use torture. In their seminal work on state crime, Green and Ward (2004: 129) suggested that torture is more likely to appear in states where there has been a historical devaluation of a section of the population; where there is a strong respect for authority; where the culture is both monolithic and enjoys a high degree of popular identification; and where there is a clear designation of an enemy embodied within the dominant ideology. In his social-psychological analysis of the policy context of torture, Kelman (2005: 128) emphasised that the conditions conducive to the rise of torture as an instrument of state policy are: the authorities' perception of an active threat to the security of the state from internal and external sources; the availability of a security apparatus, which enables the authorities to use the vast power at their disposal to counter that threat by repressive means; and the presence within the society of groups defined as enemies of or potential threats to the state.

Furthermore, Cohen and Golan (1991: 110), in their work for the Israeli human rights group B'tselem, identify a set of social and political conditions under which torture is likely to become institutionalised: a national emergency or other perceived intense threat to security; the need to process large numbers of suspects; the dehumanisation of an out-group (national, religious or ethnic); a high level of authorisation to violate normal moral principles; and the presence of a 'sacred mission' which justifies nearly anything. Martha Huggins's (2003: 527–528) study of police torture in Brazil identifies six conditions that are associated with systemic torture: unchecked and arbitrary executive rule; ideology of war against evil (or communism, etc.); secrecy of interrogation locations and procedures; hidden identities of interrogators and those interrogated; a social control division of labour, giving plausible deniability and obscuring the perpetrator's relationship to the violence; and a public rendered impotent by fear. Finally, in his research on torture and democracies, Rejali (2007a: 46) notes three situations which generate powerful demands for torture and which can result in democracies employing it: security bureaucracies overwhelm those assigned to monitor them; judicial systems place too great an emphasis on confessions; and neighbourhoods desire civic order on the streets, whatever the cost.

There seem to be three essential conditions for the opportunity for institutionalised torture within states to present itself: (1) a part of the population has been historically scapegoated, devaluated or dehumanised (being for political, religious or ethical reasons) and presented as enemies of – or potential threats to – the state; (2) the relevant authority is both respected and in possession of an efficient security apparatus to counter the supposed enemies or threats by repressive means; and (3) the supposed enemies or threats are depicted as such by means of a 'sacred mission' defined by the dominant ideology of war against evil, communism, terrorism, etc.

These three conditions were met in Argentina. The Argentine military regime held dominance in a geopolitical context of superpower confrontation (Aguila 2006: 169; Alves 1992: 188; Koonings and Kruijt 1999: 10). According to the anti-communism ideology of the French counter-insurgency doctrine, in a nuclear age shaped by the language of the Cold War, traditional concepts of warfare no longer applied. 'The communists would no longer risk a direct military confrontation with the West. Instead they would attempt to encircle it, by slowly gaining control of peripheral nations through *subversion*' (Rock 1993: 196, emphasis as in original). Thus, the main danger to 'National Security' would come from an 'internal enemy', rather than from direct foreign aggression. This created an inclusive definition of subversion that encompassed anybody, from members of left-wing armed organisation to students (Carlson 2000: 76; Fagen 1992: 43; Feierstein 2010: 46; Lopez 1987: 137–148; Navarro 2001).[9]

As Gurr points out, historical traditions of state violence encourage elites to use terror and torture, irrespective of structural factors (1986: 66). Furthermore, he argues that 'once rulers find terror to be effective in suppressing challenges, they are likely to regard it as an acceptable tactic in future challenges [...] and they are likely to regard it as an acceptable tactic in future conflicts' (1986: 55). That said, states are also able to learn techniques of repression from other countries. One of the main propositions of this monograph is that French counter-insurgency methods developed in Algeria through the 1950s appear to have not only influenced Argentina, but were also explicitly taught to the Argentine military (Fagen 1992: 43; Hey 1995: 144).

Social control

According to Kauzlarich and Kramer, a highly motivated state with easy access to illegal means of goal attainment may be blocked from exercising terror – and thus torture – by the operation of social control mechanisms (1998: 151). Thus, in order to be successful, the criminal state has to make its citizens feel uninformed, separate, fragmented, and powerless. This also means that the most significant force in thwarting state criminality – once all other important safeguard institutions have been corrupted – is a strong organised civil society (Risse *et al.* 1999).[10] This is in line with one of Gramsci's (1971) most important insights: the emphasis he placed on civil society as the terrain of political struggle.[11] Indeed, as Green and Ward suggest, civil society 'can also play a crucial role in defining state actions as illegitimate where they violate legal rules or shared moral beliefs' (2004: 4). A strong civil society can 'provide effective checks against the abuse of state authority' (Edwards 2009: 15).

In Argentina, for example, the movement of the *Madres de Plaza de Mayo* (the Mothers of the May Square) – composed of mothers and grandmothers who decided to join forces in their quest to obtain information about their 'disappeared' children (Calderon *et al.* 1992; Franco 1992; Navarro 2001) – succeeded in mobilising opposition to the authoritarian regime by contacting international organisations outside of the country. This provides an example of Risse, Ropp and Sikkink's 'boomerang pattern' of influence and change, 'when domestic groups in a repressive state bypass their state and directly search out international allies to try to bring pressure on their states from outside' (Risse *et al.* 1999: 18). It was very difficult for the mothers to achieve this dynamic because – in contrast to Chile – the Catholic Church itself supported the state terror (Marchak 1999: 321; Verbitsky 1988: 146). However, as a result of such movements, Argentine civil society reasserted itself to the point where it had room for organisation and self-expression. This constituted the 'resurrection of civil society' which could, in turn, block the highly motivated state with easy access to illegal means of goal attainment (O'Donnell and Schmitter 1986: 48).

A transnational dimension?

Torture across borders

So far, we have reviewed the literature on *why* and *how* states – such as Argentina – decided to institutionalise torture within their own territory. Yet it appears that there is no such thing as 'localised torture', since gross human rights violations are frequently reinforced by the global economic system and connected to international structures of dominance (Ackroyd *et al.* 1980; Amnesty International 2001a; Chomsky and Herman 1979; Crelinsten 2007b; Galtung 1994; Staub 1995). As Green and Ward point out, 'Individual perpetrators of torture and their political masters are not the only culpable actors in the realm of torture. Hypocrisy is a central feature of foreign policy and practice' (2004: 142).

Chambliss (1989) demonstrated how state networks can be crucial to the organisation and support of activities that violate their own laws and international laws, and, in so doing, fulfil their own broader political and economic objectives. The 2010 report of the UN Special Rapporteur on torture explained that ill-treatments were widespread practices in the majority of the countries and established a list of states that cooperated with human rights violators (Human Rights Council 2010). These included, *inter alia*, Austria, Canada, France, Germany, Italy, Spain, Sweden and the United Kingdom (Commission on Human Rights 1997; Human Rights Council 2013). By exporting torture instruments or expertise, *foreign* rather than *national* governments can also institutionalise torture in a given territory (Grewcock 2008; Grey 2007; Thompson and Paglen 2006; Tomasevski 1998). The 'West/North' seems to be leading this profitable business (Tomasevski 1998: 199).

Torture equipment such as stun guns, leg shackles, trauma-inducing drugs, electroshock weapons and chemical gases is moved through trade lines, and is designed and made regularly in European or North American states. This is carried out notably by companies in France, Germany, the United Kingdom and the United States, the products shipped to other perpetrating states around the globe (Amnesty International 2001a). The export of torture expertise to police, military and security forces throughout the world is also undertaken through transnational transfers, via training manuals, courses and practical instruction, which are offered by 'Global North' professionals from the US, China, France, Russia and the UK (Weschler 1998; Stanley 2008). This shows how the unscrupulous transfer of military training and expertise helps create professional torturers (Amnesty International 2001a: 2). According to Amnesty International:

> [...] much of this training occurs in secret so that the public and legislatures of the countries involved rarely discover who is being trained, what skills are being transferred, and who is doing the training. Both recipient and donor states often go to great lengths to conceal the transfer of expertise which is used to facilitate serious human rights violations.
>
> (2001a: 41)

For example, the United States Army School of the Americas (SOA) played a pivotal role in the training of Latin American torturers (Green and Ward 2004: 133). The public disclosure of its training manuals – which were distributed for training purposes in Colombia, Ecuador, El Salvador, Guatemala and Peru (Kepner 2001) – in 1996 forced the Pentagon to admit

> that its students were taught torture, murder, sabotage, bribery, blackmail and extortion for the achievement of political aims; that hypnosis and truth serum were recommended for use in interrogations and that the parents of captives be arrested as an inducement for the prisoner to talk.
>
> (Feitlowitz 1998: 9)

It is little surprise, then, that ten of the school's graduates became the presidents or dictators of their countries, 23 became ministers of defence, and 15 went on to be ministers of various departments (Gareau 2004: 30). Brian Smith, who has undertaken research on the SOA, explains that 'The technology and training, while not in itself an encouragement to repression or violations of citizens' rights, included many skills and materials that could be used for repressive purposes' (1982: 293). Indeed, the United States set up 'an institutional structure of domination built to violate human rights' (Herman 1991: 91). According to the Guatemalan Historical Clarification Commission, which was set up to investigate human rights violations during the period of civil conflict, the U.S:

[...] demonstrated that it was willing to provide support for strong military regimes in its strategic backyard. In the case of Guatemala, military assistance was directed towards reinforcing the national intelligence apparatus and for training the officer corps in counterinsurgency techniques, key factors which had significant bearing on human rights violations during the armed confrontation.

(Cited in Amnesty International 2001a: 44)

Similarly, this monograph argues that France also played an important role in this 'globalisation of torture', notably in Argentina. For many years, it was the fashion to insist the counter-insurgency foreign influence in Latin America was entirely 'Made in the USA' (Weschler 1998: 119). While recognising that, in the current literature in English on the subject, most authors refer to the *American* influence and only 'to a lesser extent' to the *French* one, many Argentine and French authors argued that the French influence appears to have been much more important in Argentina than the others (Heinz 1995: 67). Indeed, it seems that the doctrine of 'National Security' was nourished by the Americans but, above all, by the French. General Ramón Camps, former chief of police of Buenos Aires province, described these foreign influences in a newspaper interview:

In Argentina, we were influenced first by the French and then by the United States. [...] They organized centers for teaching counterinsurgency techniques [...] and sent out instructors, observers, and an enormous amount of literature.

(La Razón, 4 January 1981, quoted in CONADEP 1985: 442)

Indeed, between 1976 and 1983, anti-communist ideology gave the armed forces of the region a 'messianic mission' to rebuild their societies by eliminating 'subversives' (Feierstein 2010: 44). Thus, the first necessary step would have been to update traditional military planning by developing an operational capacity based on the hypothesis of 'Revolutionary War'. Yet, as Potash explained, 'This concept was not new to the Argentine army. Actually, the idea had been introduced by visiting French officers in 1957 and had been the subject of lectures and discussions in military circles' (1980: 320).

Following their experience in Indochina (1946–1954) and Algeria (1954–1962), the French military adapted the old conceptualisation of Revolutionary War and then theorised on a methodology of counter-revolutionary warfare they applied in their colonial theatres, all of which they transmitted to the Argentine military. Indeed, during the Indochina war, guerrilla warfare[12] proved to be effective in confronting and defeating a stronger and more technically advanced army, that of France. This example was a very significant precedent for the military strategy that would guide the class struggle in Argentina and 'other parts of the world dominated by imperialism' (Aguilera Peralta and Beverly 1980: 91–92). Because of the importance of the guerrilla concept to modern warfare, ruling-class military thinking had given priority to the development of a 'counterguerrilla strategy'. The so-called doctrine of Revolutionary War, for example, consists of a group of strategies and tactics developed in the late 1950s by the French armed forces as a response to guerrilla warfare on a world-wide scale (Aguilera Peralta and Beverly 1980: 92).

According to French experts in counter-insurgency war, in a nuclear age traditional concepts of warfare no longer applied: 'The communists would no longer risk a direct military confrontation with the West. Instead they would attempt to encircle it by slowly capturing control of peripheral nations through *subversion*' (Rock 1993: 196, emphasis as in original). The French experts viewed the subversives as a 'hidden enemy' who would not just be members of left-wing armed organisation (Lopez 1987: 137–148) – who together never numbered more than 1,000[13] – but could be anyone 'with vaguely left-wing views, including labor union militants, students, doctors, lawyers, and social workers running soup kitchens and neighbourhood centers' (Feierstein 2010: 46). One of the key elements in the counter-revolutionary struggle was the obtaining of information – or *renseignement* – enabling one to know the enemy's organisational structure. Consequently, according to the drafters of the doctrine of Revolutionary War, interrogation of the guerrilla force and the civilian population which supports it is the main tool for obtaining information, and recourse should be made to any means to get it, including the torture of those who are merely suspects (Mazzei 2002: 125; Vidal-Naquet 1963: 41). Because the Franco-Argentine conception of the 'hidden enemy' was 'broad and all-inclusive', the response to 'subversion' was generalized and torture became widespread (Carlson 2000: 76). In this manner, 'a new form of war, lateral war, revolutionary war' began and would help shape the future course of the world (Goyret 1980: 132).

Willing to share the *savoir-faire* it gained first in Indochina and later in Algeria, the French military started advising the Argentine army in the ways and means of dealing with internal subversion. Those contacts appeared mainly in the form of (a) training courses at the Paris Higher School of War, the *École Supérieure de Guerre*, and (b) the establishment of a French military mission into its Argentine equivalent, the *Escuela Superior de Guerra* of Buenos Aires Algeria (Abramovici 2001; Carlson 2000: 71; Feierstein 2010: 45; Frontalini and Caiti 1984: 31; MacMaster 2004: 8; Potash 1980: 320; Rouquier 1978: 471–472). These exchanges would allow the French to 'pass their experience from Indochina and Algeria on to Argentine officers' (Oliveira-Cézar 2002: 27). French specialists in torture were able – 'with the authorisation of their superiors in the cabinet ministries and the military general staff' (Alleg 2006a: 101) – to pursue new careers well beyond the borders of Algeria. Ironically, Pontecorvo's famous 1965 movie, *The Battle of Algiers*, which was intended to denounce the excesses of the Algerian War, was shown as part of the training of Argentinian officers at the Naval Higher School of Mechanics – *Escuela Superior de Mecánica de la Armada (ESMA)* – in Buenos Aires, to familiarise them with both the tactics employed by the French in Algeria and their justifications (Robin 2003; MacMaster 2004: 10; Weschler 1998: 121).

For a long time, however, that training 'had no practical relevance for Argentina' (Heinz 1995: 75–76). In fact, the 'New War' described by the French assessors did not exist in Argentina at the beginning of the 1960s: 'It was an anticipated war that the Argentine military would actually fight less than twenty years later' (Carlson 2000: 73). However, even in the 1960s 'Argentina and its people constituted an objective that was too important for international Marxism to overlook' (Ranalletti 2010a: 56). As the Argentine government was looking for an effective way to stop rebellious Peronists, who were supposedly taking part in the communist 'conspiracy' against the established order (Feierstein 2010: 44), the counter-insurgency doctrine managed to find in Argentina a 'fertile ground' early on (Amaral 1998: 183). With its ups and downs, this influence would continue well into the start and organisation of the 1976 dictatorship.

But why do democratic governments such as France become 'torture traders' or 'torture trainers' in authoritarian regimes, despite their claims that they take human rights seriously? Does democracy end at national borders? Facilitation and condemnation are sometimes exercised with astonishing ease by the same government at the same time, in relation to the same country (Green and Ward 2004: 142–143; Tomasevski 1998: 183–184). As Human Rights Watch aptly noted:

> Some of the Governments that are denouncing torture before [the United Nations Commission on Human Rights], including the United States, are at the same time providing extensive international assistance to the authorities which consistently engage in this practice.
>
> (Human Rights Watch, as cited by the Commission on Human Rights 1995: para.1)

According to Kelman, 'There are social conditions under which democratic cultures that ordinarily respect human rights may sanction torture, just as there are social conditions under which ordinary, decent individuals may be induced to take part in it' (2005: 128). The sale of and training for torture technologies may be 'a means by which more powerful states can tie weaker states into violence' (Stanley 2007: 50). Indeed, torture does not happen in a vacuum: 'The social and political context, and the supply of tools and techniques for inflicting pain rely on a failure of political will' (Amnesty International 2001a: 1). According to Galtung, the structures of the world of the 1960s, which took the form of two Western–Eastern blocs, capitalist imperialism and socialist imperialism, were so important to the ruling elites in the centre countries that they would have done almost anything to maintain them (Galtung 1994: 130). Thus, to prevent changes in the geopolitical division of the world at the time, the central elites established their bridgeheads on the periphery and tied them closely to the centre so that they would carry out counter-insurgency in their own interests and in those of the centre (Galtung 1994: 131; Tomasevski 1998: 199). These chains of repression across borders were created, for example, in the Latin American military and in Africa, particularly in the former French colonies. They can be defined as a process by which repression across borders is created through a kind of 'sub-imperialism' (Galtung 1994: 131). As Green and Ward noted, 'To create torturers who will be unrestrained in their delivery of violence against targeted populations is always part of a wider strategy of counter-insurgency and provides a lethal tool in the cultivation of fear and control' (2009b: 170). This raises the question of imperialism and the export of violence through counter-insurgency strategies.

This monograph argues that France's strategy for the transfer of counter-insurgency practices such as the use of torture to Argentina was to maximize its military influence abroad. One of the most important aspects of controlling the world military structure, in turn, is related to the 'research and development establishment' (Eide 1977: 99). In *Torture: The Role of Ideology in the French-Algerian War*, Rita Maran explains that the French use of torture in Algeria was justified through the propaganda of the *mission civilisatrice*, 'civilizing mission' (Maran 1989), which was 'paradoxically [founded] on the Universal Rights of Man of 1789' (MacMaster 2004: 5). France's colonial history was marked by the self-perception and notion of France as transmitter of the 'essence of French civilization, presumed to be the noblest in existence' (Confer 1966: 3). Consequently, French initiatives abroad were justified on the basis of the understanding of its uniquely valuable contribution to the world: French culture (Maran1989: 11). The peculiarly French interlinking of politics and culture led to the development of the 'civilizing mission ideology' (Maran 1989: 12). The main assumption was that France – by virtue of its status as an enlightened civilization – had a duty to disseminate these concepts widely. The ideology of the civilizing mission covered the field, motivating soldiers and generals, providing the government with another patriotic banner to wave, and slowing criticism of the policy on, and practice of, torture. This ideology had 'the flavour of received wisdom; unquestioned, it prevailed so long as the conditions in which it flourished prevailed' (Maran 1989: 12).

Only with the end of colonialism did actions in the name of the civilizing mission dissipate, to be replaced by neo-imperialist and anti-communist ideologies in the discourse of 'development' (Maran 1989: 12). Indeed, just as French trainers professed to believe that losing the war in Algeria would be 'synonymous with the decline of Christian civilization' (Maran 1989: 16), Argentine soldiers believed that if they were defeated in their own country 'world-wide communist domination would result' (Carlson 2000: 74). By sharing their own *savoir-faire* in the art of turning ordinary soldiers into official torturers who would – in turn – make 'subversives' talk,[14] the French appear to have prepared the ground for the institutionalisation of torture that would be implemented in Argentina between 1976 and 1983.

According to Eide, the use of violence against the domestic population – such a prominent feature of the role of military in the Third World – was an outgrowth of counter-insurgency strategies developed in the West in the 1960s: 'A combination of a vast training program for officers from the Third World, and the pushing of weapons sales, was the substance of this policy' (1977: 99). Paraphrasing Lenin, Eide further explained that 'imperialism is the monopoly stage of violence' (1977: 100). The period from the 'great' explorations, through the setting up of trading posts and missionary stations, to the establishment and exploitation of colonies, was characterized by violent European conquest. European conquest of the Third World during the history of colonialism meant the elimination of all independent Third World armed forces. These were replaced by subservient colonial armies, controlled by the colonial metropolis. Their main function was to suppress resistance to the accumulation of wealth through exploitation by colonial powers (Grimal 1985). It is easy to understand the psychological factors underlying the demand for independent armed forces by Third World regimes. Political independence, as a result of the elimination of colonialism, made it possible to break the monopoly of violence.

However, the process of militarisation in the Third World did not lead to autonomy or to independence from the former imperial masters and from any new imperial pretenders. As Eide explained,

> For this to be the case, it would require, first of all, that the armed forces being developed have as their prime function the defence of their country from external attack, primarily from the industrialized countries. But this is clearly not so.
>
> (1977: 100)

The notion that Argentina was developing its forces in order to prepare against external attacks in the early 1960s was ridiculous (Ranaletti 2005). Studies of armed conflicts in the Third World show that most of them were internal, not international (Grimal 1985): they were 'sub-imperial actions of expansion' (Eide 1977: 100). Far from being used to protect their countries from imperial onslaughts, most Third World forces served the same main function as the colonial army of the past: the repression of its own population. It is therefore plausible to use a hypothesis which is the exact contradiction of the 'autonomy' assumption. This would be that the Third World militarisation *intensified* the domination by the industrialized world: 'It is possible that such militarization served to facilitate further penetration of external capital and technology, bringing the international and unequal division of labor to apply even to the remotest corners of the Third World' (Eide 1977: 100).

On the political level, there might have been a façade of autonomy. On the economic level, however, there was an increasing subordination, not necessarily by serving some former colonialist industrialized metropolis, but rather 'by serving the totality of the old international economic order' (Eide 1977: 100–101). While it is true that the personnel who actually carried out torture in the Argentine military were not French, these officers had however been trained or influenced by France in their choice of weapons and strategies, as well as in the selection of targets. They were not tools of any outsiders in the direct sense of the word, but they responded to the domestic contradictions and tensions with means and methods not of their own making.

In the postcolonial era, it remained a major concern that local forces should be equipped, in order to help them defend and expand imperial interests, increasingly important in the context of the Cold War and the bipolar imperial confrontation between the United States and the Soviet Union. The arming of the 'forward defense areas'[15] (the very notion shows the continued impact of imperial thinking) by the United States in the 1950s and the 1960s was aimed at the containment of the Soviet Union and China (Galtung 1994: 131). The militarisation process which was initiated or accelerated by this effort quickly created its own demand. Local military forces wanted further expansion and modernisation: 'What started as geopolitical supplies thus became transformed into an expanding market which could be used – and cynically *was* utilised – for commercial purposes' (Eide 1977: 102).

This illustrates what Herman calls the 'institutional structure of domination built to violate human rights' (1991: 91). Torturers are not born, they are nurtured, trained and supported. In many countries 'they rely on the willingness of foreign governments to provide not only equipment but also personnel training and know-how' (Amnesty International 2001a: 41). It follows that the use of torture as part of human rights dialogue has to be discussed in its international structural context, and not merely as an issue regarding the infraction of human rights in the country where it is employed.

Complicity and responsibility

María, an Argentine law student at the time, was abducted from outside the University of Buenos Aires on 4 November 1976. She 'disappeared' for three months. During that time, she was repeatedly tortured by Argentine officers. During the interview, she stated:

> I was abducted from the back yard of the School of Law in Buenos Aires by members of the Argentine military. They took me to a clandestine

centre where I was tortured repeatedly. My back and chest were burned with cigarettes. I had electric shocks applied to my feet and hands for so long they had to change the batteries. [...] I was lowered into an open pit packed with human bodies – some dead, some alive – and all swarming with rats. [...] My torturers professed that they were concerned about the people of Argentina and consequently were working to liberate them from communism. [...] At that time I thought I would never survive. I was in the hands of professionals. They did everything as part of a routine. One day, after hours of torture, I was returned to 'my' room. There, I saw a man of lighter complexion. My torturers referred to him as their 'mentor'. That man cursed in unmistakable French and told them that they now had to stop torturing me because my disappearance had become public. [...] I asked him what would happen to the other people I saw tortured. At this point, he told me in his broken Spanish not to concern myself with them [...].

(María, Interview #7 – see Appendix 3)

I did not manage to fully confirm that French mentor's identity. However, data obtained in this research confirmed that French military advisers had aided Argentine military forces by reinforcing their national intelligence apparatus and training the officer corps in brutal counter-insurgency techniques as early as the late the 1950s, key factors which had a significant bearing on human rights violations during the Dirty War. This testimony illustrates that responsibility for and complicity in the torture of María spreads much further than her individual torturers. It includes all those who supported them inside and outside Argentina: all the individuals and the governments that supplied them with ad hoc *savoir-faire* and trained them.

Complicity in torture conducted by other states or their agents is recognised to be unlawful under general international law principles of State Responsibility for internationally wrongful acts, as it is recognised to be an internationally wrongful act under the Universal Declaration on Human Rights, the International Covenant on Civil and Political Rights, regional human rights treaties such as the European Convention on Human Rights, the UN Convention Against Torture and Other Cruel, Inhuman or Degrading Treatment or Punishment, and as part of customary international law (House of Lords *et al.* 2009: 13). The prohibition against torture is recognised as what international lawyers call a 'peremptory norm of general international law', that is, one which is 'accepted and recognised by the international community of states as a whole as a norm from which no derogation is permitted and which can be modified only by a subsequent norm of general international law having the same character'.[16] With regard to responsibilities, Article 2.3 of the UN Convention Against Torture and Other Cruel, Inhuman or Degrading Treatment or Punishment specifically stipulates that: 'An order from a superior officer or a public authority may not be invoked as a justification of torture'. On the other hand, the International Law Commission's Draft Articles on State Responsibility (2001) make quite clear that the acts of empowered individuals can be directly attributable to the state that empowered them. Furthermore, the principles of international law, as formulated by the International Law Commission (1957: 374–378), dictate that complicity in the commission of a crime against peace, a war crime, or a crime against humanity is a crime under international law.

The general principles of state responsibility in international law are now conveniently set out in the International Law Commission's Articles on the Responsibility of States for Internationally Wrongful Acts, which were approved by the UN's General Assembly on 12 December 2001.[17] They recognised that internationally wrongful conduct often results from the collaboration of more than one state, rather than one state acting alone. Article 16 deals with the situation where one state provides aid or assistance to another with a view to facilitating the commission of an internationally wrongful act by the latter. It states:

> A state which aids or assists another state in the commission of an internationally wrongful act by the latter is internationally responsible for doing so if: (a) that state does so with knowledge of the circumstances of the internationally wrongful act; and (b) the act would be internationally wrongful if committed by that state.
>
> (Article 16 of the International Law Commission's Articles on the Responsibility of States for Internationally Wrongful Acts)

In international law, particular consequences also flow from 'serious breaches' of obligations under peremptory norms of international law.[18] A breach of such an obligation is 'serious' if it involves 'a gross or systematic failure by the responsible state to recognise the obligation'.[19] States are under a positive obligation to co-operate to bring such serious breaches to an end,[20] and are required not to recognise as lawful a situation created by such serious breaches, nor to render aid or assistance in maintaining that situation.[21] However, these positive obligations with regard to torture, not to acquiesce in it or to validate its results, are not fully appreciated by states, which often give the impression that they are only under a negative obligation not to torture (House of Lords et al. 2009: 14–15).

There is thus 'no room for doubt' that complicity in torture, if proven, would be a direct breach of France's international human rights obligations, under the UN Convention Against Torture and Other Cruel, Inhuman or Degrading Treatment or Punishment, under customary international law, and according to the general principles of State Responsibility for internationally wrongful acts (House of Lords et al. 2009: 15). For the purposes of state responsibility for complicity in torture, it has been established that 'complicity' means simply 'one state giving assistance to another state in the commission of torture, or acquiescing in such torture, in the knowledge, including constructive knowledge, of the circumstances of the torture which is or has been taking place' (House of Lords *et al.* 2009: 16).

It is not alleged that the French government or its agents themselves engaged in torture, or directly authorized torture. The essence of the allegations is that France has been complicit in the use of torture by the Argentine military. Indeed, this monograph alleges that training in counter-insurgency strategies that heavily rely on anti-communist ideology that, in turn, justifies the use of torture amounts to complicity in torture by the various French military agents concerned, which is in direct breach of France's human rights obligations. Both recipient and donor states often go to great lengths to conceal the transfer of expertise which is used to facilitate serious human rights violations (Amnesty International 2001a: 41–42). While it can be fully accepted that intelligence cooperation is both necessary and legitimate in countering terrorism, there must, however, be mechanisms for ensuring accountability for such cooperation (House of Lords *et al.* 2009: 23). It is undoubtedly true that the inadequate international control of transfer of French counter-insurgency expertise to Argentine military and security forces contributed to gross human rights violations in that country (Amnesty International 2001a: 40).

However, the question of whether states can be criminally responsible continues to be highly controversial, for example with regard to the enactment of penal sanctions for states (Jorgensen 2000; Brownlie 1963). Unless there is evidence to demonstrate that a government has exercised 'effective control' over absolutely prohibited conduct – such as torture – in another jurisdiction, governmental responsibility cannot be extended beyond national borders (The International Court of Justice 1986: para.115). This legal gap has significant implications when we consider states that export torture instruments and expertise in pursuit of an important foreign policy objective. In this setting, 'the legal responsibility of a country involved in the manufacture and/or export of torture devices and technologies ends at the border of the importing state' (Green and Ward 2004: 145), and governments are able to 'alternate between facilitation of torture abroad and condemnation of governments on whose territory torture takes place' (Tomasevski 1998: 183), and to 'operate beyond public scrutiny and thus accountability' (Tombs and Whyte 2003a: 4). In line with Cameron's (2009) research, however, this book argues that state responsibility and complicity can better be studied through criminology, rather than international law, and through a literal use of the concept of state crime, as applied to the use of state power for deviant purposes in ways that unambiguously violate human rights. It contends that criminology offers a varied and useful set of perspectives on the study of the 'transnational institutional torturer'.

Conclusion

The literature suggests that anyone could become an official torturer, given certain conditions. It does not mean that those who have tortured should be absolved by the notion that anyone in the same situation would have done the same. Rather, it means that it is essential to 'collectively strive to first expose these socio-political conditions wherever they appear and then to join others in denouncing and challenging them' (Huggins *et al.* 2002: 267). Systematic torture appears to be impossible to sustain without a network of officials working towards a common aim (Herman 1982). For this reason, Rejali argues that 'there is no such thing as "THE torturer" [...] to speak of the torturer abstracts the fact that the torturers are all situated in an institution known as the State' (1994: 9). It is clear thus far that the human rights tradition should not only condemn the torturing state, but also the structures enabling torture, thereby promoting a greater human right 'to live in a social and world structure that does not produce torture' (Galtung 1994: 134).

Torture is an individualised form of violence that tends to be 'embedded in entrenched structural violence' (Farmer 2003: 219). Since it presupposes the deterioration of a whole set of social relations within a given situation, 'a holistic approach to the phenomenon, rather than considering torturers to be acting in an aberrant manner within an otherwise healthy society' needs to be taken (Sottas 1998: 73). Therefore, an adequate explanation of torture perpetration requires looking beyond the level of the torture chamber, or even of the states in which the torture is practised, and also focusing attention on *transnational perpetrators*. There are important ethical–normative reasons for retaining the term 'torture' in describing some acts of the state. Accordingly, labelling certain states as '(transnational) institutional torturers' – a term with powerful connotations – could be a relevant means of advancing a progressive political project aimed at protecting marginalized and vulnerable populations from indiscriminate and oppressive forms of 'national', but also 'transnational', state violence.

The aim of this monograph is to explore France's role in the Argentine Dirty War. This is not to argue that torture would not have been effective without 'French training', but it appears to have been enhanced by it (Heinz 1995: 67; Carlson 2000: 82). After all, 'Torture is neither civilian nor military, nor is it specifically French [or Argentine]: it is a plague infecting our whole era' (Sartre 2006: xxxvi). However, torture does not occur without ideological or logistical preparation and, from 1957 onwards, it seems that France performed an integral role in the architecture of the Argentine Dirty War.

The point is to write '*against* rather than simply *about*' human rights violations (Sim 2003: 247). If French complicity is demonstrated, France should come to accept that 'it is always useful for those who retain a belief in peace, and a hope for a better future, not to forget the lessons of the past' (Alleg 2006a: 102). 'Not to look, not to touch, not to record, can be the hostile act, the act of indifference and of turning away' (Scheper-Hughes 1992: 28). As Sartre put it, 'I have always detested those books that involve us in a cause mercilessly and yet offer no hope or solution' (2006: xxxi). Thus, I shall endeavour first to present a sufficient body of evidence in order to expose the extent to which the *savoir-faire* shared by the French and the Argentines shaped the perception of the soldier, the enemy and the legal system, influencing the very specific application of torture in the Argentine Dirty War; and second to inspire condemnation of its actions by labelling it as a 'transnational institutional torturer', through criminological analysis.

Notes

1 It has to be noted that there exist criticisms of the Milgram and Stanford Prison experiments: on the former see Orne and Holland (1968), Shanab and Yahya (1978), Smith and Bond (1998) and Perry (2012); on the latter see Banuazizi and Movahedi (1975) and Prescott (2005); as well as the references to source papers contained therein.
2 See Milgram (1963, 1974) but also Browning (1998: 171–173), Green and Ward (2004: 140, 178), Huggins *et al.* (2002: 252–254), and Lankford (2009: 390).
3 See Haney *et al.* (1973) but also Browning (1998: 167–168), Green and Ward (2004: 140, 180), Huggins *et al.* (2002: 261–263), Lankford (2009: 390), and Zimbardo (2007).
4 The film is a vivid re-enactment of the French army's method of brutally crushing the insurgency in Algiers in 1957, and shows the place of torture in its strategy (Ray 2006: ix).
5 Lawrence Weschler has explained that, during the Uruguayan repression in 1985, a significant number of medical personnel were involved in torture (1998: 127). Had they refused to participate in these activities, they would have suffered the consequences (Stanley 2008: 162–163). As Scarry highlights, the doctors who refused to cooperate with the regime 'disappeared at such a rate that [...] medical and health care programs entered a state of crisis' (1985: 42).
6 As we will see later, *La Cité Catholique* also played a significant role in spreading justifications of anti-subversive doctrine abroad through the creation of an Argentine branch and in arranging refuge for rebellious officers and members of the *OAS* after 1961 (Lazreg 2008: 206; Robin 2004: 158–164).
7 Reserve Police Battalion 101 was a unit of the German Order Police that played a central role in the implementation of the 'Final Solution' against Jewish people and the repression of the Polish population during the Nazi occupation of Poland.
8 According to Arendt (1965), the Nazi torturers were normal people who, either under pressure from superiors, or from twisted values and twisted thinking, had reached the conclusion that torturing and killing innocent human beings was the right and normal thing to do. It had become a banality: the banality of evil.
9 It has to be noted that these conditions were met in other dictatorships of the Southern Cone of South America as well in the 1970s (Corradi *et al.* 1992: 1). As one civilian government after another fell to the military, political refugees flowed across borders, in some cases seeking safe haven to organise revolutionary movements against the military. This situation led to a system of international cooperation among the dictatorships, known as Plan Condor – an intelligence organisation in which multinational teams tracked down dissidents outside their home countries, captured and interrogated them, and in many cases delivered

them back to the disappearance apparatus of the military governments they had fled (see McSherry 2005 and Robin 2004).

10 Adamson defines civil society as: 'the public space between large-scale bureaucratic structures of state and economy, on the one hand, and the private sphere of family, friendship, personality and intimacy, on the other' (1987/1988: 320). Drawing from works by Diamond (1996) and Roberts (1998), Brysk suggests that civil society comprises 'human activity outside the market and the state' (2000: 153). Thus, civil society appears to be made up of a range of independent associations capable of articulating norms against which the legitimacy of state actions can be judged (Green and Ward 2004: 187).

11 For detailed accounts of the history of civil society see, for example, Seligman (1992); Keane (1998); Cohen (1999); Ehrenberg (1999); Chambers (2002); Chambers and Kymlicka (2002); Foley and Hodgkinson (2002); Hall and Trentmann (2005); and Alexander (2006).

12 Guerrilla, the diminutive of guerra, meaning 'little war' is actually an ancient military strategy used, for example, by the Carthaginians against the Romans and consolidated in modern times by the victory of Spanish irregular bands against the Napoleonic army in the early nineteenth century. The basic characteristics of a guerrilla war, which distinguish it from and permit it to confront effectively a regular army, are the following: the operation of small and highly mobile groups of armed persons; strategical reliance on the active and passive support of the civilian population; the waging of a war of attrition which over time inverts the relation of inferiority/superiority so that in its final stages the guerrilla force is able to transform itself into a regular army capable of defeating in open confrontation the weakened forces of the enemy (Aguilera Peralta and Beverly 1980: 92).

13 According to Graziano, 80 per cent of Argentinian torture victims had no knowledge of subversive activities (1992: 37–38).

14 See BBC documentary 'We Have Ways of Making You Talk', broadcast on Tuesday, 5 April 2005 at 2100 BST on *BBC Two*.

15 None of the 'forward defense areas' ever used the weapons for what they had been intended: defence against attack by Soviet Union and China. All the areas made use of their military training, directly or indirectly, for internal control (Eide 1977: 102).

16 Vienna Convention on the Law of Treaties 1969, Article 53.

17 The Articles on State Responsibility are annexed to United Nations Resolution 56/83 adopted by the General Assembly on 12 December 2001. The Articles are recognised as an authoritative statement of the principles of State responsibility in international law (House of Lords *et al.* 2009: 14).

18 Articles on State Responsibility, Articles 40 and 41.

19 Articles on State Responsibility, Article 40(2).

20 Articles on State Responsibility, Article 41(1).

21 Articles on State Responsibility, Article 41(2).

Chapter 3

France's military relationship with Argentina

The transfer of an ideology that justifies torture

Despite the wealth of historical evidence of the occurrence of torture, among other state crimes, in Argentina during the Dirty War, there have been only limited scholarly efforts to investigate the role of France in such atrocities. This chapter explores ongoing debates in relation to France's complicity in the making of Argentine torturers. In order to address this transnational complicity, this chapter affords an analysis of primary data from my own fieldwork in Argentina and France supported by secondary data drawn from authors such as Périès (1999), Ranaletti (2005), Robin (2003), Trinquier (1964), and Vidal-Naquet (1963).[1] These thereby furnish the reader with a detailed study of France's military relationship to Argentina, with a particular focus on the period from 1957 to 1962.

It is now established that, on the basis of its National Security policy, the United States worked tirelessly on the development and counter-insurgency training of Latin American military personnel to give them the necessary skills for fighting the 'Third World War', which was allegedly taking place between West and East (Blakeley 2006; McClintock 1992). The struggle between Christian and atheist civilisations, between individualism and collectivism, between capitalism and communism – whose respective leaders were the United States and the Soviet Union – kept the mentors of the doctrine of National Security in a permanent state of alert. As such, prior to the start of the Argentine Dirty War in 1976, several thousand Argentinian officers had been trained in the military bases of the United States on its own territory or in the Panama Canal Zone, or they had listened closely to the recommendations of advisers who had come as part of the US military mission to Argentina (Oliveira-Cézar 2003: 70).

Equally undeniable – as I shall demonstrate in this chapter – but much less well known is the role played by the French military in training their Argentine peers in so-called Revolutionary War theory. As well as the Argentine literature that has suggested that: 'Argentina imported from France the theory and practice of the anti-subversive war well before the Americans finalized it' (Llumá 2002a: 6), documents recently declassified by the French government, the French Ministry of Foreign Affairs and the French army confirm that the theory surrounding 'Modern Warfare' came from the hands of French military assessors (see Appendix 1). As a result of their experience in Indochina and Algeria, French counter-insurgency experts had reconceptualised their understanding of Revolutionary War and developed a methodology of counter-revolutionary warfare that they applied in their colonial theatres, all of which they then transmitted to the Argentine military (see Appendix 2). As this chapter and the following shall demonstrate, the transfer of French expertise started in 1957, remained important throughout the 1960s and found a new significance in the middle of the 1970s.

One of the main theatres for these French praetorians was the *École Supérieure de Guerre* (Higher School of War) in Paris. This was where the Argentinian officers who were soon to occupy senior positions in the de facto governments were trained, as well as in the *Escuela Superior de Guerra*, its Argentine equivalent. Officers from the French military mission had a significant impact in the *Escuela Superior de Guerra* by means of courses, lectures, theoretical writings and specific case analyses of the struggle against subversion. From 1963, this institutional relationship between the two armies would have grafted onto the informal influence of a group of French military or paramilitary senior ranks who had been members of the bloodthirsty *Organisation Armée Secrète (OAS)*, a secret French armed organisation formed of men who had fled justice in their home country and settled in Argentina with the blessing of Argentine senior military commanders.

In the first part of this chapter, I shall explain the genesis of the French doctrine of Revolutionary War by describing the particular situation of the French army after the Second World War and the lessons it subsequently learned from its significant defeats in Indochina (1946–1954) and Algeria (1954–1962). In doing so, I shall develop the concepts of Revolutionary War, which will enable me to then discuss the role of civil population in this specific type of warfare with the redefinition of enemy, the development of the 'intelligence' gathering and, finally, the arguments that brought the French first and then the Argentinians to justify the practice of torture.

The second section of this chapter will reconstruct the significance of the emigration that was a consequence of the end of the Algerian War in 1962. Here I shall highlight the plan to bring in Algerian settlers and terrorists from the *OAS* and the Argentine settlement context, characterised by a furious anti-communism and magnified Catholicism. The arrival of French nationals in Argentina, on top of a Franco-Argentinian rapprochement at the institutional level, may be insignificant in terms of the numbers of people involved but it is important for its contribution to the corpus of ideas that were to form and sustain state terrorism under the last military dictatorship (1976–1983).[2]

In the third part, I shall assess the changes undergone by the Argentine army after the overthrow of General Perón in September 1955. These changes meant the incorporation of the French doctrine of revolutionary war, whose internalisation of principles and practices would have dramatic consequences for Argentine society during the late 1970s and early 1980s. I shall attempt to reveal the doctrinal and methodological influence of the French advisers on the Argentine army, not only from the experience of Argentine personnel who took courses in Paris (France being the favourite destination of those officers who were trained abroad at this time) but also from the actions of a French military mission in Buenos Aires at the *Escuela Superior de Guerra* from 1957 to 1962.

The genesis of the doctrine of Revolutionary War

> La théorie de la guerre révolutionnaire est évidemment séduisante pour notre armée. Elle offre á la fois une excuse, une justification et surtout un adversaire á la hauteur de son amour-propre.
>
> (Prevost 1960: 78)

During the first of these decolonisation wars (Indochina 1946–1954), the French army had to fight a different breed of enemy: the Viet Minh guerrillas who, led by Ho Chi Minh, had the support of Mao Tse-Tung's China and the Soviet Union. During this war, torture was employed, unsystematically perhaps, but very widely nevertheless (Grimal 1985: 121). A journalist who visited Indochina at that time gave the following account of a meeting with a French officer in his quarters. The latter explained:

> Here is my desk, [...] my table, my typewriter, my washbasin, and over there, in the corner my machine for making people talk. [...] The dynamo, I mean. Very handy for interrogating prisoners! You attach the positive pole and the negative pole, turn the handle, and the prisoner squeals.
>
> (French officer in Indochina, as quoted in Vidal-Naquet 1963: 24)

However, these practices did not constitute a national problem, as the Indochina war itself was extremely unpopular in France (Llumá 2002a: 12–13). Therefore, the French judicial system had no need to cover the practice of torture that took place in Indochina with the mantle of its authority. After seven years, in May 1954, the war ended with the surrender of the French garrison at Dien Bien Phu and the humiliating French acceptance of the Geneva Accords, which divided the territory of Vietnam into two sectors separated by the 18°N parallel. This was to be a very hard lesson that the French set out to analyse in depth to ensure it did not happen to them again. They understood that there was nothing conventional about the type of warfare practised in Indochina, at least in its early phases. It was a guerrilla war with swift strikes or fast offensive incursions into enemy or neutral territory; these tactics were undertaken either by well-trained commandos or assault groups, or by civilians with little military training but armed with an unshakeable faith in what they were doing as militias. As Oliveira-Cézar states, 'It was precisely this mass participation by civilians that was new' (Oliveira-Cézar 2003: 71). French Colonel Roger Trinquier explained it further:

> Since the liberation of France in 1945 [...] the French army has not been able to halt the collapse of our Empire. And yet, the effort the country has made for the army is unprecedented. No French military man ought to rest until we have created an army at least capable of assuring the defence of our national territory. We still persist in studying a type of warfare that no longer exists and we shall never fight again, while we pay only passing attention to the war we lost in Indochina [...]. Since the end of the Second World War, a new form of warfare has been born. Called at times either *subversive warfare* or *revolutionary warfare*, it differs fundamentally from the wars of the past in that victory is not expected from the clash of two armies on a field of battle. [...] Warfare is now an interlocking system of actions – political, economic, psychological, military – that aims at the *overthrow of the established authority in a country and its replacement by another regime*. To achieve this end, the aggressor tries to exploit the internal tensions of the country attacked – ideological, social, religious, economic – any conflict liable to have a profound influence in the population to be conquered.
>
> (Trinquier 1964: 3–5, emphases as in original)

Consequently, French officers began to study the texts that nourished their adversaries: Marx, Engels, Lenin, Lawrence of Arabia and, most significantly, the one that summarised and surpassed them all: *Problems of Strategy in China's Revolutionary War*, written in 1936 by Mao Tse-Tung for the instruction of his officers in the Red Army. According to the latter, a guerrilla organisation must permeate the population 'like fish in water' (Vidal-Naquet 1963: 42). To understand this theory in practice they drew on the painful but enriching experiences of many French military personnel in the prisoner-of-war camps of Indochina. Here, prisoners had been able to observe in their guards' behaviour the terrifying effectiveness of profound convictions, or brainwashing, which was achieved after years of the application of intelligent psychological action (Oliveira-Cézar 2003: 71).

On 10 November, less than six months after the fall of Dien Bien Phu and while France's defeated army was returning home, a nationalist rebellion broke out in Algeria. It was led by the *Front de Libération Nationale (FLN)* – National Liberation Front – a guerrilla movement that played the leading role in the war against French domination. The situation in the North African 'province' had not been favourable to the colonisers since 1945: in addition to financial problems, tensions were germinating between the two ethnic groups that made up its population. On one side were the *Pieds-Noirs* – that is, nearly one million French nationals born on Algerian soil – and, on the other, the Muslim community. In 1947, a special constitutional clause was voted in the French parliament, which set an electoral 'trap' to guarantee a greater number of European than Muslim representatives in the local parliament. From this arose several *nationalist* currents, one of them, led by Ben Bella, advocating a revolutionary path and direct action. Ben Bella became gradually more radicalised until he founded the *FLN* the following decade. Algerian nationalism was subjected to fierce repression in which members of the *Pieds-Noirs* civilian population took part at times, further exacerbating the ethnic nature of the conflict. With international decolonisation processes under way in other latitudes, tensions also took on an ideological perspective (Grimal 1985: 146).

This conflict was another example of the process of disintegration of the French colonial empire; it committed the unstable French Fourth Republic to a new, long war, this time waged in a vast territory close to mainland France. In 1956, socialist politician Guy Mollet assumed the Presidency, prioritising military victory over the *FLN* in his programme of government. His Minister of the Interior, François Mitterrand, was to play an important role during these years. The revolt, marked by nationalism and with an important religious element, spread from the interior of Algeria to the main cities – Algiers, Oran and Constantine – while Paris committed a force which, at one time, reached 500,000 men (Llumá 2002a: 12–13).

Both military superiority and brutal police repression failed to quell the rebellion, which extended over the entire territory of Algeria at the same time as terrorist violence increased. Facing a desperate paralysis of regular courses of action, Robert Lacoste – French colonial minister – decided temporarily to give the military extraordinary police powers. On 7 January 1957, prefect Serge Baret entrusted General Jacques Massu, Commander of the 10th Parachute Division, with the responsibility of enforcing law and order in Algiers.

> In the territory of the department of Algiers, the law and order responsibilities are transferred [...] to the military authority which will exercise, under the high control of the prefect of Algiers, the police powers which are normally within the hands of the civilian authorities.
>
> (Delmas 2007: 61–62)

The decree not only included the regulation of meetings and movements, but also the right to carry out night searches and to place every 'potentially dangerous person' under house arrest. Most of these measures were backed by a series of laws progressively voted by the National Assembly, especially the State of Emergency Act of 3 April 1955 and the Special Powers Act of 16 March 1956 (Delmas 2007: 30). As a result, 'the responsibility for liquidating terrorism in the city, and breaking the general strike called for by the *FLN*, fell not to any civil authority but to General Massu' (Vidal-Naquet 1963: 50).[3]

The *FLN* used the same techniques, followed the same gradual development and based themselves on the same tactical principles as Viet Minh guerrillas had successfully utilised (Oliveira-Cézar 2003: 71). This was more than enough for the French military to believe at that time, and for a long time after Algerian independence in 1962, that communism had opened in Algeria a new front in its quest for world domination. Or at least the threat of communism was used as a pretext to just a 'colonial' war. This was exactly the same mistake as the Argentine military made at the start of the 1960s when they interpreted the insurrectional acts of the Peronist resistance as covert manifestations of international communism (Feierstein 2010: 44; Oliveira-Cézar 2002: 27; Ranalletti 2010a: 56).[4] As French Lieutenant-Colonel Roger Trinquier revealed at the time:

> Our army in Algeria is in excess of 300,000 men supplied with the most modern equipment; its adversary numbers some 30,000, in general poorly equipped with only light weapons. If we were to have an opportunity to meet this enemy on the traditional field of battle, a dream vainly pursued for years by many military commanders, victory would be assured in a matter of hours. [...] however, victory is still uncertain. The problem is more complex.
>
> (Trinquier 1964: 7)

Fresh from the disastrous experience in Indochina and armed with the lessons learned from it, the French army went on the 'offensive' in Algiers less than a week after General Massu had received his orders (Keenan 2003: 2001). Backed up by the new police powers and the extended freedom to act, as given by the civilian authority, the 10th Parachute Division – members of which were called the 'parachute regiments' or paras – implemented several radical methods. Indeed, from then on, the actions of these paratroopers, many of whom were veterans of the war in Indochina, became notorious on account of their particularly repressive techniques: 'The civil power abdicated and its place was taken by a military authority, one of whose weapons was torture' (Vidal-Naquet 1963: 47).

General Massu and the other paras of the 10th Parachute Division 'waded' into the situation with a cold ferocity that made headlines throughout the world. Their first action consisted of organising a *quadrillage*, or grid pattern, system to conduct surface warfare in Algiers. To do so, the city was divided into four districts and each of them became the area of operations of a dedicated regiment: more than 200 sensitive points were thus constantly monitored, 180 patrols moved daily throughout the city, and 30 patrols each night were in the streets while many permanent as well as hasty built barricades deeply impeded the *FLN*'s movements (López Aufranc 1959). Trinquier pushed the *quadrillage* system further by developing a community policing system called the *Dispositif de Protection Urbaine (DPU)*, the Urban Protection System: every 18-man-police-station jurisdiction was divided into blocks or *îlots*, themselves subdivided into groups of houses; every *îlot* was characterised by a letter and every group by a number; and local leaders, generally French army veterans, had to give every inhabitant a special ID, the purpose of which was to link individual to a precise residency location (Trinquier 1964: 37–42).

Trinquier had begun to study in depth the principles of 'Modern Warfare', as he called the techniques of the revolutionary war in Indochina, but the years of combat in Algeria added a political dimension to his understanding that had previously been lacking. Realising that a pro-*FLN* population was the enemy's centre of gravity, he tried to disconnect the Casbah inhabitants from the insurgents, slowing down the movement of the 'fish in the water' by facilitating denunciations and replacing *FLN* propaganda with pro-French endeavours. Indeed, Trinquier also paid special attention in his writing to the ideas of Mao Tse-Tung, the 'master of the theory and practice of revolutionary war' (AMA/Mom 1959: 491).[5] As both the French military advisers and their Argentine disciples would later do, he highlighted one of Mao's maxims – that population support is 'as essential to subversion as water is to fishes' (Trinquier 1964: 6). On this basis the entire theory of revolutionary war would be developed (AMA/Badie 1957: 548; AMA/de Naurois 1958a: 116; AMA/Grand d'Esnon 1960: 343). In military terms, the *people* became the *terrain* or *battlefield*, and the frontiers that separated adversaries were no longer *geographical*, but *ideological* (AMA/Mom 1959: 505):

> In modern warfare, the enemy is far more difficult to identify. No physical frontier separates the two camps. The line of demarcation between friend and foe passes through the very heart of the nation, through the same village, and sometimes divides the same family. It is a non-physical, often ideological boundary, which must however be expressly delineated if we want to reach the adversary and defeat him.
>
> (Trinquier 1964: 24)

As a result, the French military – new-found experts on subversive warfare – interpreted the people not as the end but as the means, and their conquest was an indispensable phase in any revolutionary war: 'The stake in such a war [...] is the conquest of the minds of the population' (Vidal-Naquet 1963: 40). Indeed, if the objective of a traditional war was the conquest of enemy territory, and in revolutionary war the territory was the people themselves, it follows tha the battlefield was now the *minds* and *men's spirits* (AMA/Sánchez de Bustamante 1960: 602–603). Therefore, the conquest or neutralisation of the civilian population became a priority objective for the theoreticians of counter-revolutionary war. There was also a concomitant increase in the importance attached to 'psychological action' techniques, which became a key arm in this type of war, on a par with armour or artillery in classic war (AMA/Badie 1958d; Mazzei 2002: 129–130). As a result, the French created a department exclusively dedicated to psychological operations in Algeria, *le 5ème Bureau* – the 5th Command.

Since, according to this interpretation, the 'enemy' hides within and blends into the population with its support, an essential consequence of a revolutionary war is that any difference between combatants and civilians disappears: the entire population falls under suspicion and everybody becomes a potential enemy. This prefigures the concept of the 'enemy within', which is then extended to all opposition activity: any uprising, disturbance, protest, demand or social anxiety was founded, according to this yardstick, in Marxist infiltration. It is the generalisation and abuse of the idea that the enemy may be hidden among the population that divides the whole of society in a Manichean way, transforming any opponent, no longer into a potential ally of communism, but into a 'subversive'. As Lt-Colonel Trinquier explained it:

> [...] an army can throw itself into a campaign only when it has the moral support of the nation [...]. The army, whose responsibility it is to do battle, must receive the unreserved, affectionate, and devoted support of the nation. Any propaganda tending to undermine its morale, causing it to doubt the necessity of its sacrifices, should be unmercifully repressed. The army will then know where to strike. Any individual who, in any fashion whatsoever, favors the objectives of the enemy will be considered a traitor and treated as such.
>
> (Trinquier 1964: 24)

Consequently, in the counter-revolutionary struggle, the key problem is that of obtaining information – or *renseignement* – enabling one to know the enemy's organisational structure. According to the drafters of the revolutionary war doctrine, interrogation is the main tool for obtaining information, and recourse should be made to any means in order to get it, including the torture of those who are merely suspects (Mazzei 2002: 125; Vidal-Naquet 1963: 41). In Algeria, the insurrection was clearly developing into an Intelligence War – in the military sense of the term – for it was being waged against a closely regimented population and, in such a situation, torture by the French military and troops was accepted as an absolutely normal daily practice (García 1995: 43). Trinquier provided a Cartesian rationale for the use of torture during interrogation in revolutionary war, since it was presented as the particular bane of the terrorist, just as anti-aircraft artillery is that of the airman or machine-gun fire that of the foot soldier:[6]

> No lawyer is present for such an interrogation. If the prisoner gives the information requested, the examination is quickly terminated; if not,

specialists must force his secret from him. Then, as a soldier, he must face the suffering, and perhaps the death, he has heretofore managed to avoid. The terrorist must accept this as a condition inherent in his trade and in the methods of warfare that, with full knowledge, his superior and he himself have chosen.

(Trinquier 1964: 19)

Nevertheless, their leaders did not always use the 'T' word, turning instead to euphemisms:

If one reads what some of these men have written to justify themselves, what is particularly surprising is their attempt to justify the use of torture without having the courage to use the actual word. Even General Massu [...] never actually speaks of torture or of using water or electricity. He speaks of *clandestine and counter-revolutionary methods* and yet he is one of the most outspoken of the Generals.

(Vidal-Naquet 1963: 57–58)

Indeed, in a directive dated 16 February 1957, General Jacques Massu called for 'increased policing effort.' His subordinate in command of the Blida Atlas, General Jacques Pâris de la Bolladière, drafted a directive dated 18 February to implement this policy. In this directive he 'interpreted' General Massu's circular as follows:

We must not be tempted, like some totalitarian countries, to regard certain methods of obtaining information as normal procedure; these procedures are explicitly forbidden and must be formally condemned.
(General Jacques Pâris de la Bolladière, as quoted Vidal-Naquet 1963: 56)

But General Massu took exception to this 'interpretation' and General Pâris de la Bolladière came into conflict with his superior officer for refusing to implement orders on the 'accentuation of police effort'. Shortly after being relieved of his command, Pâris de la Bolladière warned of:

[...] the great danger it would be for us, under the false pretext of immediate efficacy, to lose sight of the moral values that have formed the greatness of our civilisation and our army.
(General Jacques Pâris de la Bolladière, as quoted in Droz and Lever 1982: 140)

Other officials did not share the same scruples. Defenders of torture techniques based their arguments on the fearsome and unverifiable principle of immediate efficacy, according to which the suffering of those tortured could prevent attacks and save the lives of thousands of innocents (Droz and Lever

1982: 141–144). In this regard, Father Delarue, the military chaplain of the 10th Parachute Division, set at rest any religious scruples the officers might have had in Algeria by drafting a note, with the help of Colonel Trinquier, in which torture was compared to the slap which a father gives a disobedient child or to a painful but necessary surgical operation. In another note, he stated:

> Faced with a choice between two evils, either to cause temporary suffer-ing to a bandit taken in the act who in any case deserves to die, or to leave numbers of innocent people to be massacred by this criminal's gang, when it could be destroyed as a result of his information, there can be no hesitation in choosing the lesser of the two evils, in an effective but not a sadistic interrogation.
>
> (Father Delarue, as quoted in Vidal-Naquet 1963: 50–51)

It was along this line of thought that Trinquier justified the use of torture, as illustrated in the following example:

> One day, at midday, one of your patrols arrests a bomb carrier. He only has one bomb […]. It is set to explode at 18:30. He has placed one, two or three …, and you know that a bomb causes a dozen deaths and thirty wounded. The terrorist is in front of you. What do you do? [He has] planted bombs on the orders of his leaders, so the people of Algiers would suffer and die, so they would be afraid and submit to the will of the FLN. He is not going to talk. Only physical suffering and the fear of death will make him speak. [Should you] cause suffering to a terrorist who is perfectly aware of the risks he is taking by placing bombs, or let the innocent die. It is not as simple a question as you think.
>
> (Trinquier 1980: 174–175)

The 'ticking bomb' scenario argument opened Pandora's Box. It turned into a morally comfortable means of justifying various forms of excess. What was initially identified by the average French soldier freshly arrived in Algeria as an isolated act of cruelty – perhaps as something just about morally concei-vable for the greater purpose of protecting his relatives from certain death – turned rapidly into the banal routine of everyday horror. Initial justifications of the exception ended up justifying the everyday. Those who overcame their scruples ultimately found themselves unable to escape from the process they subscribed to. In the context of French disgust at the FLN's campaign of vio-lence, and of the determination not to lose Algeria, the dehumanisation of the enemy led to an irretrievable process of trivialisation of horror. There was also an attempt to legalise the use of torture, known as the Wuillaume Report, dated 2 March 1955. After demonstrating that torture had become so prevalent in Algeria and had provided effective results in neutralising the terrorists, Roger Wuillaume, the Civil Inspector-General in Algiers, argued for the legalisation of torture and recommended some techniques:

> The water and electricity methods, provided they are used carefully, are said to produce a shock which is more psychological than physical and therefore do not constitute excessive cruelty. According to the 'experts' the correct way of employing the water-pipe method is to introduce water into the mouth up to the point of near-suffocation but not to that of loss of consciousness or filling of the stomach; with the electricity method the correct way is to administer a large number of short shocks as if using a red-hot needle. I myself am in no position to assert that these practices were effective and am compelled to rely on the statements of those who assured me of this and who, it should be noted, were highly thought of by their superiors. I would merely point out that, according to a certain medical opinion which I was given, the water-pipe method, if used as outlined above, involves no risk to the health of the victim. This is not the case with the electrical method which does involve some danger to anyone whose heart is in any way affected. [...] I am inclined to think that these procedures can be accepted and that, if used in the controlled manner described to me, they are no more brutal than deprivation of food, drink, and tobacco, which has always been accepted.
>
> (Text of the Wuillaume Report, Vidal-Naquet 1963: 169–179)

The French army applied these 'Revolutionary War techniques' during the Algerian War: General Massu and the other paras of the 10th Parachute Division divided Algiers into zones, unified their files of suspicious characters, created civil defence and clandestine detention centres, and systematically used torture in order to obtain the valuable information used to dismantle the structure of Algerian nationalism (Llumá 2002a: 12–13). In the short term these tactics resulted in France winning a decisive victory in the Battle of Algiers, achieved when the French decapitated the *FLN*'s leadership. This victory would serve as a doctrinal exemplar in the development of twentieth century counter-revolutionary theory and practice. In the longer term, however, the debate on the tactics used – particularly torture – would re-emerge in the French press and, somewhat paradoxically, precipitated the loss of Algeria (Branche 2001; Fanon 1963; Lazreg 2008; MacMaster 2004; Maran 1989; Paret 1964; Vidal-Naquet 1963, 2001). Indeed, the Battle of Algiers victory did not put an end to the Muslim community's growing support for the *FLN* and war started to have a harmful internal effect in France: it unleashed inflation, increased the deficit and, in the eyes of some, became a factor in economic destabilisation. Intellectuals, students, young people and representatives of the churches joined in repudiating French colonial policy from 1957, especially on the issue of torture as a basic tool of the doctrine of psychological action. It became the main topic of debate amongst the French public, putting an unsupportable strain on the weak political coalitions of the Fourth Republic. The government's fraught existence ended on 13 May 1958 when the parachute regiments in Algiers rebelled, demanding the return of General de Gaulle to power. Both the paras and the *Pieds-Noirs* believed that only the old general would ensure a French Algeria. Yet the war dragged on and its cost and unpopularity grew in mainland France. In 1959, de Gaulle, by now President of the Republic, was changing his position and took a pragmatic approach to the Algerian question, turning his back on the paras and the *Pieds-Noirs*, moving forward with the idea of Algerian independence (Maran 1989; Paret 1964).

At that time the paras were no more than a minority in the French army, but an active one that, after its success in the Battle of Algiers, came to be a genuine army within an army. Mazzei argues that it was 'nearly a sect with its own rites and legends, and a strong feeling of superiority' (2002: 110). The majority of its members had fought in Indochina, where they had confronted communism, which they considered to be the true enemy of Western civilisation and the Christian religion. Convinced that they could only achieve victory by using the same weapons as their adversaries, they put military regulations to one side and used a series of tactics known as counter-revolutionary war (Droz and Lever 1982: 291–292). Their idea was to save what remained of the French colonial empire from the advance of international communism with which, they alleged, Charles de Gaulle himself was complicit (Mazzei 2002: 110–111).

Defeated by de Gaulle's policy, their reaction was not long in coming: they advanced into the creation of paramilitary groups such as the violent *Organisation Armée Secrète (OAS)* – Secret Armed Organisation – which simultaneously fought against the Algerian rebels and the Fifth Republic; and, in April 1961, they organised the so-called Generals' Putsch and attempted a *coup d'état*, to the cry of *'Algérie Française!'* – 'French Algeria!' (Lazreg 2008: 5; Peters 1985: 133). The *OAS* made assassination attempts against de Gaulle on several occasions. Nonetheless, their attacks and indiscriminate violence could not prevent the Evian Agreements (AMA/Orfila 1962), which culminated in independence of Algeria in July 1962. As a consequence, 700,000 Europeans had to leave North Africa (Mazzei 2002: 111; Vidal-Naquet 1963: 45–46).

It is now common knowledge that, throughout most of the Algerian War, France made general use of the practices of torture, summary execution, and large-scale deportation. The current debates focus more on the scale of the methods employed and on the involvement of senior French officials, as well as on the effects of the use of torture on perpetrators (Fanon 1986).[7] These debates reveal the vicious circle that led an increasing number of officers to commit illegal acts, while most of the political leaders, in Algiers as well as in Paris, gave the military a free hand while abdicating their own responsibility.

Torture was not an epiphenomenon of the Algerian War: it was central to the army's defence of a colonial empire in its waning years (Branche 2001;

Fanon 1963; Lazreg 2008; MacMaster 2004; Maran 1989; Paret 1964; Vidal-Naquet 1963, 2001). Its systematic use was the direct outcome of the French theory and doctrine of Revolutionary War – *Doctrine de Guerre Révolutionnaire* – that developed in the 1950s.[8] As Lazreg explains:

> Even though the theory did not initially advocate torture, it informed an anti-subversive war doctrine that could not be implemented successfully without its use. Without the theory, torture could not have been systematized. Similarly, without torture, the anti-subversive war doctrine could not have been implemented
>
> (2008: 15)

Having set the theoretical and operational context, torture easily became institutionalised, in the sense that its use by the French military was not simply an instance of violence committed by a few isolated rogue individuals acting according to their personal whims (Fanon 1965).[9] The part played by torture throughout the Algerian War '[...] started as a police method of interrogation, developed into a military method of operation, and then ultimately turned into a clandestine state institution which struck at the very roots of the life of the nation' (Vidal-Naquet 1963: 15).

In Algeria, the French torturers had good reasons to feel that they were acting within legal bounds (Droz and Lever 1982: 139; Vidal-Naquet 1963: 60–75). The fact that some of them may have gone well beyond their instructions out of sadism or a spirit of initiative is a difference of degree, not of kind (Vidal-Naquet 1963: 15; Fanon 1963). Indeed, in 1962, during the trial of a prominent member of the OAS who had been accused of violating human rights in Algeria, Captain Joseph Estoup, another leading player in the Algerian War, testified to the institutional nature of the mass application of torture against detainees:

> In just one night in January 1957 the four regiments of the 10th Parachute Division all set to follow the order of 'gathering intelligence' [...]. Your honour, what military jargon calls 'gathering intelligence' is in everyday language 'interrogating' and in ordinary French it is 'torturing'.
> (Captain Joseph Estoup, as quoted in Vidal-Naquet 2001: 157–158)

At the hand of officers such as Lieutenant-Colonel Roger Trinquier, torture became an everyday practice, operating everywhere with techniques similar to those to be applied two decades later in Argentina: blows, body suspension, cigarette or blowtorch burns and, most especially, torture using electricity or the bathtub (Alleg 1958; Droz and Lever 1982: 141; Vidal-Naquet 1963). Indeed, Trinquier's theoretical writings on 'Modern War' and his experience in Indochina and Algeria would become bedside reading in Argentina for several officers who became leaders in the dictatorship of the

Argentine Dirty War and the *Proceso de Reorganización Nacional* – the 'National Reorganisation Process' (Oliveira-Cézar 2003: 73).

The French doctrine of Revolutionary War was intended to deal with both colonial and civil wars (Paret 1964: 9). It constructed 'a transnational conception of war that wove together a number of factors aimed at rallying a diverse audience comprised of recruits, politicians, and the public at large' (Lazreg 2008: 32). Furthermore, the ensuing doctrine did not distinguish 'insurgents' from 'population', and consequently merged civilians into a generic, dehumanized, 'satanic' enemy (Garrigou-Lagrange 1959: 515). The fact that France had lost its colonial wars in Indochina and Algeria apparently did not matter: the anti-subversive war doctrine 'provides a key for reading reality that makes intelligible a complex and changing reality and enables the armed forces, an institution that sinks its roots in medieval values, to cope with social complexity and change' (Perelli 1990: 101). It became very attractive to other governments and went far beyond the borders of Algeria. As Périès explained, the expansion of the application of the French doctrine of Revolutionary War far beyond France and its colonial territories confirms its 'transnational dimension' (1999: 697). It is the transnational dimension of the doctrine that made possible the transfer of the French *savoir-faire* in torture practices.

Migratory movement between Algeria and Argentina

> Mexicans descended from the Aztecs, Peruvians from the Incas, and the Argentines from boats.
>
> (Common Argentinian Proverb)

According to the Preamble to its Constitution, Argentina is a country open to 'all the men of the world who wish to dwell on Argentine soil', regardless of race, ideology or religion.[10] Laying the foundations for the policy of support of immigration, this preamble also asks 'for the protection of God, source of all reason and justice' for all people who desire to inhabit Argentina. These statements should come as no surprise since, after Spanish colonisation and independence, Argentina formed its social and demographic structure via various waves of external and internal migration. The process was complemented by the extermination and marginalisation of the original indigenous population, first displaced by European settlement and then by the territorial expansion of their heirs. This human and spatial reconfiguration of the young nation, in turn, created its own myths of the '*melting pot of races, Europeanization, and the promised land,* which quickly found their way into people's minds, particularly due to public education' (Ranaletti 2005: 286).

True to the lines set down by the Preamble, Argentina has received people from the most diverse places in the world and for the most varied reasons:

Jews persecuted by every variant of tenacious European anti-Semitism; temporarily defeated anarchists; entrepreneurs; and criminals from every European war fleeing changing circumstances. Indeed, its various governments have not discriminated against these persons, opening their frontiers even to many Nazi war criminals and French nationals linked to the Nazi power (Otero 2012). History was to repeat itself at the end of the Algerian War, when the French collaborators already exiled in Argentina were to be the pathfinders for people with similar criminal backgrounds.

The end of the Algerian War generated different views, solidarities and passions in Argentina and had a considerable impact on its society. On 19 March 1962, the Evian Agreements concluded between the Algerian National Liberation Front and the government of General de Gaulle ended the French colonial presence and a war which cost more than a million lives, most of them Algerian civilians. The evacuation of the colony meant enforced repatriation for a large number of people who left Algeria for fear of reprisals and anti-colonial sentiment. The *Pieds-Noirs* or 'French of Algeria' – considered as second-class citizens by those living in mainland France – had to seek new horizons. Argentina was among their favourite destinations (Palacio 1968: 30–32). Far from constituting a 'political' exile, the departure of these French of Algeria was a very different matter: 'More than a simple repatriation, this movement may be considered a true migration, since it includes the very present feelings of exodus and exile in the individuals involved' (Jordi 1993: 7). The majority of the French who arrived in Argentina with the defeat of colonialism in North Africa behind them presented two characteristics: furious anti-communism and magnified Catholicism. And the country they encountered was one where those two features also coincided; this turned Argentina into a particularly favourable space for the social insertion of the new arrivals.[11] Indeed, it enabled the most politically engaged of them easily to link their North African past with the new reality of Argentina, 'not for any dream of restoring colonialism, but rather to update their narrative and go back to old ways, such as clandestinity, code names, apocryphal reports, megalomania, contacts with the military world, the intelligence community and the crusade spirit' (Ranaletti 2005: 293).

In 1963, tripartite negotiations began between individuals and the two states to reach a definitive agreement on the settlement in Argentina of a significant number of persons repatriated from Algeria. The French government had no solutions to the problem of reintegrating the French of Algeria, focused as it was on stopping a bloody aftermath to a colonial war (Vidal-Naquet 1963). Encouraging a wave of migration seemed the best option to avoid adding elements of discord to an internal situation that was becoming troubled again. This is how, according to French historian Geneviève Verdo, 'The organisation of this emigration was as much a political act as it was a financial agreement [...]; at the beginning of January 1964, a group of sixty families disembarked in the port of Buenos Aires' (1989: 34–39). Once again, as in the case of the collaborators, Argentina became a safety valve for the French government. During the following two years, another five groups would be added, making a total of 'one hundred and fifty families officially registered as part of this migration' (Verdo 1989: 13):

> As from 1945, the structure of the French community underwent significant change. Apart from those of our compatriots who arrived before 1940 and remained French, it is important to distinguish political refugees, several hundreds of who arrived after the Second World War [and] the farmers repatriated to France after the Algerian War and who came and settled in Argentina between 1963 and 1967. [...] This French community in Argentina, undoubtedly the biggest in terms of numbers in Latin America cannot – truth be told – be compared in absolute numbers with other ethnic groups such as the Italians or Spanish. Nonetheless, it did exert influence and it continues to do so effectively and sustainably in nearly every area. Among the first in Argentina, the French demonstrated initiative, imagination and entrepreneurial spirit. They brought their ways of thinking and a culture which has left its mark on the country. Because, if it is true that Italy and Spain mostly sent workers, Great Britain mostly capital, and Germany mostly machines, *the French contribution was not only to work, as far as its means permitted for the material and economic development of Argentina but also to send its ideas.* At a time when technology sometimes seems to overtake the mind, this harmoniously balanced contribution to the future of Argentina must be highlighted, earning the French community the right to benefit from a choice position in the esteem of the elite and the people of the country.
>
> (ADF/Doc. 177/3, emphases added)[12]

As a result of those negotiations and in order to organise this 'migration', an inter-governmental agreement was signed on 19 October 1964, which included exciting benefits for the 'settlers' (ADF/File #177): On the Argentinian side, the agreement consisted of facilitating the administration for the import of moveable assets and capital, in addition to offering free land on generous terms, exemption from customs duties, help with education and health, and free availability and transfer of currency from France, setting maxima for transactions and fees. The French government, for its part, made itself responsible for the costs of transporting people and their property. It was also to provide a cash financial grant to each family to help it get through the initial period. Nonetheless, what had been conceived as a colonisation experiment turned into a series of individual undertakings. On the French side, near-total ignorance of the environment into which families were going to settle, the incompetence of the consular authorities and the French charged with organising the departure of those repatriated (freezing their funds and *French-style* bureaucratic obstacles), unrealistic expectations – for some a new

'El Dorado' – and unpleasant colonial aftertastes meant that disorder and incompetence prevailed. From 1965, the French *Bureau pour le Développement de la Production Agricole (BDPA)* – Office for the Development of Agricultural Production – worked on facilitating a long-lasting implementation of the *Pied-Noir* families who disembarked at the port of Buenos Aires, hoping to find as many opportunities as in Algeria (ADF/Doc. 177/1, 177/2, 177/4).

Nonetheless, for some French nationals with long criminal records, this agreement was their discreet entry door to the country: several *OAS* terrorists managed to benefit from the advantages offered to settlers. French journalist Marie-Monique Robin demonstrated that *OAS* members and sympathisers received the same benefits as those who enrolled at French consular and migration offices for the Franco-Argentinian colony creation project (Robin 2004: Chapter 22). Other members of the *OAS* had no need to enrol on a colonisation plan in order to settle in Argentina: once the de Gaulle government reached an agreement with most of the members of an organisation that had made several attempts on his life: 'The support of their compatriots and their prestige as *counter-insurgency specialists* was enough' (Ranaletti 2005: 295–296). The proposed agreement included an end to Franco's tolerance of these terrorists' activities in Spain. Those who agreed to abandon all conspiratorial activity against de Gaulle were amnestied and shortly after allowed to return to France; those who did not accept the agreement were immediately expelled from Spain to Venezuela, Paraguay, Uruguay, Argentina and Portugal (Blanquer 1992: 87; Kauffer 2002: 388–389; Segura Valero 2004).

Even though the presence of ex-*OAS* members in Argentina has been reported in various sources and studies, little is known about their specific activities (Ranaletti 2005: 303–304). They are, however, mentioned as instructors in interrogation and counter-insurgency techniques (Hodges 1991: 134–135) and as members of paramilitary groups dedicated to the suppression of dissidents from 1973 (Robin 2004). According to journalist Marcelo Larraquy, on the basis of direct testimony he obtained, José López Rega – former Minister of Social Welfare, personal assistant to Perón and creator of paramilitary group the Anti-communist Alliance of Argentina and personal assistant to Perón – had an escort comprising former *OAS* members, although Larraquy does not state their names (2003: 235, 251).

According to Argentinian historian Mario Ranaletti, the French nationals displaced by decolonisation found themselves in a

> society characterised by a state of tension over the social and financial advantages secured by the workers some years earlier, and by a state of agitation over what it thought were indicators of the presence of an internal enemy and the *expansion* of communist *subversion* within the social fabric.
>
> (Ranaletti 2005: 296)

This climate was familiar to them and they too believed in the same phantoms, interpreting colonial independence as the result of a manoeuvre orchestrated by 'international communism' to destroy 'Western Christian civilisation'. Those who settled in the interior of the country were distanced from national political problems, but those who moved to the great conurbations, such as Buenos Aires and Mendoza, were able quickly to reinstate old habits and practices:

> With a long tradition of welcoming the persecuted and displaced, with its European nuances that created the illusion of not being in Latin America, with its inner circles highly excited at the *imminence* of a new world conflagration and with its enormous open spaces, Argentina offered itself to those defeated representatives of late colonialism as a promised land to forget the immediate past, to dream of new authoritarian utopias or to recommence a pathway interrupted by the atrocities of French colonialism.
>
> (Ranaletti 2005: 298; emphasis as in original)

Franco-Argentinian military rapprochement at the institutional level: introducing a doctrine that justifies torture

After the overthrow of General Perón in September 1955, Argentina entered a new phase. Perón's election in 1946 had introduced more economic and social rights to the working classes (Rouquier 1978); the proscription and persecution of his political party triggered a spiral of violence that was, in reality, a confrontation between these classes and the upper/middle classes (James 1990). The basic goal of Perón's opponents was the reversal of the redistribution of wealth that had taken place during his first two governments (from 1946 to 1955). A frightened bourgeoisie launched a frenetic anti-communist campaign with the aim of cracking down on the radical activism of the Peronists; little by little, this morphed into a tragic struggle in what the bourgeoisie saw as the defence of 'Western Christian civilisation' (Ranaletti 2005: 297). This essentially local conflict then assumed international dimensions when Argentina joined the Cold War on the side of the regional bloc led by the United States (Rouquier 1978: 156–159). This meant that its true cause – social inequality – was never addressed properly: all forms of opposition and social protest came to be interpreted as manifestations of supposed communist penetration of the country. This is at the root of the association made in Argentina by so many members of the armed forces and civilian population when they placed the events of the Peronist resistance within a Marxist framework – an interpretation that was completely without foundation until the 1966 meeting of the Latin American Solidarity Organisation (Feierstein 2010: 44; Oliveira-Cézar 2002: 27; Ranalletti 2005: 291).

As a consequence, the Argentine army underwent major transformations during the second half of the 1950s. With the fall of Perón, the 'liberal' wing of the army began a profound *de-Peronisation* and reorganisation process (Lopez 1987), and sought to replace the Doctrine of National Defence by new and untraditional forms of warfare arising from the Cold War: nuclear war and revolutionary war (Mazzei 2002: 105–106). The Argentinian Armed and Security Forces began this process of renewal, on both the doctrinal and technical levels, in addition to 'stepping up their traditional politicisation' (Ranaletti 2005: 299). They moved into the role of internal political police, responsible for countering the 'communist influence' and 'subversion', relegating their function as the armed wing of the State for its external defence to a secondary level:

> For a long time, the primary mission of the army was to defend territorial integrity against any encroachments by neighbouring countries, specifically Chile, whose designs on Patagonia in particular have always caused concern to the Argentinian military. [...] But nowadays, subversive war is the key issue of concern to the military. It is a matter of defending an 'inner frontier' against the Castro-communism that has become enemy number one. This explains the great attention paid here to the vicissitudes of the guerrilla war in Bolivia and the sense of relief after the failure of Che Guevara's venture there.
>
> (ADF/Doc. 141/3)

This context saw the definitive eclipse of German influence on the Argentine army (Périès 1999: 759; ADF/Doc. 141/3), which was replaced by the dominance of North American and French traditions:

> [...] without external wars for over a century or any immediate threat from its neighbours, the Argentinian armed forces no longer had an opportunity to exercise their natural role, that of sword of the state. With studies by American and French authors on the global nature of strategy and on localised or subversive wars, the idea of frontier war practically disappeared, making way for the notion of a war to be waged against the enemy within. The hostile neighbour was no longer the subject of strategic studies, but rather the compatriot in the conscious or unconsciousness service of a revolutionary power.
>
> (ADF/Doc. 188/1)

In the North American case, this was related to the dominant position achieved by its army after the Second World War and, in particular, to the incorporation into its doctrine of the problem of nuclear war. The French military, for its part, strengthened its relationship with the Argentine army – with which it had been linked ever since the Perón government – by offering its Revolutionary War doctrine. This doctrine, already explained, had grown out of the French defeat in Indochina, after which a group of French officers, in order to avoid taking responsibility for their failure to reinstate colonial control, came to the conclusion that they were facing a new type of war which they did not have the strategic resources to fight. War was no longer the classic confrontation between opposing armed forces for control of a territory and/or its economic resources, but was total combat, waged in the 'hearts and minds' of the population: 'A modern war – revolutionary or subversive – but always *communist* in nature' (Llumá 2002a: 6). In this new kind of war, information is the key: it must be obtained at all cost. Consequently, torture becomes acceptable and is seen as the most radical and effective instrument of counter-insurgency action.

In the first phase of the fight against the communist aggression they believed to be under way, the Argentine military entrusted the essence of their training to their French colleagues. A 'process of decontextualisation' of the doctrine of revolutionary war by the French in Argentina led to a 'transformation of the objectives and methods used by the Argentine armed forces in the Cold War context' (Périès 1999: 743):

> After the fall of Perón in 1955, the dominant influence on the Argentine army tended to be that of the United States. This was the era of the Inter-American Defense Pacts, American military missions and American material. However, the traditional mistrust felt against the dominant power on the continent very quickly led the Argentinians to follow with increasing interest the thoughts of General de Gaulle, who incarnated in their eyes the policy of a country keen to preserve its independence faced with the hegemony of the superpowers.
>
> (ADF/Doc. 188/1)

This change in military tradition happened when an internal line of the Argentine army, then led by Colonel Carlos Jorge Rosas, tried to secure a degree of decision-making autonomy in the military. This prestigious Engineers Officer had been a military attaché in France and a student at the Paris *École Supérieure de Guerre* from 1953 until 1955. In 1957 he was appointed professor of Tactics and Strategy, and deputy principal of its Argentine equivalent. In that role, he is often regarded as being responsible for the 'importation' of the French revolutionary war doctrine. Indeed, in a relatively recent article in the *Revista de la Escuela Superior de Guerra*, General Isaías García Enciso asserted that 'the French influence in the Argentine army was introduced by Colonel Rosas' (AMA/Picciuolo 1996: 34). According to Lieutenant-Colonel Robert Louis Bentresque:

> It was *Chivo* Rosas who was behind the idea that the Argentinians could avoid a conflict by having the French come, who had already been

beaten. That is why they asked for a mission. And so there were two French officers permanently assigned as advisers to the Argentinian School of War. [...] It was Rosas who asked for a French officer at the General Staff to advise him and to have him close at hand to ask his opinion without delay.

(Lieutenant-Colonel Robert Louis Bentresque, as interviewed by Périès 1999: 760–761)

Samuel Amaral (1998), Ramón Camps (1981), Diego Llumá (2002a), Daniel Mazzei (2002), and María Oliveira-Cézar (2002,2003) are also of the opinion that he was responsible for introducing the Argentine army to the repressive ideas and techniques used by the French in Indochina (1946–1954) and Algeria (1954–1962). However, this point of view is not without controversy. Mario Ranaletti (2005) emphasised that Rosas's personal military education abroad should be taken into account while evaluating his influence. Relying on Rosas's articles published in the *Revista de la Escuela Superior de Guerra,* on the consultation of his personal archives and on an interview with his son, Ranaletti came to the conclusion that Rosas was not particularly interested in the Revolutionary War doctrine itself. What he really wanted was the reorientation and reorganisation of the Argentine military away from American influence, which he set out to achieve by strengthening already existing ties with France (Ranaletti 2005: 300).

This monograph supports the idea that the strategy devised by Rosas was that of seeking financing and procurement in France in order to offset US influence. The Argentine military was introduced to French military doctrine with the help of the following: (a) several other Argentinian senior rank officers who had also taken training courses in various French centres, in particular the Paris *École Supérieure de Guerre* (including Lieutenant-Colonels Pedro Tibiletti (1954–1956), Cándido Hure (1955–1957), Manrique Miguel Mom (1956–1958), Alcides López Aufranc (1957–1959), and Edgardo Daneri (1958–1960)); and (b) French diplomatic representation in Argentina (Mazzei 2002: 115–116; Périès 1999: 875–876). Indeed, as mentioned by the Military Attaché to the French Embassy in Buenos Aires, Colonel A. R. Bernard, in a secret communication with the Secretary of Defence in Paris on 29 March 1956:

> After the revolution of September [which overthrew the second Peronist government in 1955], the Argentine army is undergoing a complete reorganization process and it is interesting to note that some of its most influential members are looking at France to find inspiration, or even a reference model. [...] Colonel Rosas, recently graduated from our school, is offering to restructure the *Escuela Superior de Guerra* according to French norms.

(ADF/Doc. 74/4)

From the perspective of French interests, we are glad to see some commands entrusted to generals or higher ranks whose feelings of friendship for our country are not in doubt. Colonel Lopez Aufranc, a former student of our Schools of War and of General Staff, has for a long time had a trusting, ongoing relationship with our Military Attaché services. [...] He has always shown support for the arrival and then maintenance of a French military advisors' mission. The same applies to General Rosas.

(ADF/Doc. 141/1)

Those 'French norms' were the very ones that had been 'applied by the French against the *FLN* of Algeria since 1954' (Llumá 2002a: 6), namely, their theories of counter-revolutionary warfare. The French military considered the *FLN* to be a communist-type revolutionary organisation because it did not understand the nationalist nature of the phenomenon (Llumá 2002b: 21). A few months later, in July 1956, the French Ambassador in Buenos Aires revealed to the Secretary of State in France, Christian Pineau, the 'exceptional political interest to increase the effort in strengthening ties and cohesion between the French and Argentine armed forces' (ADF/Doc. 74/5).

Shortly after the overthrow of General Perón, and especially after the intensification of acts by the Peronist resistance, a group of general staff officers put their trust in the visiting French officers because they were the only Western specialists in revolutionary war on account of their extensive experience in policing activities in an urban setting (Oliveira-Cézar 2003: 73–74). Military contacts between France and Argentina increased after Colonel Rosas's stay at the *École Supérieure de Guerre* in Paris (1953–1955), which can be seen as the start of a significant exchange of officers and advisers who would share the *savoir-faire* developed in the light of the French colonial wars. Those contacts appeared mainly in the form of: (a) training courses at the Paris *École Supérieure de Guerre*; and (b) the establishment of a French military mission into the Buenos Aires *Escuela Superior de Guerra* (ADF/Doc. 229/1, 229/5). These exchanges would allow the French to 'pass their experience from Indochina and Algeria on to Argentine officers' (Oliveira-Cézar 2002: 27). French specialists in torture were able – 'with the authorisation of their superiors in the cabinet ministries and the military general staff' (Alleg 2006a: 101) – to pursue new careers well beyond the borders of Algeria. With its ups and downs, this influence would continue well into the launch and organisation of the 1976 dictatorship.

Training courses at the Paris 'École Supérieure de Guerre'

Argentina has traditionally sent staff officers for training to France. Prestigious Argentine officers studied at various French military institutions, especially the Paris Higher School of War, *École Supérieure de Guerre*: the place where the elite of the French army was trained. Others received this influence during long missions to France. The goal of the *École Supérieure* was to select and train small groups of officers who would be posted to the General Staffs of their own countries later on. As the Attaché of Armed Forces at the French Embassy in Buenos Aires explained to the French Secretary of External Affairs concerning the importance of these training courses:

> [...] the direct and indirect transfer of our culture are obvious long-term investments in this country which, if we turn our back on it, will turn to other Western nations or countries [...].
>
> (ADF/Doc. 2234/6)

Joining this group was an impressive body of international students, a quarter of who came from Latin America, a further 22 per cent of who were from Argentina (Dhombres 2003; Le Sueur 2006: xxiii; McClintock 1992; Périès 1999: 709; Ray 2006: ix–x; Robin 2004: 168–169). The *École Supérieure* started training Latin American military personnel from 1951 onwards and, between 1951 and 1962, the proportion of trainees coming from South America represented more than a quarter of the foreign officers present at the Higher School (Périès 1999: 709). Right after Brazil, Argentina was the second most represented country, with nine trainees hosted in the *École Supérieure*'s 65th cohort (1952–1954) (Périès 1999: 710).

The Argentinian selection was made according to the merits in each promotion (their class ranking): the first was sent to France, the second to Spain, the third to Germany and the fourth to the USA (Llumá 2002a: 6). According to a former student, it was a 'real privilege' to be sent to Paris (General Reynaldo Benito Bignone, as interviewed by Robin 2004: 316–317). Upon their return home, the majority of these officers were politically active, though not always with the same ideology (Oliveira-Cézar 2003: 74), and fulfilled roles in the leadership of their Argentine equivalent, the *Escuela Superior de Guerra*. This was what happened in the case of Colonel Carlos Rosas, deputy principal in 1957 and 1958, and in the cases of Lieutenant-Colonels Pedro Tibiletti and Cándido Hure, the Argentine Higher School's principal and deputy principal in 1960. Others graduating from France were Lieutenant-Colonel Manrique Miguel Mom, whose teaching work in the Higher School of War was influential, as reflected in a pair of published articles on Revolutionary War (AMA/Mom 1958, 1959), and Lieutenant-Colonel Alcides López Aufranc, who described his personal experience of the Paris *École Supérieure* in these words (AMA/López Aufranc 1959):

> When the events of 13 May 1958 occurred in Algiers, precipitating the rise to power of General de Gaulle, the French students of the *École Supérieure*'s 71st cohort were sent to North Africa in order to reinforce

the general staffs, forming a new division created to direct psychological action. We foreign students were authorised to join personnel in the Theatre of Operations for two weeks, visiting from the Commander in Chief's Command Post to tiny villages with Muslim self-defence, including the electrified barriers on the borders with Tunisia and Morocco.

(AMA/López Aufranc 1959: 611)

These training courses were also used as a means of strengthening the presence of the French military industry in the Argentinian market. Indeed, on 1 June 1954, the French Chargé d'Affaires in Buenos Aires explained to the Secretary of State in France how important it was, now that German influence had waned in Argentina, for the Argentine officers staying in France to witness all French military accomplishments so that France could be chosen above American and English 'suppliers' (ADF/Doc. 74/1). In other words, France was trying to further its arms sales and technological exports as well as improve its diplomatic ties with Argentina.

These exchanges were seen as essential to the military collaboration between the two countries. This extended to the point where, on 16 March and 6 April 1956, the French Ambassador in Buenos Aires revealed to the Secretary of State in France that Colonel A. R. Bernard, Military Attaché to the French Embassy in Buenos Aires, had extremely important reasons to support the admission of two Argentine officers (instead of one) to the École Supérieure de Guerre in Paris:

> I fully concur with the opinion of Colonel Bernard and I would be pleased if the department wanted to make a case with the Ministry of War for the political interest attached, at a time when the Argentine army is being completely reorganised, to an exceptional effort being made to promote its incorporation of our methods and military norms.
>
> (ADF/Doc. 74/2)

> [C]olonel Bernard asks that a certain amount of information be sent to him on our logistical military institutions, in order to send them to a French trained general of the Argentinian artillery. I would be grateful to the Department if it would kindly support this request with the Minister of National Defence, the importance of which goes without saying.
>
> (ADF/Doc. 74/3)

On 3 September 1958, the very recent simultaneous influence of the French military advisers at the Escuela Superior de Guerra (as we shall see in the next section) gave birth to an official document which described the planned visit of 120 Argentinian officers to France; these students would also go to Algeria in the middle of its liberation war:

The Command of the Argentine army has made known its desire to organise an end-of-course visit to Europe and Africa at the end of 1958 for officers: (1) of the Argentinian Higher School of War (60 officers); (2) of the Army Higher Technical School (30 officers); (3) possibly, of the Higher School of Intelligence (30 officers). The plan for the visit provides: (a) for the Higher School of War: − A stay in France from 10 to 26 November 1958 [...], − a stay in Algeria from 17 to 19 December 1958 [...].

(ADF/Doc. 74/6)

A few days later, the French Secretary of State had 'the honour to inform the French Ambassador in Buenos Aires' that the plan made by the command of the Argentine army to organise an end-of-course visit for pupils of three military schools had met with his 'full approval' (ADF/Doc. 74/7). A few days later, the French General Staff of National Defence would also have 'the honour of informing the General Staff of the Argentine Armed Forces that in principle agreement can be given to the command of the Argentine army for the planned visit to France' (ADF/Doc. 74/8).

Argentine General Alcides López Aufranc was a student at the *École Supérieure de Guerre* between 1957 and 1959. Then a Lieutenant-Colonel, he explained his training course in France and Algeria in the following terms:

> At the Argentinian General Staff, we heard talk of French doctrine, which was very much in vogue at the time. That is why I was selected to train in counter-revolutionary war. The teachers [at the French Higher School of War] talked about nothing else! And for me, that was something completely new. We did not yet know of this kind of problem in Latin America. There were political struggles and they were sometimes violent, but they were not subversive in nature, because the Communist Party had not begun its infiltration work. [...] We were convinced that World War Three was imminent and that the Soviet Union was going to try to open a front on Argentinian territory... it was thanks to the teaching of the French that I understood that the enemy could be the people and that to win the war, we had to win minds. [...] After the events of 13 May 1958, the 71st class of the Higher School of War, of which I was a member, was sent to Algeria to strengthen the general staffs in a new division created to direct psychological action.
>
> (General Alcides López Aufranc, as interviewed by Robin 2004: 167–168)

As French political analyst, Georges Gabriel Périès, explained:

> It's not any officer who would start teaching and spreading the doctrine of Revolutionary War at the *École Supérieure de Guerre*, but frustrated

soldiers who just came out of two wars that they lost [...]; one can easily imagine the impact that their attitude and mindset were going to have on Argentine officers attending their conferences.

(Périès 1999: 786)

As for the content of the course they followed in Paris, Argentine officers were obviously exposed to the doctrine of Revolutionary War. One of the first French theoreticians on the subject, along with Trinquier, was Colonel Charles Lacheroy (Villatoux and Villatoux 2012: 45). A French army officer who spent most of his career in the African colonies, Lacheroy was sent to Indochina from 1951 to 1953, where he began to discover and appreciate this new type of warfare and its techniques, in particular the methods of psychological action. These became his speciality upon his return to France, where he was to drive the creation of a 5th Command dedicated to this task in every military unit. A typical example of the French praetorianism so common at the time, he was constantly involved in coups: he took an active part in the civilian and military rebellion of 13 May 1958 which, from Algeria, caused the fall of the Fourth Republic and the appointment of Charles de Gaulle; he was then personally involved in the failed Generals' Putsch of April 1961 against de Gaulle himself; and, finally, at the end of 1961, he became leader of the OAS and exiled in Spain where, paradoxically, his ideological ally Francisco Franco arrested him and sent him as a prisoner to the Canary Islands. Sentenced to death *in absentia* in April 1961, Lacheroy was granted an amnesty in 1968 and returned to Paris, where he retired (Villatoux and Villatoux 2012: 47).

In 1958, while the situation in Algeria was still tense, he was made Director of Information and Psychological Action Services in Algiers and, in December of that year, he started to hold conferences at the *École Supérieure de Guerre* and at the *Centre d'Études Asiatiques et Africaines* – Centre of Asian and African Studies – in Paris (Oliveira-Cézar 2003: 71–72). During his lectures at the *École Supérieure*, he structured the fundamentals of the knowledge on Revolutionary War available at the time, which would be used as a model for later analyses. In doing so, he would teach Argentine officers, among others, a theory that they would themselves apply later.

According to Lacheroy (Lacheroy 1958), this new type of war was a total war: it involved women, children and the elderly. Traditional rules of war were dead: conventional armies no longer confronted each other – not even in the form of an army against bands of guerrillas – because it was a war in which the main objective was not simply to take power but to 'take' the population. By conquering the body and soul of every individual, the population would be controlled and victory assured. And to control it, Lacheroy explained that it was necessary to use the same methodology as one's enemies – to incorporate, infiltrate, intimidate and turn the population. Among the revolutionary techniques he addressed, he spoke first of the appropriation of physical persons, which necessitated taking account of, and controlling in depth, the different worlds to which each person belonged – family, work, culture, social group, religion, age, home, village or town. Then he moved on to the appropriation of souls, which would be achieved through psychological means to 'channel the energies, desires, enthusiasms, loves and hates' (Lacheroy 1958: 317). This would also be used for the rehabilitation or conversion of prisoners after having broken them by means of 'brutality' and total isolation involving the loss of one's initial system of references and its gradual substitution (Lacheroy 1958: 319).

Lacheroy set out five phases in the development of Revolutionary War (1958: 322–328). In the first phase nothing happens; nobody asks themselves questions, giving rise to the need to create a problem, which may be galvanised through terrorist attacks. The second phase is characterised by specific attacks against alleged 'traitors', in which individuals who are usually seen as humble and ordinary (rather than the famous or politically engaged) are publicly identified in order to scapegoat them. Others then become fearful that they will be the next victims, while repression is simultaneously imposed by the established order: 'terror is implanted and silence instilled' (Lacheroy 1958: 323). In the third phase, the first military groups are formed and the first political commissars infiltrate the mass of the population to 'transform passivity into activism and then into pressure' (Lacheroy 1958: 324). The fourth phase is marked by the specialisation of civilian militants and the first actions by militarised groups. The fifth and final phase leads to the 'professionalisation' of the revolutionaries: former militia members are now full-time soldiers, supported by the revolutionary party of government opposition, which in turn is largely financed by the people. Lacheroy ended by giving his formula for this new type of war, which he believed would be the war of the future: the nature of the new war saw the population as the axis, for which reason it has to be reached by psychological action, which is, in reality, the new, essential weapon since a social error or success is more effective than a bomb (Lacheroy 1958: 330).

The Algerian experience encouraged the French to adopt and extend Lacheroy's theory and they added to it the characteristics pertinent to the urban environment. As we have seen, military victory in the Battle of Algiers was based on two pillars: the psychological approach mentioned above and total control of the population. To achieve this, they created the Urban Protection Unit (DPU) which enabled them effectively to gather intelligence; they divided the city into districts by means of their grid system, the districts into islets, the islets by groups of houses and the houses by the families living in them until they got down to the individual; they registered every resident, recording their routines and regular journeys. At each level there was an administrator who, at any time of day or night, had to be able to report to the military on any possible changes to the sector for which he was responsible – for example, a visitor who spent the night in a home that was not his own. Islets were frequently randomly searched, houses raided and individuals detained as a preventive measure, to ensure that everything was working as planned:

> Acting on the idea that the *FLN* obtained its collaborators through terror, the military resolved that *terror had to change sides*. To do this they sought information *by all means* and used rehabilitated prisoners to infiltrate the *FLN*, which would have the dual result of getting to *FLN* militants, poisoning their minds and making terror spread.
>
> (Oliveira-Cézar 2003: 72–73, emphases as in original)

French military mission at the Buenos Aires 'Escuela Superior de Guerra'

In 1957, a French military mission – which came from the troubled army that had fought the Battle of Algiers the same year – arrived in Buenos Aires (ADF/Doc. 74/16). It was originally composed of Lieutenant-Colonels François Pierre Badie and Patrice de Naurois, who were later joined by Lieutenant-Colonels Robert Louis Bentresque and Jean Nougués (see Appendix 2). Their advisory work concerning the gradual conversion from the Doctrine of National Defence to that of Revolutionary War began in the *Escuela Superior de Guerra* – the 'army's principal theoretical training centre and the natural ambit for these changes to appear the most and the most quickly' (Mazzei 2002: 106) – and was immediately reflected in a series of articles and lectures always translated by General Rosas and published in its main organ, the *Revista de la Escuela Superior de Guerra*, the Higher School of War Review (Llumá 2002a: 7; Rouquier 1978: 471). Up to that point, articles in this quarterly publication had largely been dedicated to nineteenth-century Argentinian military history and the Second World War. Starting in 1957, topics broadened and more attention was paid to nuclear war and Revolutionary War. In the latter case, which is what this monograph is concerned with, the hypothesis of conflict studied at the Higher School changed: the focus moved from the old 'Plan BC' – that is a potential war against Brazil and/or Chile – to the Revolutionary War, i.e. internal/civil war (Llumá 2002a: 7). Indeed, from 1958 to 1962, the *Revista de la Escuela Superior de Guerra* published a large number of articles on revolutionary and counter-revolutionary war. These were written by the French military mission advisers, even before their presence as advisers became official at the end of 1959 (ADF/File #74), as well as by other French guests inspired by their own military experience. These articles associated total control of the population with the methods of dividing the territory into sectors, intelligence or 'seeking information by any means', psychological action and civilian-military action (López 1987: 144–160; Oliveira-Cézar 2002: 27–28; Oliveira-Cézar 2003: 74).

Both this series of publications and the physical presence of this group of French military assessors at the *Escuela Superior de Guerra* was the starting point of the course on counter-insurgency that came to set the scene for the humanitarian disaster that would take place two decades later. They built the pillars that would uphold the doctrine of the 'Dirty War' and ideologically trained some of the men who would become generals in the 1970s. To understand the true scale of the prestige this military mission achieved among Argentinian officers, we can quote three of those who studied at the School of War during those years. According to a former Lieutenant-Colonel of the Argentine army:

> I had known Patrice de Naurois well, a great professional in [the field of Revolutionary War] and Pierre Badie. But the one I was closest to was Robert Bentresque. [...] The main thing that [the French] taught us was that to fight revolutionary or subversive aggression, you must have a good intelligence machine [...]. The problem is that in this type of war there are no longer any differences between combatants and the civilian population and that is how errors can be made [...]. It is not for nothing that one speaks of a dirty war.... In any case, it was thanks to the teaching we received on the Algerian Revolutionary War that we were able to wage our own war in Argentina. [...] We can try to live in denial, but to win an anti-subversive war, torture is unavoidable.
>
> (Lieutenant-Colonel Federico, Interview #5 – see Appendix 3)

According to General Ramón J. Camps:

> [...] the French approach was more correct than the North American one; the French pointed to the overall design, whereas the North Americans focused exclusively or nearly exclusively on military aspects [...]. So far as they were concerned, the ongoing world conflict was not ideological, psychological, cold, warm or hot. It was war, war in which each opponent employed every force available, violent and non-violent, to make the other belligerent surrender, to conquer him or make him renounce his political goals.
>
> (Camps 1981: 2)

Another disciple of the French doctrines, General Acdel Vilas, recalled:

> I admit, and I say this with pride, that from a long time back I had been paying attention to work on this subject published in France – translated in Argentina or in Spain – produced by *OAS* and French army officers who had fought in Indochina and in Algeria. [...] On the basis of the experience gathered through these classics in the field [...] I started issuing orders [...].
>
> (General Acdel Vilas, as quoted in Anderson and López Crespo 1986: 3)

Lieutenant-Colonel François Pierre Badie

The first articles by the French advisers were published in the last quarter of 1957, and they continued steadily until 1962. In every case they referred to recent experiences of the French army. One of the most prolific, Lieutenant-Colonel Badie, began his contribution by undertaking an analysis of the French Resistance during the Second World War (AMA/Badie 1957). This text, on the face of it, had no direct relationship with the East–West conflict and the Cold War. Nevertheless, he chose to study this kind of subversive war as an excuse to explain a specific form of resistance used, that of guerrilla warfare. According to one of Badie's students:

> The French Resistance was a subversive war. It used resources that were in the *population*: action and support were in the *population*, communications were by the *population*, logistics by the *population*, with a pistol shot from time to time. It was a subversive war against the Vichy government.
>
> (Lieutenant-Colonel Federico, Interview #5 – see Appendix 3)

And although the topic related to the recent past, it had an abundance of descriptions of guerrilla tactics with a specific teaching goal: to show how to use them to their best advantage, since it was only 'by knowing them well that we shall learn how to adapt to them' (AMA/Badie 1957: 550). Badie's subsequent articles specialised in the analysis of specific situations in which modern war had been applied, such as the Suez intervention, in which he analysed the actions of French paras in Port Said during the taking of the Suez Canal in November 1956 (AMA/Badie 1958a, 1958b).

His first direct reference to the Algerian situation was in a lecture on the protection of frontiers (such as the Great Wall of China, the Iron Curtain), a particularly sensitive matter for the French who, during those very years, had set up electrified barbed wire barriers to prevent rebels entering Algeria from Tunisia and Morocco (AMA/Badie 1958c). In another publication, Badie also theorised an aspect considered central to all revolutionary wars – that of psychological war, which he defined as 'the systematic use of measures and various means dedicated to influencing the opinion, feelings, attitude and behaviour of the adversary (civil authorities, armed forces, population), with a view to modifying them to support the objectives sought' (AMA/Badie 1958d: 667). He acknowledged that violating spirits in this way was valid only in times of war, but he did not clarify that in a revolutionary conflict it is not easy to define when one is at war. He then pointed to the effectiveness of the 5th Bureaux (Command) responsible for conquering the soul of the Algerian population and said that those involved gave a three-week course to every officer who arrived at a Psychological and Anti-guerrilla Training Centre in Algeria (AMA/Badie 1958d). Later on, he theorised about the subversive war in China (AMA/Badie 1959).

Lieutenant-Colonel Patrice de Naurois

Lieutenant-Colonel de Naurois wrote technical studies in several areas: the use of the rapid mechanised division (AMA/de Naurois 1957); the method of reasoning and situational appraisal and resolution (AMA/de Naurois 1958e); and the organisation and main actions of NATO (AMA/de Naurois 1958c). These three articles were about the techniques of modern war, but another three referred more directly to Revolutionary War. De Naurois described the strategy and tactics of the Viet Minh, emphasising the conquest of the masses (AMA/de Naurois 1958a). He also studied the theory of Subversive War, in which he distinguished the external enemy or infiltrated guerrilla commandos from the internal enemy; he explained the specific difficulties of identifying the internal enemy when it was in every organ of national activity, and against which one has to fight using its own methods, using single political/military command in each administrative division of the territory (AMA/de Naurois 1958b).

In his last theoretical work, de Naurois analysed the difference between two very similar types of war: Subversive War and Revolutionary War (AMA/de Naurois 1958d). According to him, although they used the same methods and they both set out to win power, Subversive War was not the same as Revolutionary War: the former aimed to change not the system but the authorities in commamd for which end it was sufficient to win over part of the population; by contrast, 'communist revolutionary war' had the objective of 'the transformation of humanity, the victory of communism over capitalism' (AMA/de Naurois 1958d: 688), for which reason it was necessary to conquer the entirety of the masses. In both cases, however, 'subversion is implanted into a society that is already organised; it grows within it, it feeds on it and at the same time, little by little, it undermines it, it destroys it, to replace it with its own organisation' (AMA/de Naurois 1958d: 695–701). To combat it one needs to destroy its political and administrative organisation. For this one had to divide the territory into 'as tight a grid as possible', and place 'each part under the responsibility of a unit of the armed forces' (AMA/de Naurois 1958d: 688). Each unit would have to control the residents, procure the maximum information about them and secure 'the active participation of the population in the fight' – in other words either militias of local auxiliaries or supplementaries, or armed self-defence groups, should be organised in every district, in every group of houses (AMA/de Naurois 1958d: 688). This is an evident reference to the repressive model applied in the Battle of Algiers the year before, which later on would be partially applied during the Argentine Dirty War. De Naurois ends by defining communist revolutionary war as 'total, permanent, universal and multiform' (AMA/de Naurois 1958d: 701). In a dramatic warning, issued in the light of its 'underground, insidious' character and its capacity to spread, he says that, 'communism has agents everywhere in the world, and anywhere that there is an agent, the revolution has already begun' (AMA/de Naurois 1958d: 702). This fits perfectly with the Junta's belief that the Third World War had already started; on opposing sides were the atheist communist totalitarianism of the East and the Catholic individualist liberalism of the West (Oliveira-Cézar 2003: 75).

Lieutenant-Colonel Robert Louis Bentresque

Around 1960, Lieutenant-Colonels Bentresque and Nougués took over the posts of Badie and de Naurois. As the former explained:

> The French army sent me to Argentina [...]. I was sent a travel order, a tricolour piece of paper on which was written in regulation fashion: 'Lieutenant-Colonel Bentresque is to report to Buenos Aires; he will return when he has completed his mission.' I was paid by the Argentinian government [...]. When I arrived there they told me, 'You are going to the *Escuela Superior de Guerra*'. [...] So I asked what I had to do. [I] was told: 'Listen, we know that back home you have studied the problems of subversive war, but we don't really have any idea of what that means or what it is. Would you be able to help us in the courses we are going to give?' [...] We very quickly got on to the problem of subversion. I [...] explained everything: a) the systems for organising populations; b) propaganda; c) psychological warfare [...] I took my examples firstly from Indochina [...] and then from Algeria [...]. I [...] taught at the *Escuela Superior de Guerra*, [...] even at the *Escuela Superior de Mecánica de la Armada* [ESMA].
>
> (Lieutenant-Colonel Robert Louis Bentresque, as interviewed by Périès 1999: 765, 783)

Bentresque published only two articles in the *Revista de la Escuela Superior de Guerra*, but both of them were significant. In the first, he developed a method on the reasoning that should be pursued in subversive war that enabled him to establish the basis of a resolution and determine the way forward in a situation where every aspect of total war was applied, unlike the line followed in classic or nuclear war (AMA/Bentresque 1959). His other article was an exhaustive study of the confrontation between 'pro-West' and 'pro-Communist' forces in Laos, set out to show how the conflict was waged in one of the many 'battles of the Revolutionary War' (AMA/Bentresque 1960).

Lieutenant-Colonel Jean Nougués

Two articles by Nougués were also published. The first of these was the only one to refer to the repressive methods used by the French in during the Algerian War (AMA/Nougués 1960). In it, Nougués developed the idea of placing the Algerian conflict in the context of the Cold War, which has the characteristics of being 'ideological' and 'global', since 'the Algerian War [...] appears to be a source of knowledge applicable to other circumstances [...]' (AMA/Nougués 1960: 201). Nougués also referred to the controversy unleashed in France by the revelation of the repressive practices of the police and the military – in other words, torture – in Algeria. With pride, he explained that:

> The French army does not merit this excess of honour or this indignity. The operations successfully conducted in Algeria are a very different thing from blind repression. Our forces, in the face of a revolutionary assault, were impelled towards a counter-revolutionary war which, far from tarnishing their honour, was to represent one of their finest glories.
>
> (AMA/Nougués 1960: 174)

In his second article – probably the most interesting article in the *Revista de la Escuela Superior de Guerra* signed by a French officer – Nougués developed, by way of balance, the achievements of the Argentine army in counter-insurgency warfare. He provided very valuable information about the Argentine Higher School's advances in this arena, especially those of the Army General Staff, as well as the first experiences of this type of war in Argentina (AMA/Nougués 1962). First, he acknowledged that Argentina did not present 'favourable conditions to the development of communist subversion' (AMA/Nougués 1962: 30), describing the social and cultural conditions in Argentina – a significant middle class, a high level of culture and education, a homogeneous, mostly white population, religious and linguistic unity, a satisfactory standard of living, and much lower levels of social inequality than in other Latin American countries – as being ones in which the advance of a revolutionary movement would be difficult, even while the country somewhat lacked notions of social justice. However, he warned that, in any operation similar to those carried out by French troops with Algerian nationalists, Peronism could turn into the spearhead of Marxism: 'Nevertheless, the danger exists' (AMA/Nougués 1962: 30) because 'the most effective and most insidious means of transmission of communism in Argentina is Fidelism, which may take advantage of the maintenance of anti-US feelings and the availability of Peronist masses which are still imperfectly integrated into political life' (AMA/Nougués 1962: 31). One must not underestimate the importance of the intellectuals in Argentina, no matter how small they may be in number, 'as they are likely to be the leaders of the revolution. After enlisting the masses under a national flag they could, more or less progressively, divert the movement towards Castroism, popular democracy and communism' (AMA/Nougués 1962: 32). Since the great majority of the population was concentrated in the cities, 'Revolutionary War could take the form of mass demonstrations, sabotage and urban terrorism, much more than rural guerrilla warfare' (AMA/Nougués 1962: 32). In other words, 'a more or less socialist and pro-Fidel nationalism could be a Trojan horse for the communist penetration of Argentina' (AMA/Nougués 1962: 33). Nougués' allusions to Peronism and its resistance are crystal clear here.

He then analysed what the Argentine army had achieved so far: it had formed and developed doctrine on Revolutionary War, in addition to preparing 'imaginary but believable' exercises for its application (AMA/Nougués 1962: 34). Ernesto López later makes clear that these were undertaken by the group of specialists under the command of General Rosas in operations *Hierro* (Iron) and, later, *Hierro Forjado* (Wrought Iron) (1987: 158). These operations aimed at dividing and reorganising the territory in a certain way in order to control Argentina's population and it was this territorial division that would be used from 1976 onwards by General Videla (Robin 2004: 208–209). They also led to the creation of an actual theoretical textbook in 1962 called *'Points of View – the Conduct of Revolutionary War'* (García 1995: 96–102), which was used as preparatory material for the writing of real regulations on the fight against subversion (Mazzei 2002: 130–131). Nougués then went on to list other Argentine successes, such as the organisation of the 1961 Inter-American Course on Counter-Revolutionary War (ADF/Doc. 74/19). He highlighted the fact that 'with the creation of a military territorial organisation (defence zones, sub-zones and areas), Argentina had acquired the anti-subversive infrastructure it needed' (AMA/Nougués 1962: 38). This was the scheme applied in Algeria that was then adopted in Argentina during the Dirty War to optimise 'counter-revolutionary' repression.

In this study, Nougués acknowledged the Argentine army's 'important theoretical and practical work, which merely needs to be built on' (AMA/ Nougués 1962: 33). According to him, among the steps that needed to be taken were: giving greater importance to the Gendarmerie and broadening its work from the frontiers to the whole country; the establishment of a counter-guerrilla-war training centre; territorial commands separated from units' operational commands, to increase the speed and effectiveness of manoeuvres; and a match established between the military and civilian hierarchies[13] (AMA/ Nougués 1962: 39–41). One wonders if Nougués were not imagining the militarisation of all levels of Argentine society, as carried out by the *Proceso de Reorganización Nacional* ('National Reorganisation Process') 14 years later.[14] Nevertheless, one cannot deny the almost premonitory acuity of his analysis.

The French military mission in Argentina is made official

It was the success of this French military mission in Argentina that led to its institutionalisation on 11 February 1960. General Rosas had initially organised this mission by facilitating the individual contracts of French advisers Lieutenant-Colonels François Pierre Badie and Patrice de Naurois. In 1959, Military Attaché François Serralta succeeded in arranging the signing of an official agreement between the French and Argentinian armies, institutionalising the French military mission:

> [...] I have the honour of forwarding to you enclosed the translation of the draft agreement that the Argentinian General Staff has presented for the approval of the Secretary of State for War. This agreement, which would be made between the Armed Forces Minister and the Argentinian Secretary of State for War, would replace the individual contracts made up to now by the advisers and would give their mission a more official character.
>
> (ADF/Doc. 74/9)

On 20 November 1959, the French Ambassador in Buenos Aires, Armand Blanquet du Chayla, would give his total support to the draft agreement:

> I have the honour to forward to you herewith the French translation of the draft agreement placing a French military mission at the disposal of the Argentinian army [...]. The new formula, fortunately developed by Colonel Serralta, has definite advantages compared to the old system of individual contracts. Indeed, the planned agreement commits the Argentinian army and the French army Ministry, giving it an official character that previous contracts did not have to the same degree. On the other hand, with the notice period for any termination going from one month to one year, our officers will benefit from a situation whose stability and continuity can only strengthen their authority and influence. I therefore approve the contents of the attached documents on all points.
>
> (ADF/Doc. 74/10)

This was followed, on the same day, by the full approval of the French Prime Minister at the time, Michel Debré:

> [...] I have the honour of informing you that I give my approval without restriction to the planned agreement. As the agreement, however, must be made between the French Armed Forces Minister and the Argentinian Secretary of State for War, it is your responsibility to make this decision known to our Military Attaché. I also see no objection to Colonel Serralta being authorised by you to sign this agreement on the spot in Buenos Aires on behalf of the Armed Forces Minister.
>
> (ADF/Doc. 74/11)

The agreement signed between the French Armed Forces Minister and the Argentine Republic's Secretary of State for War with immediate effect was about the technical assistance that the Argentine army had already been receiving from the French army. In this way the French instructors who had been in Argentina for several years were given legal status. In the terms of the provisions of the agreement:

> In accordance with the request made to the French government by the Argentinian government, with the aim of benefiting from French technical military assistance, and further to the desire to strengthen the bonds of friendship and cooperation existing between the French and Argentinian armed forces, the Armed Forces Minister of the French Republic and the Secretary of State for War of the Argentine Republic have agreed the following: [...] The Armed Forces Minister of the French Republic will make available to the Argentinian army a mission of senior officers of the French army, which will provide technical assistance to the army of the Argentine Republic and its officers, with the aim of increasing the technical effectiveness and preparedness of the Argentinian army. [...] This agreement shall enter into force on the date of its signature and shall replace the individual contracts made with French military advisers currently posted to Argentina. It will remain in force until the expiry of one year from the date upon which either contracting party officially notifies its wish to stop its effects. Moreover, in the event of foreign hostilities, the mission may be immediately cancelled at the initiative of either government.
>
> (ADF/Doc. 74/12)

According to the provisions of the agreement, the mission consisted of three senior officers of the rank of Lieutenant-Colonel or Colonel in the French army that were to pass the benefit of their technical and professional knowledge on to the Argentine army (ADF/Doc. 74/12/Article 2). Their role consisted, in particular, of providing teaching within the *Escuela Superior de Guerra* – the Buenos Aires equivalent of the Paris *École Supérieure de Guerre* (Article 3). In addition to these three senior officers, and upon the request of the government of Argentina, other French army personnel were to be assigned to the mission on a temporary basis at the expense of the Argentine authorities (Article 4). The length of each mission member's stay in Argentina was normally 24 months, starting from the date of his journey to Buenos Aires (Article 1). He had an obligation not to divulge or reveal, in any way, to a foreign government or to any person, secrets or confidential matters of which he may become aware as a natural consequence of his role, or by any other means, it being understood that this obligation was to remain wholly in force after the roles as advisers to the Argentinian army had ended (Article 6). The Argentine government, by the offices of the Secretariat of War, was to pay the remuneration of the members of the mission (Article 12) and the costs of their and their families' travel to Buenos Aires (Article 13). Furthermore, during their stay in Buenos Aires, the members of the mission enjoyed immunity from the civilian jurisdiction of Argentinian courts for acts or infractions inherent to the exercise of their official duties (Article 9) and the same tax exemptions as members of the diplomatic mission of France to Argentina (Article 10). The instruction French teachers gave at the *Escuela Superior de Guerra* was 'highly appreciated in Buenos Aires' (ADF/Doc. 74/17).

Other French visits to the Escuela Superior de Guerra

Meanwhile, on the occasion of the celebrations for the 150th anniversary of the May Revolution in 1960, President Arturo Frondizi and the Commander in Chief of the Army, Carlos Toranzo Montero, invited his French counterpart and hero of the French Resistance, General André Demetz, to Buenos Aires, with the idea of inspecting and consolidating the action of the French military mission (ADF/Doc. 74/13). Demetz arrived accompanied by three officers: Lieutenant-Colonel Henri Grand d'Esnon, Captain Carron de la Carrière and Colonel Philibert (ADF/Doc. 74/14, 74/15), all veterans from Algeria. Toranzo Montero had been invited to follow a training course in Paris earlier that same year, where he met with Demetz. He had been accompanied by the then-promoted General Rosas, who was obviously already familiar with the French military methods, materials and organisation, and received for the occasion the ultimate decoration: *Commandeur de la Légion d'Honneur*, Legion of Honour Commander (ADF/Doc. 141/1):

> General Demetz, Chief of Staff of the Army, specially invited by General Toranzo Montero, Commander in Chief of the Army, has just spent a week in Buenos Aires. His stay coincided with 150th anniversary celebrations in which, in addition to our official delegation, twenty Flying School cadets took part. This means that French uniforms were present in the various events that took place on this occasion. The contacts made between General Demetz and General Toranzo Montero during the latter's visit to Paris last February were renewed here in, it seems to me, an atmosphere of real trust and warmth. General Demetz and the officers accompanying him will be able to testify to this. If the relationships we have with the Argentinian General Staff are so good, the credit for this goes largely to the excellent work done by our Military, Naval and Air Attaché, Colonel Serralta who, sadly, is at the end of his posting, and by the presence of our advisers at the School of War. The three officers we have here on a constant basis are extremely popular. One of the most remarkable, Colonel de Naurois, is also leaving Argentina after a three-year stay. I should like the Department to pass on to the Armed Forces Minister the appreciation I have for the activity of our officers in Argentina and in particular for that of those I have just named and who are leaving this country for good. The work they have done there deserves to be taken into account for their future careers.

(ADF/Doc. 74/16)

On this occasion, one of the officers who accompanied General Demetz, Lieutenant-Colonel Henri Grand d'Esnon, gave an extensive lecture on subversive war in the *Escuela Superior de Guerra*, at the end of which his superior offered some concluding thoughts. In his paper, Grand d'Esnon ratified de Naurois's statements with regard to the difference between Revolutionary War and Subversive War. Both expressions reflect, in their origins, conflicts of a different nature, which, with the passage of time, became synonyms (Mazzei 2002: 117). In this respect, he referred to an official text of the French army of 1956, which defined Subversive War in these terms:

> War waged within a territory under the control of a legal or de facto authority, considered an enemy by part of the inhabitants of the territory, which may be supported and reinforced from abroad or not, with the goal of wresting control of the territory from the authority in question or, at least, paralysing its action in the territory.
>
> (AMA/Grand d'Esnon 1960: 339–340)

This broad definition could include '[…] the War of American Independence, […] your own War of Independence, […] and the French Resistance against the forces of occupation' (AMA/Grand d'Esnon 1960: 340). In contrast, Revolutionary War was:

> In its most literal sense, […] an operation undertaken not only to change a group of leaders and the political orientation of a government, but also, and most especially, to bring down the pre-existing social order, with the aim of establishing another system built on a different basis. Of course, this definition applies especially to actions which, directed from Moscow or Peking, are intended to extend the communist regime, with all the upheaval this brings to established organizations and social relationships.
>
> (AMA/Grand d'Esnon 1960: 340)

It can be inferred from these definitions that, originally, all revolutionary wars were subversive, but not all subversive wars were revolutionary. Nevertheless, a careful reading of texts published by the *Revista de la Escuela Superior de Guerra* evidences an indiscriminate use of both categories.[15] According to Argentine Lieutenant-Colonel López Aufranc, the use of both terms as synonyms 'is a common error that should be avoided', since 'their goals are completely different' (AMA/López Aufranc 1959: 612). In his opinion, the confusion arises because 'Revolutionary War uses the forms and procedures of Subversive War', such as guerrilla war (AMA/López Aufranc 1959: 612–613). In his lecture, Grand d'Esnon explained this confusion as arising from the fact that 'the subversive argument is nearly essential in order to fulfil the revolutionary goal', and that 'subversive wars are becoming more and more likely to pursue revolutionary aims' (AMA/Grand d'Esnon 1960: 340). This is because

> Marxist studies of subversive war, by going deeply into the complete ana-
> lysis of this phenomenon, have completely renewed their conception
> while modernising their procedures [...] and there is no subversive action
> today which is not profoundly characterised by the Marxist contribution.
>
> (AMA/Grand d'Esnon 1960: 340–341)

The source of this confusion is deeper and can be found among the
French paratroopers who were veterans of the Viet Minh prisoner-of-war
camps. For these soldiers, the Algerian conflict was a continuation of this
revolutionary war, forming part of a war on a world scale: 'Hard Indochina experience turned those who were left from the contingent defeated
at Dien Bien Phu into genuine experts in Revolutionary War' (Mazzei
2002: 119–120). Indeed, for them, communism was (always) behind every
enemy. One of those veterans, Captain Jacques Mercier, maintained – in a
pamphlet which can still be found in the library of the *École Supérieure de
Guerre* – that the Algerian *FLN*'s extreme nationalism was not real, but a
long-term artificial creation of 'Marxist theoreticians', which followed the
following process: (1) Artificially create, if necessary, an aggressive nationalism; (2) Place the colonial power in the role of the accused; (3) Ensure
the triumph of the nationalist movement through dispossession of the capitalist power, if necessary through armed insurrection; (4) Some time after
recognition of independence, provoke an economic and social crisis ensuring the success of the local communist party, enabling Sovietisation
(Mercier 1958: 9–10).

Grand d'Esnon also added some new points when mentioning characteristics of subversive war, such as: (a) the importance of the psychological
aspect, since 'directed by the weaker against the stronger, subversion can
only succeed when the psychological factor multiplies the strength of the
weaker party and reduces the strength of the stronger'; (b) the difficulty in
identifying the enemy, since 'some of its members are intermingled with
the population and nothing can allow distinguishing them'; (c) the temporal
aspect of such a conflict which is 'always going to imply a long duration,
marked by violence and the spread of terror' (AMA/Grand d'Esnon 1960:
344–345). General Demetz approved of his subordinate's speech in his concluding comments, underlining the essential and indispensable virtues that
military leaders should present in order to succeed in fighting a subversive
war: constancy, self-control, firmness and intellectual discipline. He also
mentioned that, in such a war, officers of every rank are obliged to act in
ways that are normally foreign to them. He finished by highlighted the
importance of 'information' in wars centred on the population (AMA/
Grand d'Esnon 1960: 361–363).

Argentine theoreticians in the Escuela Superior de Guerra

It seems that Captain Mercier's arguments were transferred to the Argentine army, where many officers adopted his narratives as their own. Indeed, there were also Argentinians who created their own literature and published works on Revolutionary War and the fight against subversion in the *Revista de la Escuela Superior de Guerra*, from 1957 to 1962. This included officers who had studied at the *École Supérieure de Guerre*: Colonel Carlos Jorge Rosas (1953–1955) on *Strategy and Tactics* (AMA/Rosas 1958); Lieutenant-Colonel Alcides López Aufranc (1957–1959) on *Revolutionary War in Algeria* (AMA/ López Aufranc 1959), in which article he brings a direct vision of operations during his two weeks *in situ*; and the two works by Lieutenant-Colonel Manrique Miguel Mom (1956–1958) on *Revolutionary War* (AMA/Mom 1958; 1959), both based on courses he had taken in Paris. These writings were later developed by Colonel Guillermo Osiris Villegas (1962) in his book *Guerra Revolucionaria Comunista* ('Communist Revolutionary War'), the publication of which formed the basis of his reputation as the main Argentine theoretician on the subject.

For instance, when Lieutenant-Colonel Manrique Miguel Mom returned from Paris, he published a veritable manual of Revolutionary War, enabling us to appreciate the extent to which the concept had become generalised. Mom himself acknowledged that his text was not original, but a 'translation and adaptation of concepts and/or paragraphs and/or complete texts' taken from the *Revue Militaire d'Information* ('Military Information Review') – the main organ of publication of the French army – as well as class notes of conferences or lectures that took place in the *École Supérieure de Guerre*, or the writings of Mao Tse Tung (AMA/Mom 1958: 641, 1959: 489).

In the first of these it is notable that after establishing the difference between the revolutionary and subversive processes we have already seen, Mom offered as examples of subversive war the Argentine Revolution of May 1810, the San Martín campaigns of Independence, the Revolutions of September 1930 and September 1951, the so-called Liberation Revolution of September 1955, and the Algerian Revolution of 13 May 1958 (AMA/ Mom 1958: 648). The eclectic mix of situations he selects and the fact that he calls these processes *subversive* is interesting. For him they are clearly positive, which is diametrically opposite to the negative way in which subversion would later be perceived. Mom continued by describing the phases of revolution, where the influence of Lacheroy's work on the instructors of the French military school becomes clear. Following Lacheroy, Mom explained that the nature of the new war saw the population as the axis, for which reason it has to be reached by psychological action, which is, in reality, the new, essential weapon (AMA/Mom 1958: 652). Among the associations Mom names as having the revolutionary aim of destroying established society are the Union of French Mothers, the Fighters for Peace, and the Human Rights League (AMA/Mom 1958: 655). He ended his first report by stating that the successes of communism were due to the fact that it had taken advantage of the 'surprise factor', since the societies in which it had become established did not detect it in time (AMA/Mom 1958: 664).

In his second article, imbued with the crusade mysticism that characterised his French peers, Mom included, for the first time for an Argentinian officer, every ongoing war or conflict (large and small) among Revolutionary Wars:

> The conflict *currently under way* throughout the 'free' world is nothing other than a REVOLUTIONARY war, conceived, prepared and conducted by Marxism–Leninism with a view to the conquest of total world power.
>
> (AMA/Mom 1959: 489, emphases as in original)

Mom continued, as did all followers of the French theoreticians, by expounding the revolutionary phases. He concluded by calling on his counter-revolutionary colleagues to 'do likewise before it is too late' (AMA/Mom 1959: 515).

Thus, all conflicts were conceived as being one, a generalised Revolutionary War conducted by 'Marxism–Leninism' against the 'free world', whose ultimate goal was the conquest of the world. Along this same theoretical line, Lieutenant-Colonel Tomás Sánchez de Bustamante gave a historical development of the tactics and strategies of Revolutionary War, re-stating the idea of one sole war on a planetary scale, 'a conflict between two civilisations' – the Christian West and the atheist East – whereby the aim of one of the sides (the 'Reds') was 'the gradual implementation of communism the world over' (AMA/Sánchez de Bustamante 1960: 602–603, 1961, 1962).

It seems from reading these texts that there was little interest in whether the wars mentioned were originally wars of independence or decolonialisation, or whether, according to official texts, every war of liberation was a subversive war but only some were revolutionary. In practice, as far as the French theorists and their Argentinian disciples were concerned, if all the conflicts globally formed part of one single war for the conquest of the world, every subversive war was, at the same time, revolutionary and, therefore, the terms became synonymous. Similarly, to combat this type of warfare the interchangeable terms of 'fight against subversion' and 'counter-revolutionary war' were used. According to Mazzei, in Argentina, 'the adjective *revolutionary* was the preferred usage to refer to this type of war, whereas for the techniques used to fight it, the sadly infamous phrase *fight against subversion* was preferred' (2002: 122).

Beyond the conceptions of paratrooper veterans, it is valid to ask why the French army institutionally made these theories – all of which gave excessive weight to Algerian communism over the nationalist and religious aspects of the Algerian *FLN* revolt – its own. One possible answer to this question is provided by an Argentinian officer, Lieutenant-Colonel Alcides López Aufranc:

> If the Algerian War was exclusively *subversive*, that is, its aim was to shake off the yoke of the mother country, solely to achieve independence, this struggle would have enjoyed the moral and material support of countries that believe in the people's right to self-determination. […] However, describing it as *revolutionary* immediately associates it with communism and this justifies France before world opinion. […] The Western powers were disqualified from supporting the Algerians. […] Part of the divisions that France was obliged to keep mobilised at the disposal of NATO were taken to Algeria on the understanding that red aggression had already occurred, albeit through intermediaries.
>
> (AMA/López Aufranc 1959: 613–614, emphases added)

The religious or colonial origins of particular conflicts mattered little. Behind them the 'wolf in sheep's clothing' always lurked. However, some years later, an editorial by the leadership of the *Escuela Superior de Guerra* opened up, recognising that:

> Insofar as Algeria was concerned, even though it did demonstrate a commencement of hostilities based on procedures congruent with Soviet doctrine, there was no evidence of a clearly defined communist goal. It was more a case of a revolutionary and subversive force from the point of view of its techniques, but politically geared towards emancipation.
>
> (AMA/Prefacio de la Dirección 1963)

Conclusion

We have covered a phase of the French presence in Argentina that resulted from the transfer of French experience with subversion, set against the backdrop of the Cold War and the loss of the Algerian colony. Having arrived at this point, we must ask ourselves what verdict stands regarding the presence of the French military mission in the Argentine army from 1957 to 1962. It can reasonably be stated that it established the theoretical, methodological and even semantic basis that informed the repressive actions of the Argentine army during its Dirty War in the 1970s. The institution of the *disappeared*, the use of torture, the random searching of towns, the death flights, turning activists to infiltrate armed organisations and territorial division to 'control the population' are French creations applied in Argentina, about which Trinquier (1964) theorised in his book, *Modern Warfare: A French View of Counterinsurgency* (Llumá 2002a: 15). Although the French military advisers did not refer to 'torture' as such, they certainly brought a vision in which this practice was accepted: they transferred the ideology of counter-revolutionary war; they provided the bibliography to justify its techniques; and they taught Argentine officers the importance, in this particular type of war, of gathering information at all costs. During those five years, the Argentine army developed its entire structure of 'anti-subversive' repression and the basis was established for the development and internalisation of the so-called 'Doctrine of National Security' (Mazzei 2002: 137).

Willing to share its experience, the French military started advising the Argentine state in the ways and means of dealing with internal subversion. Indeed, following the establishment of an important French mission in 1957, it has been proven that Argentina's armed forces were trained by French advisers at the *Escuela Superior de Guerra* in Buenos Aires to wage a 'new type of war'. As we have seen, their training focused on counter-insurgency methods developed by the French in Indochina and Algeria, such as interrogation techniques – meaning, torture (Abramovici 2001; Carlson 2000: 71; Feierstein 2010: 45; Frontalini and Caiti 1984: 31; MacMaster 2004: 8; Potash 1980: 320; Rouquier 1978: 471–472). From the late 1950s until the early 1960s, articles about the doctrine of Revolutionary War written by French officers appeared in the Argentine Higher School of War's official magazine – *La Revista de la Escuela Superior de Guerra* – and Argentinian soldiers drew upon these ideas in their own publications (Carlson 2000: 71). In other words, through conferences, lectures, articles in military reviews, and technical training exercises, the French advisers, followed by their Argentine disciples (who would end up surpassing their masters), emphasised from 1957 onwards that the battlefield would now be the population itself and that information on potential subversives had to be gathered at all costs, even through the use of torture (Robin 2004: 201).

For a long time, however, that training 'had no practical relevance for Argentina, especially in the urban areas' (Heinz 1995: 75–76). In fact, the 'New War' described by the French assessors did not exist in Argentina at the beginning of the 1960s: 'It was an anticipated war that the Argentine military would actually fight less than twenty years later' (Carlson 2000: 73). Yet, even in the 1960s, 'Argentina and its people constitute[d] an objective that [was] too important for international Marxism to overlook' (AMA/Nougués 1962: 30). It was precisely because the Argentine government was looking for an effective way to stop rebellious Peronists, who were supposedly taking part in the communist 'conspiracy' against the established order (Feierstein 2010: 44; Ranalletti 2005: 291), that the French counter-insurgency doctrine quickly found 'fertile ground' in Argentina (Amaral 1998: 183; Robin 2004: 202).

By sharing their specific *savoir-faire* in Revolutionary War, the French prepared the ground for the institutionalisation of torture that would be implemented between 1976 and 1983 in Argentina. They therefore deserve the label of 'transnational institutional torturers'. Yet their influence did not end in 1962. Indeed, according to French political analyst Georges Gabriel Périès, the 'process of decontextualisation and adaptation' of the doctrine of Revolutionary War in Argentina was a two-stage operation: theoretical between 1958 and 1962, and practical between the end of the 1970s and the early 1980s. At this point, the Argentine 'students' of the French advisers would make their entrance onto political stage by launching the *Proceso de Reorganización Nacional* – the 'National Reorganisation Process' (Périès 1999: 768). And this is what I shall discuss in the next chapter.

Notes

1 Often faced with difficult choices in the presence of a huge, disparate subject area and unable to give an equal share to every issue, I considered it sensible to give the greatest share to problems for which English-language sources are, up to now, the least accessible.

2 This research was triggered by documents and associated interest in them relating to the Argentinian–French connection with regards to the French export of 'torture'. If the research had been started in France (i.e. not in Argentina), it might well have given rise to a rather different, or wider, pattern of linkages, and a slightly more 'globalised' picture. Although the question of this monograph was *not* 'To what parts of the world did France export its savoir-faire on torture', it is interesting to note that a large number of *Pieds-Noirs* settled in continental France, while others migrated to different countries, such as Spain, Italy and other South American states (Verdo 1989; Palacio 1968). Indeed, the end of the Algerian war did lead to some return migration, and the Algerians resident in France were forced, as a result of the 1962 Evian Accords that ended the war, to leave (Alba and Silberman 2002). According to British social anthropologist, Professor Jeremy Keenan, there are certainly networks-linkages-associations operating between France, Algeria and South Africa, with the 'return flow' of South African Apartheid torturers who came and worked for the Algerian regime of the 1990s when it was inflicting massive torture – just 40 years on from Massu's activities (2009, 2013).

3 A highly decorated officer who had fought for France in every major conflict since World War I, Jacques Émile Charles Marie Massu joined General de Gaulle's Free French forces in 1940. After liberation, he spent years commanding troops fighting nationalist forces in Indochina. But General Massu's greatest fame and notoriety rested on his role in Algeria, where his harsh measures resulted in the defeat of the *FLN* and caused him to be revered by soldiers and veterans' groups, who called him the 'father of paratroopers', *'le père de paras'*. It is interesting to note that, for much of the ensuing 40 years, General Massu was confronted, even haunted, by the tactics of torture systematically used in Algeria. Following the publication in French newspapers of the account of Louisette Ighilahriz – who described the months of physical assaults she endured during the Algerian War, when he was in command (see Chapter 1) – he was asked to respond and publicly apologise for the use of torture, acknowledging that: 'It was not necessary' as they 'could have gotten along without it very well', thereby confirming that torture had been institutionalised in Algeria (Beaugé 2000). However, he insisted that he personally had not been involved in imposing torture (Kaufman 2002).

4 With regard to the fear of Communist ideology, it has to be noted that, Daniele Ganser revealed in his book, *NATO's Secret Armies: Operation Gladio and Terrorism in Western Europe*, that the alliance's own secret history had links to terrorism in

the context of the 'War against Communism' (Ganser 2005). The existence of Operation Gladio came into light at a time when experts were debating whether NATO wass suited to deal with the 'Global War on Terror'.

5 Military articles of the *Archivos Militares Argentinos (AMA)*, Argentine Military Archives – see Appendix 2. Hereafter, reference to articles of the AMA will be made as follow: AMA/Name of the author + date + page number. For example here, 'AMA/Mom 1959: 491' refers to a quote found in the article of the Argentine military archives, written by Mom in 1959 at page 491 – that is, Mom (1959) 'Guerra Revolucionaria: Causas-Proceso-Desarrollo', *Revista de la Escuela Superior de Guerra*, No. 334, p. 491.

6 French Lieutenant-Colonel Roger Trinquier was an officer in the colonial infantry. He led counter-guerrilla units against the Viet Minh, including thousands of Montagnard tribesmen in the climatic battle of Dien Bien Phu. Narrowly escaping being purged as a Vichy sympathizer, he rotated between training assignments in France and duties as a paratrooper in Algeria, including with the 10th Parachute Division under General Jacques Massu during the Battle of Algiers in 1957 (Trinquier 1964: xi–xviii).

7 Frantz Fanon was born in the French colony of Martinique in 1925. His family occupied a social position within Martinican society that could reasonably qualify them as part of the black bourgeoisie. Fanon was raised in this environment. Politicised and torn between the assimilationism of Martinique's middle class and his racial identity, Fanon left the colony in 1943, at the age of 18, to fight with the Free French forces in the waning days of the Second World War. After the war, he stayed in France to study psychiatry and medicine where he encountered bafflingly simplistic anti-black racism, so different from the complex, class-permeated distinctions of shades of lightness and darkness one finds in the Caribbean. As a psychiatrist, Fanon came to realise the profound emotional and psychological toll colonialism can have on the psyche of the colonised – a realisation that led to the publication of his *Black Skin, White Masks* (1952). The next year, Fanon moved to Algeria to head the psychiatry department at Blida-Joinville Hospital – a post that profoundly impacted his outlook on what can, and what he felt must, be done about colonialism. The following year, 1954, marked the eruption of the Algerian war of independence against France. At the still segregated hospital, Fanon found himself treating both the Algerian victims of torture and the French officers who had administered this torture. In the village of Tebessa, for example, most men were killed and stuck on poles all along the road going out of town, with their genitals cut off and stuffed in their mouths. As Fanon wrote, survivors lived in a state of trauma for many years and the impact on young French soldiers was also hugely damaging. The war was creating an increasingly hostile environment in Algeria and Fanon began to feel unable to act according to his conscience and knowledge: he believed that to truly promote mental health, he needed to support political and economic changes in the larger society and decided to help the *FLN*. In 1957, he was expelled from his position in Algeria by the French government. All of Fanon's ideas about the complex role of colonisation on the colonised came to fruition in his ground-breaking book, *The Wretched of the Earth* (1963) – a work that addressed the psychic consequences of torture that were perpetrated in Algeria.

8 The conceptual groundwork for the theory was laid out by Colonel Lionel-Max Chassin and Colonel Charles Lacheroy, after both havingc completed a tour of duty in Indochina and written about the manner in which Mao Tse Tung led the revolution in China and assumed power (Ambler 1966: 308; Lacheroy 2003: 19, 68–69).

9 In *Algeria Unveiled* (1965), Fanon takes the veil as a starting point for an exploration of the new Algeria that was being created through the revolution. According

to him, the veil stood as confirmation of Algeria's backwards patriarchy, of its primitive insularity and of the passivity of Algerian women. However, Fanon also inverts the veil and shows how by fighting the French, women also asserted their place in Algerian society. Behind the veil, their thoughts were unknowable: they could be observing the colonial administration with contempt, calmly plotting its downfall or carrying grenades rather than pliantly accepting its reign. The veil also stirred less pragmatic concerns: it spoke to a highly sexualized realm of 'exotic themes deeply rooted in the unconscious' (Fanon 1965: 173). The Algerian women's privacy, in which their thoughts and feelings were hidden from the coloniser, invoked a frantic response. Occupation became a conduit for the most basic and vicious of human impulses: torture, dehumanisation, and sexual assaults. It shifted the rules of the game and empowered the allegedly placid: Algeria became a playground for phobias and sadism. This was also witnessed during the Abu Ghraib scandal.

10 The Constitution of Argentina was adopted on 1 May 1853 and has been amended many times starting in 1860. It was last amended and revised in 1994. The reformed Constitution entered into force on 24 August 1994.

11 Interestingly enough, this ideological component was also a legacy of the French political right, the origins of which date back to the nineteenth century (Llumá 2002a: 9). In 1959, this trend would be taken up by *Ciudad Católica* (Catholic City), an Argentinian version of *Cité Catholique* founded in France by Catholic traditionalist propagandist Jean Ousset, which had influenced the psychological development of the military in Algeria. Ousset's publications became vitally important to complement, adapt and legitimise the French military approach to the management of subversion and state terrorism in Argentina as they constituted a bulwark of Catholic justification for the use of torture against prisoners considered to be 'subversives'. The actions of the *Ciudad Católica* were widely disseminated in the Argentinian military world: they constituted a 'revitalisation of the militancy of traditionalist Catholics and the extreme right in the spaces where the military gathered socially, such as training institutes, parishes, Catholic lay associations and groups' (Ranaletti 2005: 301). A surge of writings, lectures, talks, courses, private study groups, periodicals and spiritual retreats promoted by 'trainers' such as priest Julio Meinvielle (leader of Catholic anti-Semitism), Carlos Sacheri (president of the *Ciudad Católica*) and Jordán Bruno Genta (an agitator enrolled in the Catholic extreme right) also reproduced the French analyses. The *Cursillos de Cristiandad* (Short Courses in Christianity) movement succeeded in giving the local right wing a mysticism (Llumá 2002a: 9). Its members (*Cursillistas*) took inspiration from the *Coopérateurs du Christ Roi* (Cooperators of Christ the King), a French Catholic ultra-right-wing organisation with the magazine *Verbe* at its centre, led by two priests, Sarat and Grasset, who had also sided with the *OAS* insurrectionists in Algeria.

12 Diplomatic documents of the *Archives Diplomatiques Francaises (ADF)*, French Diplomatic Archives – see Appendix 1. Hereafter, reference to documents of ADF will be made as follow: AMF/File nimber + Document number. For example here, 'ADF/Doc. 177/3' refers to a quote found in Document #3 of File #177 of the French diplomatic archives – that is, Dossier 177 – Cote 18–12–1; No. 403/AS; A.s. Communauté Francaise d'Argentine; Buenos Aires, le 28 Septembre 1970, L'Ambassadeur de France en Argentine (Jean de La Chevardière de La Grandville), à Son Excellence Monsieur Maurice Schumann, Ministre des Affaires Etrangères, Direction des Conventions Administratives et des Affaires Consulaires. (Doc.177/3)

13 This was recognised as difficult in light of of the country's federal organisation since it seems impossible for the legal administrative divisions to match all the zones, sub-zones and areas (AMA/Nougués 1962: 39–41).

14 The generals who seized power on 24 March 1976 proposed to carry out a complete reorganisation of the Argentine economy, society and polity. They labelled this transformation the *Proceso de Reorganización Nacional* ('National Reorganisation Process'). What this 'process' meant in fact was unlimited power for the military to do anything it wished (Potash 1980).
15 An example of the interchangeable use of the two terms can be found in Bentresque (1959).

Chapter 4

Continuing education

The implementation of French *savoir-faire* during the Argentine Dirty War

As we saw in Chapter 3, archival documents found in Paris and Buenos Aires revealed how French soldiers who had been operating in Algeria in the early 1950s went on to teach their *savoir-faire* in revolutionary warfare to the Argentine military prior to the Dirty War (1976–1983). Indeed, the French contribution was to be crucially important in fashioning the techniques and ideas behind Argentinian state terrorism. It was to play a defining role in conditioning the Argentine military to the use of torture. A detailed analysis of the archival material clearly gives evidence of instances of French state criminality as a 'transnational institutional torturer'.

This chapter challenges the idea that the intensification of French influence and the beginnings of state terrorism in Argentina should be taken as a mere spatio-temporal coincidence (Abramovici 2001; Ranaletti 2005). Rather, it argues for a causal relationship. Central to the main argument of this research is the view that an adequate explanation of torture perpetration requires us to look beyond the torture chamber, or even beyond the states in which the torture is practised, and focus attention on the larger policy context in which it is embedded. For many years, it was the fashion to insist that any counter-insurgency of a foreign nature in Latin America was entirely 'Made in the USA' (Weschler 1998: 119). While recognising that, in the current English language literature on the subject, most authors refer to the *American* influence and only 'to a lesser extent' to the *French*, this monograph argues that the French influence appears to have been much more important than others in Argentina. Indeed, the counter-insurgency doctrine adopted and developed by the Argentine generals was nourished by the Americans but, above all, by the French. General Ramón Camps, former chief of police of Buenos Aires province, described these foreign influences in a newspaper interview:

> In Argentina, we were influenced first by the French and then by the United States. [...] They organised centers for teaching counterinsurgency techniques [...] and sent out instructors, observers, and an enormous amount of literature.
>
> (La Razón, 4 January 1981, quoted in CONADEP 1985: 474)

According to General Reynaldo Benito Bignone, who became the last military president of Argentina on 1 July 1982:

> In the early 1960s [...] the Americans had no such doctrine, and certainly no experience. Afterwards, they had the School of the Americas, but in the meantime, we had already written our own military regulations to combat subversion [...] thanks to the teachings of the French advisers, who had given us documents from the Algerian War.
>
> (General Reynaldo Benito Bignone, as interviewed by Robin 2004: 316–317)

On 25 April 1995, the Argentine Army Chief of Staff, General Martín Antonio Balza, admitted in a speech broadcast on a TV news programme that the military persecuted and killed political opponents during the Dirty War against 'subversives' from 1976 to 1983. According to him, the Argentine army 'employed illegitimate methods, including the suppression of life, to obtain information'.[1] It was the first time a high-ranking military official had acknowledged that the army tortured and killed political opponents during the Dirty War. Later, when asked about the consequences that the French training in counter-insurgency warfare had in shaping the minds of Dirty War Argentine torturers, General Balza replied as follows:

> [...] It was a political, ideological, military and religious cocktail that engendered the most criminal regime in our history. And for this cocktail to be mixed, the teaching provided by French military advisers from the end of the 1950s played a fundamental role. That was added to – but the damage was already done – by the influence of the North Americans [...] the French took a harmful, pernicious concept to Argentina which literally poisoned the minds of officers of my generation: that of the 'enemy within'. [...] For reasons specific to Argentina, which long resisted any form of allegiance to the North Americans, the influence of the famous 'doctrine of national security' only became effective at the end of the 1960s, and I would say that it played a role of consolidating the teachings of the French.
>
> (General Martín Antonio Balza, as interviewed by Robin 2004: 200–202)

This chapter also reveals the connection between the circulation of 'French ideas' that helped form a certain way of thought related to the issues of political protest and violence in Argentina from 1957 onwards on the one hand, and the use of torture during the Argentine Dirty War on the other. Indeed, the French contribution was crucial to the development of the legitimising narrative used by the dictatorship to justify, both within the Armed Forces and to society, the repressive actions they deployed. As seen in Chapter 3, this collaboration awoke great interest on the part of the Argentine military and Catholic traditionalists: any social protest would be seen as concealing, behind the social, financial or political demands, an action aimed at weakening the 'Catholic West'. This, in turn, made it possible to put any manner of actions into practice – no matter how cruel and inhuman – to defend a civilisation threatened with 'destruction'.

In the first section of this chapter, I shall explore the reasons for the departure of the French military mission from the *Escuela Superior de Guerra* in 1962. It might indeed seem paradoxical that at that very time that the Argentine military had arrived at a mutually agreeable doctrinal understanding with their French colleagues, the influence of the French started to decline in this institution.

The second part of this chapter explains how the rise of armed organisations in Argentina at the beginning of the 1970s and the return of Peronism to government encouraged the Argentine military to prepare decisive action – and how, to this end, they again sought military advice from the French. I shall also briefly draw up an assessment of the amendment to the Agreement of 11 February 1960 signed between the government of the French Republic and the government of the Argentine Republic, concerning the mission of French military advisers to the Argentine army.

In the third part of this chapter, I shall reveal why in 1981 only the agreement was 'put on hold', by suspending its de facto application. Indeed, the last two French military assessors would leave Buenos Aires on 15 July and 4 November 1981 respectively.

Finally, in the fourth part of this chapter, I shall explain how the movement of the *Madres de la Plaza de Mayo* provides a paradoxical example of Risse, Ropp and Sikkink's civil society 'boomerang pattern' of influence and change (Risse *et al.* 1999: 18). These *Madres* – 'Mothers' – in exchanging information about the fate of their children, bypassed the state that had institutionalised torture (Argentina) to seek help in the state that had contributed to its institutionalisation (France).

A decline of French influence from 1962 onwards?

Following the establishment of an important French military mission in 1957 in Buenos Aires, Argentina's armed forces were trained at the *Escuela Superior de Guerra* by French advisers to wage a 'new type of war'. As we have seen, this training focused on counter-insurgency methods developed by the French in Indochina and Algeria, such as interrogation techniques, or in other words, torture (Abramovici 2001; Carlson 2000: 71; Feierstein 2010: 45; Frontalini and Caiti 1984: 31; MacMaster 2004: 8; Potash 1980: 320; Rouquier 1978: 471–472). From the late 1950s until the early 1960s, around 20 articles about the doctrine of Revolutionary War written by French officers appeared in the Argentine Higher School of War's official magazine – *La Revista de la Escuela Superior de Guerra* – and Argentinian soldiers drew upon these ideas in their own publications (Carlson 2000: 71). In other words, through French-led conferences, lectures, articles in military reviews, and technical training exercises, the French advisers emphasised from 1957 onwards that the battlefield would now be the population itself and that information on potential subversive activity had to be gathered at all costs (Robin 2004: 201). During the Dirty War, their Argentinian military disciples would end up surpassing their masters.

In 1962, however, Lieutenant-Colonel Jean Nougués' last article (AMA/Nougués 1962) marked the end of the French military presence in the *Escuela Superior de Guerra*. It may appear surprising that, at the very time that the Argentine military had arrived at a doctrinal symbiosis with their French colleagues, the presence of the French in the Argentine Higher School of War started to decline. The reasons that may explain the Argentinian officers distancing themselves from their teachers are twofold: a new alignment with the United States and the French themselves abandoning the doctrine of Revolutionary War, as I discuss in the next two sections.

Change of influence: an alignment with United States policies?

At almost the same time, North American influence was growing. According to Belgian specialist Joseph Comblin (1977), the United States established 500 main military bases and nearly 3000 secondary bases from 1947 to 1961 to guarantee its national security. Many of these were located near socialist countries and prevented them from expanding ideologies outside their borders, while the United States brandished the threat of atomic war if they did so (Comblin 1977: 83–84). During the Second World War, the United States had formed the Inter-American Defense Board; in 1947 they succeeded in having a majority of Latin American countries sign the Inter-American Treaty of Reciprocal Assistance; in 1948 they set up the Organisation of American States; in 1949 they created the North Atlantic Treaty Organisation; and in 1951 the signing of the Mutual Security Act created the Military Aid Plan, through which the States of Latin America received military equipment, arms and instructors. At this time, since conflict hypotheses provided for the possibility of an extra-continental Soviet invasion, the United States supplied the Latin American militaries with heavy weaponry and naval aviation equipment through the Military Aid Plan so that they could fight the invasion.

The whole strategy of the United States had to be re-thought between 1960 and 1961 when the USSR also became a nuclear power, because if a total conventional war could destroy one of the adversaries, an atomic war would destroy both. As López explains, the new strategy of dissuasion gave rise to the formulation of an indirect global strategy, 'fruit of the gradual *nuclear stalemate* which cancelled out the possibilities of direct confrontation between the two superpowers', while in Latin America the notion of 'hemi-spherical defence against external attack was becoming out of date and con-cerns about internal security and the control of internal subversion in each country became enthroned' (López 1987: 51; emphasis as in original). These concerns grew stronger when faced with the almost simultaneous beginnings of decolonisation and revolutionary activities, which highlighted the import-ance and effectiveness that guerrilla warfare could have, on its own or in concert with conventional military operations. 'Without distinguishing between the very diverse forms of these processes, national security experts only paid close attention to the techniques used, bundling all the processes together as *revolutionary* and *terrorist* wars', whose common denominator was their supposed alliance with Moscow' (Oliveira-Cézar 2002: 26; emphasis as in original).

Argentina had kept its distance from the United States, with its neutrality during both world wars and its delay in ratifying the treaties and pacts pro-posed by them. Among the military there was a strong feeling of anti-imperialism, but this antipathy did not mean that they would not have adopted the concept of bipolarity and that they would not have lined up with the 'Christian West' against 'Marxist atheism'. On the contrary, stimulated by Catholic integrism,[2] the Argentine military embraced the new crusade against those who set out to destroy their value system, 'the worst enemies to our way of life', as General Carlos Túrolo put it in 1961 when Cuba declared itself socialist (ADF/Doc. 74/19). Indeed, under John Fitzgerald Kennedy, the training of Latin American officers then became a priority for the United States: the US Army changed its policy towards Latin American armies with the creation of the Inter-American Defense College, the invitation to Con-ferences of American Armies and, fundamentally, the exponential growth in the number of Latin American officers trained in US and Panama Canal col-leges (Mazzei 2002: 136–137).

However, even in this context, it appears the French remained influential. Indeed, they had also reached the Panama Canal College and would, as a consequence, introduce the French doctrine of Revolutionary War to a larger public during the first Conference of the *Escuela de las Americas* (School of the Americas) in 1961 (Périès 1999: 875). Both French and Argentinian theoreti-cians who had been trained at the *École Supérieure de Guerre* or at the *Escuela Superior de Guerra* during the Algerian War were present (including Lieutenant-Colonel Roger Trinquier) and would give conferences and lec-tures in this institution, where more than 100 would-be torturers were trained by the mid-1970s, before 'performing' in Vietnam, Bolivia, Guate-mala, Peru, Chile, Venezuela, Salvador, Nicaragua and Uruguay, among others (Llumá 2002a: 10; Robin 2003).

This is how French and new Argentinian experts taught some of their techniques of counter-revolutionary war – including torture – to the next generation of Latin American officers. Returning from this conference, Chief of the Argentine Army, General José Pablo Spirito, created a secret 'committee to fight against the Marxist expansion' which would be managed by Colonel Alcides Lopez Aufranc, an ex-student of the Paris *École Supérieure de Guerre*, as we have seen, who would be chief of the army between 1972 and 1973. Lopez Aufranc actively collaborated with Lieutenant-Colonel Robert Louis Brentesque in the design of the military exercises 'Hierro', 'Hierro Forjado' and 'Azucena' from the 1960s (Llumá 2002a: 10). As Bentresque explained:

> Regarding the reorganisation of the Argentinian army [...] it was mainly an operational army without territorial bases. So we mounted an exercise called *Hierro* [Iron] and *Hierro Forjado* [Wrought Iron] with Rosas and Mom, to see if, firstly, territorialisation could work in Argentina and secondly to accustom military minds to a territorial system. [...] Rosas listened to me, and Mom too. The exercise lasted nearly a year and it worked.
>
> (Lieutenant-Colonel Robert Louis Bentresque, as interviewed by Périès 1999: 788)

French influence culminated in the organisation in October 1961 of an Inter-American Course on Counter-Revolutionary War in the *Escuela Superior de Guerra* of Buenos Aires, attended by 14 Latin American countries from the continent. Indeed, the programme of study had been elaborated by the French assessors. According to the French Ambassador at the time, Armand Blanquet du Chayla, the French and their experience were so influential that the US advisers 'were seen to be jealous' (ADF/Doc. 74/19). The new French Military Attaché, Colonel Notelle, had informed his ambassador that the objective of the course was official recognition that communism was the common enemy and official acceptance of an action plan against Marxist subversion (ADF/Doc. 74/18):

> A course on the fight against communism is currently taking place in Buenos Aires, benefiting officers from the USA and Latin American republics. The idea of the course was born during a visit by the School of War of the Argentinian army to Peru. A French adviser was one of the leaders from the School of War. General Spirito, Chief of Staff of the Army, representing Argentina at the Panama Conference held last July had taken up the idea with the aim of: (1) Having communism officially recognised as a common enemy; (2) Having an action plan against Marxist subversion accepted and gaining agreement that a study, as defined in Annex II, would be developed as part of the Inter-American courses due to take place in Buenos Aires. Annex II was written by the General Staff of the Argentinian Army with the close collaboration of the French advisers.
>
> (ADF/Doc. 74/18)

Further to the Panama discussions, General Spirito, upon his return, created the Committee to Combat Marxist Expansion, placing former student of the *École Supérieure de Guerre*, Colonel Lopez Aufranc, at its head. The course was taking place under the authority of the Commander of the School of War. It included 39 officers as course members representing the following countries: Bolivia, Brazil, Colombia, Chile, Ecuador, United States, Guatemala, Honduras, Mexico, Panama, Paraguay, Peru, Uruguay and Venezuela. Among the leaders and lecturers, 'the French advisers were playing one of the most important roles, albeit discreetly' (ADF/Doc. 74/18). On 6 October 1961, in a note to the French Minister of Foreign Affairs, the Military, Naval and Air Attaché to the French Embassy in Argentina explained the role played by the French assessors in the Inter-American Course on Counter-Revolutionary War, which had recently been inaugurated at the *Escuela Superior de Guerra* in Buenos Aires, and the 'jealousy' of the American military delegation:

This Argentinian initiative had 14 American states sign up for it, each state represented by two or three officers. The General Staff of the Army and that of the Higher School of War are very pleased with this significant participation, which seems to bear witness to a certain respect for this country's armed forces. The roles of the French military advisers in the design and preparation of this course were instrumental and the presence of United States military personnel among the participants on this course must be highlighted, the course reserving a special place for the study of the anti-Marxist struggle in a spirit and ways that largely benefit from the experience acquired in this area by the French army. It can be especially welcomed that North American military circles [...] have recently shown a certain jealousy of the influence of French advisers in the Argentinian General Staffs and in the Buenos Aires Higher School of War.

(ADF/Doc. 74/19)

This was a 'jealousy' reinforced by Argentine General Alcides López Aufranc:

To prepare this course [Inter-American Course on Counter-Revolutionary War], I worked in close collaboration with three advisers of the time, and mainly with Robert Bentresque, who was a real expert in anti-subversive warfare. [...] [The Americans] were even very jealous, to the point of calling for the departure of the French military mission! But, hey, everything the Americans knew about Revolutionary War, they learned from us!

(General Alcides López Aufranc, as interviewed by Robin 2004: 213)

Still on the same topic, the French Ambassador in Argentina, Armand Blanquet du Chayla, explained that the nature of the Course on Counter-Revolutionary War and its Inter-American character demonstrated 'quite an intention of anti-communist engagement' (ADF/Doc. 74/19). But it was even more significant that the opening of the course was actually presided over by President Frondizi. In his presence, General Carlos Túrolo, Principal of the *Escuela Superior de Guerra*, developed in his inaugural speech the theme of the indispensable coordination between the American countries to anticipate and possibly wage a 'ruthless war' that guards as much 'against the mind as against the body ... the greatest enemy of our way of life' (ADF/Doc. 74/19).

Along with the Inter-American Course on Counter-Revolutionary War, there were other indications of the degree of mutual understanding reached between French and Argentinian officers and other examples of their contribution to the system of repression in the hemisphere. One example is the development and implementation of the CONINTES Plan (*CONmocion INTerna del EStado*) – which spoke of a 'national menace' from an 'internal political enemy' – from 1958 to 1960, according to which people accused of terrorism were subject to military jurisdiction (Llumá 2002a: 8; Périès 1999: 808; Ranaletti 2005: 300–301). During these years, the Argentine army had also developed a territorial organisation method based on a grid pattern, or *quadrillage*, of dividing the terrain on a model similar to that used by French troops in Algeria. In this way, the whole country was divided into areas, zones and sub-zones, forming a network that extended over the entire territory, based on the concept that the population was the terrain to be conquered and defended.[3] The application of the CONINTES Plan in 1960 was the first practical application of this territorial schema and of this new role for the army as the guardian of internal order (Llumá 2002a: 15–16; Mazzei 2002: 131–132; Ranaletti 2005: 300–301).

Although the plan of training military to the doctrine of Revolutionary War was spreading, the French military mission in Buenos Aires began noticing a change in the Frondizi government, which wanted to align more closely with the United States, a direction with which Charles de Gaulle had strategic problems (Llumá 2002a: 9). As we saw earlier, the Argentine army had moved from German influence to French, because they could not bring themselves to accept US leadership in spite of the many officers already training in United States bases. But all this changed from 1962 when Juan Carlos Onganía became Commander in Chief of the Argentine Army and brought it closer to the viewpoints of the United States, with the support of General Alejandro Agustín Lanusse.[4]

According to the French Ambassador, Jean-Paul Boncour, General Juan Carlos Onganía had never favoured the French teachings – too intellectualised for his taste, in particular on account of the importance they gave to psychological action – and had evinced irritation because the IV Annual Conference of American Armies held in 1963 in Fort Amador had concentrated on French theories of psychological warfare instead of dedicating itself to a discussion on collective armed resistance to possible Cuban aggression. This prevented him from repeating his request for modern armaments and equipment for possible Caribbean intervention brigades:

> From the descriptions of the economic and socially-themed anticommunist debates and from the theories of psychological warfare which sum up the work of the IV Annual Conference of the American Armies, we can taste a particular flavour from our knowing that General Onganía, Commander in Chief of the Argentinian Army, went to Fort Amador with the illusion that there, one would be talking sufficiently about collective armed resistance to any Cuban aggression, for him to be able to repeat with more success than on the occasion of his visit to Washington […] the Argentinian demand for modern armaments and equipment for possible 'intervention brigades' in the Caribbean.
>
> (ADF/Doc. 74/20)

Consequently, it was thought that: 'It is other than in the United States, and particularly in France, that the Argentine high command would be looking to procure the material in question' (ADF/Doc. 74/20). Therefore, when on 27 August 1963 General Onganía said that he was going to stay for about a month in Europe, the French Minister of Foreign Affairs decided that 'an official invitation should be rapidly formulated for several reasons', the most important of which is that General Onganía, the top military leader in the country at the time, 'could be called on to play an important political role' in the next couple of years (ADF/Doc. 141/2). Additionally, the 'fate of the three French officers acting as advisers in Argentina', in balance in 1963, depended in part on him (ADF/Doc. 141/2). Despite those efforts, neither General Onganía nor General Lanusse were 'in favour of the presence of the French military advisers' (ADF/Doc. 141/1). As the new French Ambassador, Christian de Margerie, explained in January 1964:

> […] this attitude is undoubtedly inspired by the American military missions with which he is in close contact and which have never had a very positive view of the permanent presence of French instructors in the Argentinian army.
>
> (ADF/Doc. 141/1)

Finally, in May 1964, Argentina signed the Military Aid Plan with the United States, which provided new equipment on advantageous financial terms but, as French Chargé d'Affaires Dimitri de Favitski explained, the Plan came with too many political conditions which removed sovereignty from the Argentine military:

> The Agreement on Military Assistance signed on 10 May 1964 with the United States permitted Argentina to have a certain quantity of equipment

at financially advantageous prices. Nonetheless, the political conditions sometimes attached to their provision, the delays in delivery, and the out-of-date nature of some materials disappointed the Argentinian military, who decided to turn more towards Europe to carry out the modernisation of their armaments. As a result of this new orientation, France was able to sell around sixty AMX13s and a certain number of howitzers. Argentina also planned to purchase surface ships, submarines, helicopters and inter-ceptor aircraft.

(ADF/Doc. 141/3)

As from 1964 and the signing of the Military Aid Plan that institutional-ised the training of Argentinians in US bases and increased the importance of instructors from the United States in Argentina, General Juan Carlos Onganía only supported the dissemination of US counter-insurgency doc-trine and the presence of advisers from the US military mission (Oliveira-Cézar 2002: 28–29). But the French advisers had already prepared the ground for the Americans: 'the Argentinian military class was readier to adopt the doctrine of national security because it had already taken on the integrist Catholic tendencies of French Catholic ultra-conservatives' (Almirón 1999: 33). Indeed, in Argentina, the strategy of counter-revolutionary war came directly from France. That is why the Argentinian army adopted the theories of the internal front and ideological frontiers, along with the practice of the war against subversion, even before the Americans developed it. As from 1957, this was all part of Argentine military doctrine: 'To a certain extent, American Doctrine of National Security was no longer needed, because they already had its equivalent imported from France. But otherwise this French import was an excellent introduction: attitudes were ready' (Comblin 1977: 146).

The crisis of the French army: the abandonment of the doctrine of Revolutionary War?

The departure of the French military mission from the *Escuela Superior de Guerra* can be related to the profound crisis that was affecting the French army.[5] Defeated in Indochina and disillusioned by the Algerian conflict, the French military had lost all discernment of hierarchy, subordination and authority (Mazzei 2002: 136). The last events in Algiers, especially the so-called Generals' Putsch in April 1961, had given rise to a re-think on foreign policy. These events demonstrated that it was possible to win not only battles but entire campaigns and still lose a war; that several of the architects of the doctrine of Revolutionary War had rebelled against the constitutional gov-ernment and even against their own senior military commanders and, finally, that many officers had gone underground with the *Organisation Armée Secrète* (*OAS*) – thus forming what they themselves had defined as a terrorist, subversive association, since they used sabotage, assassination and indiscriminate terrorism to attempt to retake the power they were losing in Algeria.

The only sensible thing to do for the Argentinian officers, with all this, would have been to reject once and for all the military doctrine that had evolved so badly. Indeed, it was put to one side for several years, though not completely, since on the one hand the French military mission continued to operate, and on the other hand there were Argentinian military officers who unofficially asked French former OAS officers, fleeing justice and taking refuge in Argentina, to give lectures on their counter-revolutionary experience (Oliveira-Cézar 2003: 79). However, this quasi-rejection was only temporary, since what had been learned from the French was not lost and the Revolutionary War doctrine returned in 1976 in the hands of the Junta involved in the *Proceso de Reorganización Nacional* – 'National Reorganisation Process'.

Historiography and military sociology are divided on the question of the doctrine of Revolutionary War: some take it as the most important French contribution to military thought and others think of it as an intellectual and military fiasco which met France's colonialist interests (Paret 1964; Périès 1999). As French journalist and expert on the topic, Pierre Abramovici, explained:

> Counter-insurgency ideology has its origin in the colonial war that France waged in Indochina at the end of the Second World War. French strategists designed a system to combat an enemy that was disseminated throughout the population. I think that they assimilated poorly determined Maoist theories on Revolutionary War and adapted this counter-revolutionary strategy to the war against the *FLN* [...] in Algeria, from the 5th Department of Psychological Action.
>
> (Abramovici, as interviewed by Llumá 2002b: 20)

This doctrine had the attraction of being an all-embracing analysis using the language of the Cold War, but also one that incorporated several traditional themes from the Argentinian military mind-set (Ranaletti 2005: 299). While the ideas of the doctrine were adopted by the bulk of the Argentine army in the course of the 1960s, some officers criticised the *en bloc* adoption of French doctrine, without eliminating significant negative factors. As Lieutenant-Colonel Mario Orsolini wrote in 1964:

> It is proposed to position Argentina, through the perspective of a world previously divided into antagonistic ideological blocs, instead of working the other way round, which is, looking at the world from the perspective of Argentina. The first approach defines us as anti-communists rather than as Argentinians; the second as Argentinians rather than anti-communists.
>
> (Orsolini 1964: 48)

The adoption of French doctrine without eliminating from it the factors that were questionable or negative for Argentina transferred to the army an unreal picture of the position of the population, which was ultimately taken to be true (Mazzei 2002: 134). According to Lieutenant-Colonel Robert Louis Bentresque:

> I can say one thing, and that is that this doctrine was useful in Argentina, but also that attention should have been paid to the Argentinian factor with Nouguès. We were wrong there, because it was applied rather harshly. That is an American temperament. They are violent in their reactions, but effective. It was a victory all in all, but one which should not have been won at any price. As a Christian I cannot accept it, but they did work well.
> (Lieutenant-Colonel Robert Louis Bentresque, as interviewed by Périès 1999: 836)

The theory of Revolutionary War was on the way to replacing the hypothesis of war between Argentina and its neighbours. It was a 'feasible and realistic' hypothesis, set in the framework of the Cold War and the division of the world into opposing blocs. Nonetheless, application of this theory led to effects contrary to those expected which, to a certain extent, were similar to those that occurred with the French army in Algeria, since:

> [...] it incessantly encouraged leaders to step beyond the specifically professional path, enriching the repertoire of arguments for chronic coups.
> (Orsolini 1964: 46)

In Argentina, the doctrine of Revolutionary War produced too violent an impact in the army, and, according to a number of commentators, psychologically unbalanced a significant proportion of the senior ranks. It also created a harmful hypersensitivity and anti-communist psychosis, manifested by impatience, intolerance, thoughtless judgement, pressure for drastic action, an overestimation of the capacity and danger of international communism, and permanent disagreement with the measures taken by civilian government; these were analysed under the distorting, one-sided magnifying glass of anti-communist ideology (Mazzei 2002: 135; Orsolini 1964: 49; Rouquier 1978: 156).

Exporting the doctrine of Revolutionary War to Argentina and internationalising the concept of the 'enemy within' also influenced the increase in levels of military autonomy.[6] This inevitably led to the inversion of the principle of military subordination to civilian power and to the militarisation of society (García 1995: 351). In this respect, Colonel Grand d'Esnon explains that:

When the degree of insecurity is very high, the other representatives of authority have, generally, been obliged to step back and the military have remained alone to maintain contact with the population; in this event, even in small increments, all administrative functions fall to the army and it is then normal that the unity of command should be certain to be in its favour. [...] But whatever organisation is adopted, unity of action in the military, administrative, political, police and economic fields has to be considered an essential rule.

(AMA/Grand d'Esnon 1960: 352)

With prophetic tone, Lieutenant-Colonel Mario Orsolini reflected on the application of the French doctrine of Revolutionary War in Argentina which, with ideology as a cause, will:

[...] lead to a holy war, with the ferocious characters peculiar to it, of neither giving nor knowing any quarter; without attributing the character of combatant to the adversary. In all ranks of the army, a tendency imperceptibly develops to share the ideas of the most extremist politicians, to imitate the procedures of the opposing terrorism and to consider anyone who raises his voice against this state of collective insanity as an enemy, refusing to support plans it considers mistaken. Hatred becomes the main motive for one's own actions and fear, fundamentally hidden. [...] With the ideological army as an instrument of Revolutionary War, good sense is impossible, sensibility is cowardice and prudence is sin. Hatred and distrust of the population are imported together with the Theory. [...] Thus, the army becomes a tool of sectoral interests [...] the promoter of revolutionary changes to the economic and social structure which, to no advantage, upturn the established order, causing the advent of the DICTATOR.

(Orsolini 1964: 52–53, emphasis as in original)

The official return of French influence in the 1970s

It is now established that Argentina's army adopted the theories and practices of the war against subversion, before the Americans developed it. We also know that the profound crisis affecting the French army in 1962 did not dissuade the Argentine military from adopting the doctrine of Revolutionary War. For a long time, however, the French training in counter-insurgency techniques 'had no practical relevance for Argentina, especially in the urban areas' (Heinz 1995: 75–76). In fact, the 'New War' described by the French assessors did not exist in Argentina at the beginning of the 1960s: 'It was an anticipated war that the Argentine military would actually fight less than twenty years later' (Carlson 2000: 73). Yet, even in the 1960s, 'Argentina and its people constitute[d] an objective that [was] too important for international

Marxism to overlook' (AMA/Nougués 1962: 30). As the Argentine government was looking for an effective way to stop rebellious Peronists who were supposedly taking part in the communist 'conspiracy' against the established order (Feierstein 2010: 44; Ranalletti 2005: 291), the counter-insurgency doctrine managed to find in Argentina a 'fertile ground' early on (Amaral 1998: 183; Ranalletti 2002; Robin 2004: 202).

Yet, their influence did not end in 1962. Indeed, as mentioned in Chapter 3, the 'process of decontextualisation and adaptation' of the doctrine of Revolutionary War in Argentina happened in two stages: theoretical between 1958 and 1962, and practical between the end of the 1970s and the early 1980s. At this point, the Argentine 'students' of the French advisers would make their entrance onto political stage by launching the *Proceso de Reorganización Nacional* – the 'National Reorganisation Process' (Périès 1999: 768).

At the beginning of the 1970s, French politician Pierre Messmer, Charles de Gaulle's Secretary of Defence from 1959 to 1970, was then Prime Minister of French President Georges Pompidou. It is interesting to note that Messmer detested the veterans of Algeria, because their redeployment became a problem at the end of the Algerian War. He used to refer to them as the 'idiots' and decided to send them abroad to be rid of them (Abramovici 2001). His official justification for this 'assistance' was that it had been requested by the Argentine government:

> It was General de Gaulle himself who decided there would be a mission, on the proposal of the Minister of Foreign Affairs. […] The United States had not yet, at that time, turned their hands to instruction and the supply of materiel to South American armies. But I think that in 1960 Argentina was particularly interested in France's experience in the field of Revolutionary War […].
>
> (Pierre Messmer, as interviewed by Robin 2004: 175)

As Messmer stated, 'Argentina wanted the advisers so we gave them what they wanted. Argentina is an independent country and there was no reason for us to deny their request', revealing that on the basis of this request a modified agreement was signed in 1970 (Abramovici 2001; Chelala 2001). The only thing that changed was that the French government would now pay the maintenance of the assessors it would send to Argentina, but it was a way of revitalising cooperation in this area. Indeed, from 1963, the presence in Argentina of the three senior French military advisers within the Argentine army, 'was periodically called into question on budgetary grounds, the Argentinian government judging that it was no longer in a position to take responsibility for their remuneration' (ADF/Doc. 179/1). Therefore, in the event that the French government did not take responsibility for their pay, the Argentine government had considered removing at least two of these adviser posts from 1971 – the fate of the third would be determined on the basis of budgets and the needs of the army (ADF/Doc. 179/2). However, on 6 May 1970, the French Ambassador in Argentina, Jean de la Chevardière de la Grandville, explained to the Minister of Foreign Affairs, Maurice Schumann, the importance of maintaining the mission of the three assessors in Buenos Aires:

> [...] the risk of seeing our military mission removed, possibly to make way for technical assistance from another European state (Germany comes to mind) willing to pay the costs of a mission, as the Americans do, the only ones along with us to have a military mission to Argentina, seems very great. Later on it would be difficult, if not impossible, to regain a position that has given us great benefits up to now in both the economic [...] and general domains on account of the friendly relations we have acquired with an army whose leaders inspire a large measure of the country's internal and external policies.
>
> (ADF/Doc. 179/2)

Understanding the high stakes, the French Minister of Foreign Affairs decided that, from January 1st 1971 his department would cover the subsistence allowance paid up to that year to the three French military advisers in Argentina: he authorised the French Ambassador in Buenos Aires to sign a new agreement amending the agreement made on 11 February 1960 (ADF/Doc. 179/3):

> On behalf of the government of the French Republic, We, Minister of Foreign Affairs, hereby empower Mr Jean de la Chevardière de le Grand-ville, Ambassador Extraordinary and Plenipotentiary of the French Republic in Argentina, to sign in Buenos Aires the Agreement between the government of the French Republic and the government of the Argentine Republic, amending the Agreement of 11 February 1960 regarding the mission of French military advisers to the Argentine army.
>
> (ADF/Doc. 179/4)

Consequently, a new wording of Article 12 of the Agreement of 11 February 1960 regarding the mission of French military advisers to the Argentine army was made necessary by French budgetary rules; it would from then read:

> Article 12 – The remuneration of members of the mission shall be borne by the government of the French Republic. This remuneration includes, in addition to the salaries and allowances provided by French regulation, a monthly subsistence allowance of one thousand and fifty dollars or the equivalent in convertible French francs.
>
> (ADF/Doc. 179/5)

By 1973, Argentina's economy had collapsed and the perception of the military was that social and political movements would threaten to take over the country and create a 'second Cuba' (ADF/Doc. 141/4). The idea of the military leadership was to make the ever-popular Perón, whose election in 1946 brought expanded economic and social rights to the working classes, return to the public arena to found a new radical social movement and thus tarnish his own reputation; in other words, Peronism would be removed thanks to Perón himself (Périès 1999: 746). Consequently, on 23 September 1973, the former populist leader was re-elected despite nearly 20 years in exile. As predicted, even Perón was unable to please everybody and, only a few days after the elections, José Ignacio Rucci, the secretary general of Argentina's largest labour union, the *Confederación General del Trabajo*, was murdered, allegedly by members of a left-wing Peronist guerrilla group. With political violence on the rise, Perón ordered his social welfare minister, José López Rega, to eliminate left-wing militants. López Rega decided to transform the *Alianza Anti-comunista Argentina* – 'Argentine Anticommunist Alliance'; an organisation initially associated with the right-wing Peronists, usually known as the 'Triple A' – into a death squad, and to enlist members of the security forces.[7]

The rise of violence in Argentina and the return of Perón to government encouraged the Argentine military to prepare decisive action. To this end, they again sought military advice from the French. As Lieutenant-Colonel Bernard Jozan, French Military Attaché in Buenos Aires, explained to the Secretary of War in Paris in 1974:

> [...] Argentinian General Staff turned to the French military mission again. [...] The Argentinian need represents a possibly important fact, in response to which the French Command may be interested in adopting a stance in favour of the Argentinian army.
>
> (ADF/Doc. 201/2)

Thus, even in 1974, the 'Franco-Argentine military relations as part of the French military mission' were 'excellent, and the official end-of-year festivities went off in a context of great camaraderie' (ADF/Doc. 201/3). An example of this military harmony between the French and Argentine armies in the 1970s can be found on the occasion of the French National Holiday, when 'General Videla, then Chief of Staff, was keen to receive the entire French mission to offer it his thanks [...]' (ADF/Doc. 201/2).

In the mid-1970s, the new chief of the French mission to Argentina had the profile required by the Argentine military: experience in counter-insurgency tactics. Consequently, Robert Servent – a veteran of the Second World War, of Indochina and of the 5th Department of Psychological Action in Algeria – disembarked in Buenos Aires:

On 5 May 1974, Colonel Servent took command of the military mission [...]. [...] The Argentine military remains very interested in everything the mission can give it in the realm of: subversive war, psychological warfare and action, French experiences in Algeria [...]. The intelligence officers' training school has submitted the written questions in Annex 2 [...] about the techniques used by the French for gaining information in subversion.

(ADF/Doc. 201/1)

But Perón died suddenly in July 1974, and his third wife, Isabel, assumed power with López Rega as her de facto Prime Minister. This was only to increase the atmosphere of violence and uncertainty. Yet, even then, Lieutenant-Colonel Bernard Jozan explained to the Secretary of War in Paris that the French military mission continued to implement teaching although the French advisers had to be discreet while explaining the problem of 'subversion':

The third quarter of 1974 opened with the key event of the death of Lieutenant General Perón, head of state. After a period of political adjust-ment that was relatively calm on the social level, Argentina went through a troubled period after certain political parties voluntarily decided to withdraw into clandestine activity. [...] In this anxious, tense atmosphere, the French military mission has continued to implement its work plan [...]; it has maintained numerous foreign contacts and has continued to receive a large number of visits from Argentinian officers, concerned about problems of subversive activities and particular professional prob-lems. Regarding subversion, the French military mission is applying the orders it received from the French Ambassador, namely not to publicly discuss subversion; and to avoid as much as possible dealing with it in private.

(ADF/Doc. 201/2)

To restore the country to order, Junta commander General Jorge Rafael Videla overthrew the failing Peronist government, marking yet another military intervention in Argentinian politics. On 24 March 1976, the powerful armed forces installed their dictatorship, launched the *Proceso de Reorganización Nacional* – 'National Reorganisation Process' – and initiated a phase of anti-insurgent warfare known as the 'Dirty War', *Guerra Sucia*, that would last until 1983 (Abramovici 2001; Carlson 2000: 71), with the violent and dramatic consequences that we now know (Oliveira-Cézar 2002: 27–28). According to General Reynaldo Benito Bignone:[8]

The influence of the French continued in the 1970s [...]. The decrees signed by Isabel Martínez de Perón are directly inspired by the experience of the French in Algeria. I would even say that the process of national reorganisation launched by the military government in March 1976 is a copy of the Battle of Algiers. [...] We took everything from the French: the division of the territory into grids, the importance of intelligence in this type of war, the interrogation methods....

(General Reynaldo Benito Bignone, as interviewed by Robin 2004: 316–317)

French journalist and expert Pierre Abramovici is also of the opinion that the National Reorganisation Process launched by the Argentine military government in March 1976 was a copy of the Battle of Algiers:

My theory is that the Battle of Algiers was conducted in an identical way to what I call the 'Battle of Buenos Aires'. In Algiers, the 5th Department concentrated files together on every suspicious person. In Buenos Aires, led by General Commissioner Antonio Villar, at that time head of the Federal Police (and one of the founders of the Triple A), a similar centralisation exercise took place, to which was added information on political refugees from the rest of Latin America.

(Abramovici, as interviewed by Llumá 2002b: 20)

Although Argentina had long been marked by the presence of armed forces in political life, through *coups d'état*, dictatorships and exceptional regimes, the military government that settled itself between 1976 and 1983 exhibited new features that were distinct from those of earlier authoritarian regimes. During this period, Argentine soldiers kidnapped, tortured, and murdered between 15,000 and 30,000 people, according to human rights organisations (Abramovici 2001; Chelala 2001; MacMaster 2004: 8). Most of these victims were non-combatant; however, subversion was specified as 'inclusive': leaders of the traditional political parties, trade unions, student organisations, as well as prominent intellectual, artistic, cultural and media figures were also targeted, since their words or actions were perceived as defending and extending legitimacy to the armed left. This level of violence may be due to the fact that General Videla's 1976 order of battle contained two theories: the traditional model anchored in territory and the French model of the 'psychological action' of the doctrine of Revolutionary War; something new in Argentina which distinguished the 'National Reorganisation Process' from the de facto regimes of neighbouring countries (Llumá 2002a: 15). As explained by Argentine General Martín Antonio Balza:

Yet again, it was French doctrine that prepared the ground for the monstrous dictatorship of General Videla – because if Argentina had already suffered five *coups d'état*, it had never known so many human rights violations, practised on so large a scale and planned as part of a new mode of the exercise of power, that is, state terrorism.

(General Martín Antonio Balza, as interviewed by Robin 2004: 200–202)

The French officer who was acting as leader of the advisory mission in Buenos Aires in 1976 was still Colonel Robert Servent. He was a friend both of General Reynaldo Benito Bignone and of General Paul Aussaresses, who played a key role in the Battle of Algiers and was a former head of intelligence under Trinquier himself. According to General Bignone, 'Servent played an important role in the National Reorganisation Process': he taught the Argentine military the importance of gathering information and, hence, the use of torture in a subversive war (General Reynaldo Benito Bignone, as interviewed by Robin 2004: 316–317). Summoned by Judge Roger Le Loire who was investigating the disappearance of some Franco-Argentine citizens in Argentina, Servent acknowledged that he taught the Argentine military about French counter-insurgency techniques:

COLONEL ROBERT SERVENT: I was a military adviser [...] assistant instructor.... The time I was there, the Chief of Staff was General Videla, with Colonels Bignone and Harguindéguy as his assistants.

JUDGE ROGER LE LOIRE: Do you know where the political prisoners were detained?

COLONEL ROBERT SERVENT: I found out at one time through public rumour that this happened in a navy building; besides, the navy were the most passionate about counter-revolutionary activities....

JUDGE ROGER LE LOIRE: This is an extract from the report of the Commission on Human Rights in Argentina published in Madrid in 1977, which states: 'Two permanent missions, North American and French, advise the Argentinian armed forces. [...] The French mission, led by Colonel Servent, advises the Argentinian military on intelligence matters, that is, the search for and rapid exploitation of intelligence. On a practical level, the tools of intelligence include informing, torture and infiltration' (CADHU 1977: 133). What do you think about that?

COLONEL ROBERT SERVENT: I challenge the term *intelligence*. It is correct that I advised the Argentinian military in the sense that I explained to them how it was done in the French army. [...] But as for the term intelligence including informing, torture and infiltration, I never saw that in the French army....

(Colonel Robert Servent, as interviewed by Juge Roger Le Loire; Robin 2004: 323–324)

This illustrates what Cohen (1993) described as a 'complex discourse of denial', in which state officers engage to deny or justify their involvement in violations of human rights, and more specifically a reclassification of what has taken place. Indeed, in Algeria, Servent was in charge of the interrogation of the *ralliés*.[9] It has also has been established that Servent, who was acting as leader of the advisory mission in Buenos Aires in 1976, was in charge of interrogating – in other words torturing – the *ralliés* in Algiers (Abramovici, as interviewed by Llumá 2002b: 23).

As a result, when General Videla launched the National Reorganisation Process, the French influence was still perceptible and the French advisers still present in Argentina. As the French Secretary of State made clear in 1976:

> Our military aid to Argentina takes two forms: 1) Military advisers in Buenos Aires and […]; 2) Training of officers on placement in Paris […].
>
> (ADF/Doc. 229/1)

Indeed, the training courses offered to Argentine officers at the Paris *École Supérieure de Guerre* continued throughout the 1970s as well (ADF/Doc. 188/2; ADF/Doc. 2234/4). By then, the placements that the relevant French authorities were offering in French schools and bases were 'too few in number' to match the number of requests received: 'The results [of these courses], however, are lasting and the training given is essential for the future' (ADF/Doc. 188/1). Indeed, these placements were seen as 'an excellent means of extending the French influence on a military society that, regardless of political organisation, will always play an important role in Argentina' (ADF/Doc. 2234/5). As Henri de Coignac, French Chargé d'Affaires in Argentina, explain to Claude Cheysson, French Minister of Foreign Relations:

> […] this form of cooperation seems the most appropriate to me nowadays to enable the continuance of fruitful relationships between the two armies. Indeed, I consider that the presence of Argentine military pupils in our schools facilitates better understanding of our policy and attitude to different world events. I would add that the discreet power behind this cooperation, widely used by the United States at a time when relations with Buenos Aires were undergoing serious difficulties, constitutes an effective way to maintain meaningful dialogue with a community that has always played a considerable role in this country. Experience has indeed shown that trainees returned from their placement in France with a very favourable impression, becoming in their army the best ambassadors for our influence.
>
> (ADF/Doc. 2234/3)

It thus seems that, even at the beginning of the Argentine Dirty War (1976–1983), the 'Algerian experience', would still be what had to be remembered from the French *savoir-faire*. As the French Military Attaché at the time explained:

I had a fairly long conversation with the Argentinian Military Attaché last night at a dinner. This senior officer – a former colleague of General Videla, whom he seemed to know quite well – developed a number of points, of which I can especially remember here [...] [that] the French military mission to Argentina, although modest, was important in the eyes of the Argentinian army. It was the only foreign mission along with that of the United States. Originally it would have been sought by Buenos Aires so that the Argentinian army could benefit from the 'incomparable' experience the French army gained in subversive war after the Algerian experience....

(ADF/Doc. 229/2)

The suspension of the French military mission to Argentina in 1981

As mentioned earlier, the French military aid to Argentina took two forms: French military advisers in Buenos Aires and the training of Argentine officers on placement in France (ADF/Doc. 229/1, 229/5). During the Dirty War, however, French public opinion became aware of the human rights violations that had been taking place on Argentine soil since 1976 and the request for placements in the *École Supérieure de Guerre* and other higher military education made by the Argentinian authorities began to be seen as a public relations issue: the French government judged it 'preferable, bearing in mind the circumstances, to refrain from accepting Argentinian trainees' (ADF/Doc. 229/4). Also, in a memorandum of 25 May 1979, the French Minister of Foreign Relations explained his annoyance concerning a visit of a significant delegation of Argentine pupil officers in Paris:

The Protocol Service has communicated a copy of a *note verbale* from the Argentinian Embassy in Paris to the America Desk on the arrival in France for a visit lasting four to six days, next November, of pupil officers from the Argentinian Army School. [...] It is hardly in keeping with diplomatic practice that the Argentinian Embassy should inform the Department of the arrival of 201 pupil officers and their leaders from the Argentinian Army School [...] without considering it appropriate to ask if these visits have been authorised by the French government. [...] Moreover, the America Desk is questioning the appropriateness of a visit by a significant number of pupil officers from the Argentinian army, [...] mindful of the ongoing sensitivity of part of French public opinion to the situation in Argentina and to the fate of our detained (4) or missing (13) nationals.

(ADF/Doc. 229/3)

But the French attitude towards the Argentinian trainees would be friendly again by the end of the Dirty War. As Jean Dominique Paolini, the French

Ambassador in Buenos Aires, explained to Claude Cheysson, the Secretary of State in France, on 20 January, 20 July and 28 Septembre 1983 respectively:

> [...] I have been made aware from experience that our best support, even if they are the only contact we could have at times of tense situations such as that caused by the recent conflict, is afforded us by those officers who attended courses in our schools. Regardless of their commercial impact, these pupils are, therefore, reliable intermediaries for our influence within the Argentinian armed forces. That is why once again this year I support the Argentinian armed forces' placement requests.
>
> (ADF/Doc. 2234/7)

> The cooperation in question has always had the advantage of training young officers who have subsequently always demonstrated personal attachment to our country and have served as a fulcrum for our efforts. At a time when the Argentinian armed forces are to be subordinated to civilian constitutional power, the placements in France by several of their best officers can only strengthen the long-awaited democratisation of their army.
>
> (ADF/Doc. 2234/8)

> The Argentinian military trainees sent to our schools have always proven dedicated Francophiles upon their return, forming one of our most reliable forms of support within the armed forces [...]. The next reorganisation of these forces, which must follow the country's return to a constitutional regime, can only give greater importance to maintaining our influence.
>
> (ADF/Doc. 2234/9)

The French military mission in Buenos Aires was 'put on hold' in 1981. Having been created through the Agreement of 11 February 1960 – amended in 1971 – signed between the government of the French Republic and the government of the Argentine Republic, the mission of French military advisers to the Argentine army was suspended:

> [...] Under an agreement that, in its original form dates back to 11 February 1960, a military mission of senior officers from our army has been seconded to the General Staff of the Argentinian Army acting as 'advisers'. The evolution of the situation in Argentina on one hand, and the limited appropriations for military aid on the other had already led the Department, for several years, to limit the number of these officers to two instead of the three provided under the Agreement. By the end of 1979 it appeared that, even in reduced form, maintenance of this mission – created in well determined circumstances which were no longer of

clear interest – was both burdensome and inappropriate. Also, the Department adopted the principle of 'putting the agreement on hold', by suspending its de facto application. To this end it was decided not to replace the two advisers at the end of their stays (15 July and 4 November 1981 respectively).

(ADF/Doc. 229/5)

The French Ambassador in Argentina was instructed to inform the Argentinian authorities that this measure was a consequence of reductions in staff and budgetary considerations. The formula adopted in this way made it possible for the French government to avoid the termination procedure provided in the text of the agreement with a notice period of one year (ADF/Doc. 229/5).

This might also be because, by the end of the Dirty War, French public opinion had become aware of the human rights violations that had been taking place on Argentine soil since 1976 and the military cooperation with the Argentina began to be seen as a problem:

The French taught us everything, starting with interrogation methods […]. They explained to us what torture was used for in anti-subversive war, where intelligence is key. […] I would say that the leaders, the highest-placed, the very top of the French hierarchy, supported us during the *Proceso*. But not at a lower level, where the matter of human rights was a real problem. You know, public opinion and the world in general are full of people who lean towards progressive centre-left or socialist ideas.

(General Matias, Interview #6 – see Appendix 3)

Eventually, however, by the end of the Dirty War the French attitude towards Argentina would be friendly again. The French Military Attaché in Argentina asked the Argentinian General Staff what direction they were thinking of taking and decided to propose to them a military mission that would help them in developing this strategy. Indeed, he sought that, 'The next reorganisation of these forces, which must follow the country's return to a constitutional regime, can only give greater importance to maintenance of the French influence' (ADF/Doc. 2234/9). As he explained in a note to the French Ministry of Foreign Affairs:

The permanent mission of two military advisers in Argentina was suspended at the end of 1981. There is no need to emphasise, in the event that such a hypothesis should emerge, its importance in the strengthening of links with Argentina where history has proved that, whatever its up and downs, the army remained one of the country's backbones. An organisation of the same type as ours with strong democratic branding would be likely to be well received by political power and should bring not insignificant impacts in the medium term.

(ADF/Doc. 2234/2)

Consequently, on 17 February 1984, Jean Dominique Paolini, French Ambassador in Argentina, emphasised the importance of trying to convince General Torres, the Argentine joint general staff at the time, to revive the military cooperation between the two countries:

If the Department and the Ministry of Defence were in agreement, [the French Military Attaché] could also be instructed to consider with his interlocutors in the joint general staff or in the Ministry of Defence if a high level French contact and information mission on these problems would be likely to interest them. In this regard, we could possibly reconsider the idea of the 'two French military advisers' whose departure has been presented, I recall, as a simple suspension of the agreement.

(ADF/Doc. 2234/1)

Yet, it seems that by the end of the Dirty War, 'The resumption of the permanent mission of two French military advisers in Argentina, a mission that was suspended at the end of 1981 is desired by neither the French Ministry of Defence nor the Foreign Ministry' (ADF/Doc. 2233f/1).

Argentine civil society's boomerang effect: a shield against a French transnational institutional torturer?

The intensity of class conflict during the period that preceded that of the last Argentine military regime, the atmosphere of armed struggle against urban guerrillas, and fear of the possible re-grouping of the Marxist opposition, made it relatively easy for the regime to gain acceptance of its 'project' amongst the upper and middle classes (Stepan 1985). Indeed, significant sectors lent their support to the regime. Aguila explains that, in Argentina,

while the legal forces were beginning to execute their sinister plan of social and political terror, the Catholic Church, the editorials of the main newspaper of the city, national celebrations, and military acts became passionate forums of the most intense justification of the repression and the legitimating of the new social order imposed on the country and the city by the dictatorship.

(2010: 144)

According to Argentine historian Mario Ranaletti, the Argentine military incorporated two French influences into their view of social conflict and politics: one was that arising from the doctrine of Revolutionary War, or the ensemble of ideas that the French military developed to explain their defeat in Indochina and the situation in Algeria, while the other was the traditionalist Catholic interpretation of the Cold War as a confrontation between civilisations (Ranaletti 2005: 305). The strong impression left by these two influences can be appreciated in the narrative used to legitimise the last military dictatorship in Argentina and the part played by some members of religious orders who, in response to officers' questions, explained that the torture carried out on detainees would be forgiven because it was done in the name of the defence of 'Western, Christian civilisation' (Verbitsky 1995: 36–37):

> In the Argentinian Navy Higher School of Mechanics (*ESMA*), torture was not viewed from a moral point of view, but was considered a combat weapon. The military chaplain justified the methods used in the Battle of Algiers, including torture. There was, let us say, religious support [...]. It must be said that here in Argentina a whole sector of the Catholic hierarchy supported practices of this nature [...].
>
> (Colonel Sergio, Interview #4 – see Appendix 3)

According to French political analyst Georges Gabriel Périès, 'National-Catholic discourse reproduced the process of logical argument for the legitimisation of the large-scale practice of torture in Argentina as a means to restore the power of the state through its militarisation' (Périès 1999: 834). Indeed, the French use of torture in Algeria was justified through the propaganda of the 'mission civilisatrice' (Maran 1989), which was 'paradoxically [founded] on the Universal Rights of Man of 1789' (MacMaster 2004: 5). They managed the 'civilising role' of France while pursuing a campaign of torture in the country (Keenan 2003).[10] Just as French trainers professed that losing the war in Algeria would be 'synonymous with the decline of Christian civilisation' (Maran 1989: 16), the Argentine soldiers believed that if they were defeated within their own country 'world-wide communist domination would result' (Carlson 2000: 74). This might be due to the fact that the French doctrine of Revolutionary War had its foundations in a range of historical components of the Catholic-military way of thought, most especially in the idea of the 'enemy within' (Périès 1999: 838; Ranaletti 2005: 288).[11] The main contribution of this 'French, Christian civilisation' ideology to Argentine military training was to strengthen the perception of political problems, especially growing violence and social inequalities (portrayed as the result of the Marxist penetration and subversion) (Ranaletti 2005: 303). This ideological support of terror was also largely responsible for what Colonel Prudencio García defined as intensive indoctrination and reactionary, anti-communist training (García 1995).

In her seminal work, *The Body in Pain* (1985), Scarry explains that pain destroys the sense of self and the world, and is, 'experienced spatially as either the contraction of the universe down to the immediate vicinity of the body or as the body swelling to fill the entire world' (1985: 35). Furthermore, when a state perpetrates or tacitly condones torture, there is a characteristic sense amongst inhabitants that there is no escape, no other world (Feitlowitz 1998: 82; Green and Ward 2004: 127; Scarry 1985: 27). This 'unmaking of the world' was certainly experienced in Argentina between 1976 and 1983 since two states were involved in the institutionalisation of torture: Argentina at the national level, and France at the transnational level. Yet, one way or another, news was disseminated and out of this massive 'unmaking' came an imaginative 'remaking' (Franco 1992: 112): Although the Argentine military regime began with phases in which the institutions of civil society were emasculated, its 'ambitious behaviourist projects' eventually failed (Aguila 2006: 169; Corradi *et al.* 1992: 2; Franco 1992: 104; Garreton 1992: 16; Stepan 2001: 75).

The threat of capture, torture, imprisonment or death was, however, not enough to dissuade resistance movements within civil society in mobilising against the Argentine military dictatorship (Dassin 1992: 170; Garreton 1992: 19). The most salient of such movements was probably that of the *Madres y Abuelas de la Plaza de Mayo* which came into existence in April 1977 (ADF/ Doc. 2228c/3),[12] after 14 mothers met to exchange information about their 'disappeared' children while parading around the central pyramid of the *Plaza de Mayo* in central Buenos Aires (Calderon *et al.* 1992; Franco 1992; Eckstein 2001; Navarro 2001). Finally recognising the political implications of the mothers' Thursday marches, petitions, and demonstrations, the Argentine military decided to strike. From December 1977 onwards, these Mother protestors were dispersed by police with tear gas and shots in the air; some were arrested and tortured while others themselves 'disappeared' (Navarro 2001: 252):

> The movement, which now has more than 2500 members, has set the search for its children as its main goal. It also provides moral and material support to the families of the disappeared in need. If the Mothers have been able to conduct their action in relative freedom for some months, it has not always been so and the police have often intervened massively to prevent the weekly demonstrations from taking place.
>
> (ADF/Doc. 2228c/3)

Vulnerable, isolated, and constantly threatened by the overwhelming power of the Junta, the *Madres* nevertheless persisted in their struggle. They established contacts with human rights organisations in other countries, lobbied for support among foreign congressmen, testified wherever they were invited to do so, and visited any president willing to receive them. This provides an example of Risse, Ropp and Sikkink's 'boomerang pattern' of influence and change: 'when domestic groups in a repressive state bypass their state and directly search out international allies to try to bring pressure on their states from outside' (Risse *et al.* 1999: 18). Chile and Uruguay, which both had an authentic tradition of democratic politics, were two of the earliest illustrations of this dynamic (Fagen 1992: 39; Heinz 1995: 68; Weschler 1998: 99), but it was much harder for Argentina to achieve because it had very few non-governmental organisations, other than the Catholic Church. And the Church itself supported state terror (Marchak 1999: 321; Verbitsky 1988: 146):

> Execrated by the military regime, the Mothers of the Plaza de Mayo Movement have never found any real support in Argentina from the Church or from the political class. Even so, they benefit from the support of eminent personalities such as Nobel Peace Laureate Adolfo Pérez Esquivel and author Ernesto Sabato and, thanks to the courage and tenacity of their members, have been able to gather large amounts of information on the 15,000 or so people who disappeared between 1975 and 1978.
>
> (ADF/Doc. 2228c/3)

Despite fears of reprisals against their abducted relatives or against themselves, they flocked to give testimony during the hearings held by the Organisation of American States' Inter-American Commission on Human Rights, which visited Argentina in September 1979 for three weeks. As Navarro noted,

> The queues outside the Organisation of American States building in downtown Buenos Aires grew to up to 3,000 people at times. The six-member team took note of denunciations of disappearances from individuals and human rights organizations, visited prisoners, a detention camp, and graveyards.
>
> (2001: 253)

Being unable to prevent the human rights organisation's visit, the military government strove to fight a battle, both internally and within international forums, against what they called the 'Anti-Argentine Campaign'. With this slogan they hoped to restore the support that significant sectors of society had previously given to the regime, and which was beginning to crack. The Junta published a book and deployed a campaign through the news media presenting its own version of events, and plastered Buenos Aires with posters proclaiming '*Somos derechos y humanos*' – 'We are right and human' (Aguila 2006: 176).

By the end of the Dirty War, the Mothers and Grandmothers also went to France to ask the French President at the time, François Mitterrand, to help them:

> The President and Vice-President of the Mothers of the Plaza de Mayo Movement, Mrs Hebe de Bonafini and Mrs Gard de Antokoletz, will

shortly be making a European tour to meet the United Nations Commission on Human Rights in Geneva. During this visit, they are planning to go to countries with nationals either detained or disappeared in Argentina in order to draw the attention of relevant governments to their action. Thus, this delegation will be in Paris for some days from 14 February after a visit to Madrid where they will be received by the Foreign Minister, Mr Fernando Morán. Mesdames Hebe de Bonafini and Gard Antokoletz have already requested an audience with the President of France [...].

(ADF/Doc. 2228c/1)

This provides a paradoxical example of the 'boomerang pattern' of influence and change (Risse *et al.* 1999: 18) since the *Madres* bypassed their state that had institutionalised torture to seek help in the state that had helped institutionalise it. Yet, on 9 February 1983, French President François Mitterrand replied positively to the President and Vice-President of the Mothers of the Plaza de Mayo Movement's request:

The President of France will receive the representatives of the Mothers of the Plaza de Mayo on 15 February.

(ADF/Doc. 2228c/2)

Also, in a memorandum of 15 February 1983, the French Minister of Foreign Relations explained the reasons behind President Mitterrand's decision to grant the representatives of the Mothers the requested audience:

[...] three mothers were abducted on 9 December 1977, along with two French nuns, sisters Léonie Duquet and Alice Domon (the latter of whom attended meetings of the group), never to reappear. Many others have been arrested or have been the subjects of harassment and various provocations. [...] In France, Solma, a solidarity movement with the Mothers of the Plaza de Mayo, was created last year. It is chaired by the mother of a French disappeared, Mrs Dauthier. In addition, the Socialist Human Rights Club organises a demonstration outside the Argentinian Embassy every Thursday.

(ADF/Doc. 2228c/3)

The Argentinian regime had always refused to provide the least indication of the fate of the disappeared and considers that this phenomenon was no more than a consequence of the fight against *subversion* and *terrorism*. However, following the discovery in October 1982 of several clandestine cemeteries, the Buenos Aires authorities were subjected to fierce attack from international public opinion demanding explanations. It seemed that the Junta disagreed with President Bignone on this point and it was difficult to see how a satisfactory response could have been given before the handover of power to civilians the next autumn. As the French Minister of Foreign Relations continued to explain in 1983:

> France has made many representations to the Argentinian authorities to demand information on the fate of its 15 disappeared nationals and to emphasise the need, purely on humanitarian grounds but also to restore Argentina's image, to get to the bottom of this matter. Even though all our actions have been in vain (we have at most the unofficial confirmation of the deaths of three of our compatriots), we are not diminishing our efforts. And that is why we [...] have also publicly expressed our sorrow at the discovery of the clandestine cemetery of Grand Bourg and facilitated the mission to Buenos Aires, last November by the Families' Association of the French Disappeared. This mission was able to meet a number of officials and representatives of humanitarian organisations, including the Mothers of the Plaza de Mayo. At the international level, we are supporting every initiative likely to move this matter forward (the United Nations working group on the disappeared was created in 1980 at our request and has been constantly renewed in spite of the opposition from numerous countries).
>
> (ADF/Doc. 2228c/3)

The main newspapers of Buenos Aires gave prominent coverage to the audience granted to Mesdames Bonafini and Antokoletz by the President of France on 15 February. Of the meeting with the President, all the daily papers have reported the statement by the Mothers according to which the President:

> [...] promised all that was in his power in the political and legal arenas to support the Mothers of the Plaza de Mayo in their efforts to clarify the fates of the disappeared detainees.
>
> (ADF/Doc. 2228c/4)

This visit, published in the Argentine daily press, had not been well received in Buenos Aires. As the French Ambassador in Buenos Aires, Jean Dominique Paolini, explained to the French Ministry of Foreign Affairs on 17 February 1983:

> After signing some exchange of letters, Mr Aguirre Lanari [Argentina's Foreign Minister] asked me to remain in his office to talk to me about the audience granted by the French President to the leaders of the Mothers of the Plaza de Mayo. This news published in the daily press had been poorly received, he told me, at the cabinet meeting. This association, which is also pursuing a political goal hostile to the government, was the only one to say

that there had been 30,000 disappeared in Argentina, a figure which, the minister added, had no relation to reality. By giving its support to this association, the French government seemed to be willing to direct a political action against the Argentinian government. He asked me to convey this point of view to my government. I replied to the Minister reminding him of *the constant concern of the French government for human rights, which was a fundamental component of its policy throughout the world and not only in Argentina*, as I had repeatedly stressed myself during our conversations. It was, therefore, perfectly reasonable that the leaders of this association should have been received by the Head of State. [...] One could not interpret that as an action directed against Argentina.

(ADF/Doc. 2228c/5; emphasis added)

As the French Ambassador in Buenos Aires, Jean Dominique Paolini, explained to France's Foreign Minister, Claude Cheysson, on 25 February 1983:

The Mothers of the Plaza de Mayo have become international symbols of Argentinian political life in recent years. Their demands have earned them recognition from the international press. [...] the complexity of the Argentine internal situation [...] has made almost total ignorance of their role in Argentina [...] while they enjoy great popularity abroad. [...] European governments [...] have not hesitated to receive and listen to the representatives of this Argentinian drama, Adela Antokoletz and Hebe Bonafini. [...] The group's leaders have acquired impressive political capacities which are reflected in their answers during their press conferences. Let us recall their harsh judgement of the Argentinian church, the scepticism that Argentinian political parties inspire in them, as do international bodies and finally, the political intervention which they demand on behalf of Argentinian exiles for them to be able to return to Argentina. [...] It should be noted, in fact, that the international action of the Mothers has only been deployed in solid Western democracies moved by the numerous victims of disappearances. *For the Western world, disappearances are unacceptable because the state should not use the methods of criminals.* President Mitterrand [...] would have focused on this point.

(ADF/Doc. 2228c/6, emphasis added)

Yet, as Llumá explained: 'The institution of the *disappeared* as an instrument of terror [...] is also a French creation applied in Argentina' (2002a: 15). Indeed, French Colonel Roger Trinquier, a veteran of the Indochina War (1946–1954) and Algerian War (1954–1962), had already started to theorise on the disappearance of individuals in Algeria (Trinquier 1964).

The movement of the *Madres y Abuelas de la Plaza de Mayo* mobilised opposition to the Argentine military regime both in Argentina and in France: by bypassing their state and directly searching out an allegedly external ally respectful of human rights, the Mothers demonstrated that civil society is the most significant force in challenging national and transnational state criminality. Although their marches and initiatives initially had a limited and very personal objective, they were the first demonstrations that denounced disappearances in Argentina and, eventually, helped in bringing down the repressive military government (Aguila 2010; Bousquet 1983; De Bonafini 1985; Eckstein 2001; Navarro 2001; Stepan 2001: 88). According to Marie Orensanz, creator of an imposing metallic memorial of Buenos Aires which reads *'Las raíces son femeninas'* – 'The roots are feminine':[13]

> The harsh position the mothers were put through when their children disappeared, the fact that they fought with the available means, without violence, just denouncing ... their requests became something people could no longer ignore ... neither in Argentina, nor in France.
>
> (Marie Orensanz, Interview #1 – see Appendix 3)

Conclusion

It has been established that the Argentine army adopted the theories and practice of the war against subversion, even before the Americans developed it. Also, it has been proven that the profound crisis that was affecting the French army in 1962 did not dissuade the Argentine military from adopting the doctrine of Revolutionary War.

Although French training in counter-insurgency techniques had no immediate practical relevance for Argentina for a long time, as it was adopted in 1957 and only applied in 1976, the doctrine of Revolutionary War managed to find 'fertile ground' in Argentina (Amaral 1998: 183). At the beginning of the 1970s, the rise of violence in Argentina and the return of Peronism to government encouraged the Argentine military to prepare decisive action. To this end, they again sought military advice from the French. This continuous training in ideological extremism would ultimately function effectively in the reactionary education of the cadres involved in Argentine state terrorism.

The two-step process of the 'decontextualisation and adaptation' (Périès 1999: 768) of the French doctrine of Revolutionary War in Argentina has thus been demonstrated: the first step was the theoretical part, between 1958 and 1962, and the second step was the implementation of the French teaching, between the end of the 1970s and the early 1980s. By sharing its specific *savoir-faire* in Revolutionary War prior to and during the Argentine Dirty War, the French prepared the ground for the institutionalisation of torture that was implemented between 1976 and 1983 in Argentina.

Indeed, systematic torture appears to be impossible to sustain without a network of officials working towards a common aim (Herman 1982): torture is an individualised form of violence that tends to be 'embedded in entrenched structural violence' (Farmer 2003: 219). As mentioned in Chapter 2, if most individual torturers are not born, it follows that they must be *made*. Having deduced this, the process by which ordinary people become perpetrators of torture at the state's disposal has been explored. In doing so, it has been shown how ideological persuasion and training contribute to the *making of an official torturer*.

By looking beyond the level of the Argentine torture chambers, or even of the Argentine state, the received explanations for the institutionalisation of torture in Argentina were unravelled and new grids of analyses were built up to better understand the phenomenon. Torture does not occur without ideological or logistical preparation and, from 1957 onwards, France performed an integral role in the architecture of the Argentine Dirty War: by training Argentine officers in an ideology that justifies torture, France contributed to the institutionalisation of torture in Argentina and, therefore, merits the label of 'transnational institutional torturer'.

Yet, despite the fact that the military regime that took place during the Dirty War tried to eliminate collective identities, collective organisations, and collective action, the *Madres y Abuelas de la Plaza de Mayo*'s 'boomerang pattern' of influence and change clearly responded to both national and transnational institutional torturers.

Notes

1　See Canal 11 TV Programme 'Tiempo Nuevo', broadcast on Tuesday, 25 April 1995 at 2100AST on *Canal 11*.
2　In particular, the actions of the *Ciudad Católica* were widely disseminated in the Argentinian military world: they constituted a 'revitalisation of the militancy of traditionalist Catholics and the extreme right in the spaces where the military gathered socially, such as training institutes, parishes, Catholic lay associations and groups' (Ranaletti 2005: 301).
3　In Argentina, see AMA/Nougués 1962: 38–39 and, in Algeria, see AMA/López Aufranc 1959: 634).
4　From 1962 to 1966 they both maintained a legalistic position, but one must not forget that, at that time, the United Stated still preferred civilian governments, on condition that they did not deviate from their guidelines (Rouquier 1978: 522).
5　To a lesser extent, the French Army has been in a perpetual state of crisis since the Dreyfus Affair, a political crisis beginning in 1894 and continuing through 1906 in France during the Third Republic.
6　The progressively pathological imbalance of Argentinian society in favour of the armed forces and the Church in the years leading up to the Juntas could be explained by Messner and Rosenfeld's (1997) 'institutional anomie theory', which advocates that even if negative socio-economic change proves to be associated with crime, the association should be lower than expected in regions where social institutions are stronger.
7　The Triple A was founded on two pillars: General Commissioner Alberto Villar and José López Rega, who both frequented exiled members of the clandestine OAS circles. For this, it had the support of French military and paramilitary personnel who had fought in Algeria. The most notable of these was Colonel Jean

Roger Gardes, condemned to death *in absentia* after the 1961 attempted putsch in Algeria and subject to an extradition request from 1963, whose men played an important part in the Ezeiza Massacre during Juan Perón's return to the country after 17 years of exile (Llumá 2002a: 15; Abramovici, as interviewed by Llumá 2002b: 22).

8 General Reynaldo Benito Bignone became the last military president of Argentina on 1 July 1982, succeeding Leopoldo Galtieri, who had to give up the presidency after his defeat in the Falklands War (2 April–14 June 1982).

9 The *rallié* was a concept developed in Indochina, where there were two indigenous types: those who were ethnically anti-Vietnamese, and so pro-French – the *alliés* (allies) – and the Vietnamese population which might side with the Vietcong. In the latter case, there was still a way of separating these from the Vietcong: through *psychological action*, which consisted of physically separating individuals, confining them and torturing them until they changed sides; hence the name of *ralliés* (Abramovici, as interviewed by Llumá 2002b: 23).

10 The mid-1950s saw the 'discovery' of one of the world's greatest archaeological finds, the prehistoric rock paintings of the Central Saharan mountains of the Tassili-n-Ajjer (Keenan 2003: 193). The 'discovery' was attributed almost entirely to the French pre-historian, Henri Lhote (see Lhote 1958). His 16-month expedition to the Tassili coincided with the Algerian War (Keenan 2003). The fact that Lhote (1958) made no reference in his book *À la Decouverte des Fresques du Tassili* (1957) to these events or the political context in which the expedition was undertaken does not mean that the expedition was an apolitical event. On the contrary, the expedition – which was supervised by former governor general of Algeria Jacques Soustelle – was no simple archaeological jaunt into the Sahara: 'It had the full backing of the French political and intellectual/scientific establishment, with both military and civil authorities in Algeria being placed at its disposal' (Keenan 2003: 201). Indeed, by the time of Soustelle's patronage of Lhote's expedition, he had come to show an uncompromising hostility to Algerian nationalism and had become the political and intellectual standard-bearer of an Algérie Française. Following his departure from Algiers, 'he became the main political and intellectual spokesman for the integration of Algeria with France, becoming a leader of the May 1958 rebellion in Algeria and a major force behind the abortive military uprising (the 'Generals' Revolt') in Algeria in 1961' (Keenan 2003: 202). In this manner, Lhote's expedition played an important 'civilising and cultural role' at a most opportune time for the integrationists. As Keenan explains, 'Lhote's press conference on his arrival in Algiers, at which he revealed to the general public the greatest centre of prehistoric art in the world, gave the European community in Algeria just the sort of fillip that it needed' (Keenan 2003: 202).

11 It is not the aim of this monograph to provide a detailed analysis of the Catholic ideological component to the import of the French subversion doctrine. In fact, the origins of the ideological and mystical apparatus associated with Catholic anti-communism has already been emphasised by other authors, such as Argentinian journalist Horacio Verbitsky (2007a, 2007b, 2008, 2009, 2010) who has significantly documented the relationship between the Catholic Church and the military in Argentina and its French influence.

12 However, it did not acquire a formal structure until 1979. That same year, it was joined by the *Abuelas de Plaza de Mayo* – the Grandmothers of Plaza de Mayo – founded by women whose grandchildren had disappeared, having either been abducted with their mothers or born in clandestine detention centres (Navarro 2001).

13 The monument to the victims of state terrorism and the sculptures installed in the *Parque de la Memoria* – such as Claudia Fontes' *Reconstrucción del Retrato de Pablo*

Míguez, Nicolás Guagnini's *30,000*, and Marie Orensanz's *Pensar es un Hecho Revolucionario*; the *Nosotros No Sabiamos* collages, by León Ferrari; the *Buena Memoria*, by Marcelo Brodsky; Gustavo Germano's set of photographs, *Ausencias*; and the *Manos Anónimas* series, by Carlos Alonso … are just a few examples of the way in which art engages in the construction of the collective memory (Foucault 1969: 248–251). Moreover, these artists show how art can emerge as a critical form of resistance.

Conclusion

> Great power and great crimes are inseparable. It is only those with great political or economic power who can, with the stroke of a pen, an utterance of an order, or even a knowing nod of the head, send thousands to their death or consign millions to lives of unrelenting want and misery. When economic and political powers pursue common interests, the potential for harm is magnified further.
>
> (Michalowski and Kramer 2006: 1)

Having reached this point, we must return to the research question. The horror that took place in Argentina during its Dirty War (1976–1983) was so extraordinary, so enormous, that it was 'unbelievable' in the prime sense of the word: one could not believe it. Human rights organisations calculated the number of 'disappeared' victims throughout this long reign of terror at between 15,000 and 30,000 (Abramovici 2001; Chelala 2001; MacMaster 2004: 8). Most of these victims were tortured. The torture techniques used included, but were not limited to: food and water deprivation; amputation; beating; burning; cutting; whipping; electro-shock; rape; water/urine/vomit/or blood-boarding; tooth or fingernail extraction; and psychological pressures such as mock executions, forced witnessing of others being tortured, or baby snatching right after delivery (since some of the victims were pregnant when they were abducted).

This research was not concerned with acts of torture as 'ordinary' crimes – that is, acts committed by private individuals or carried out by individual officials at their own initiative – but as state crimes: acts of torture that are explicitly prescribed, tacitly condoned, or at least tolerated by the authorities. It is that kind of 'institutionalised torture' that took place in Argentina between 1976 and 1983. Therefore, this monograph was about great crime. It was also a monograph about great power, namely the national (Argentine) and transnational (French) institutional perpetrators who were complicit in the great crime of torture – a behaviour which violates human rights principles and is perceived as deviant by the international community and by domestic audiences.

This book has provided a detailed insight into the intricacies of the complicity of the 'transnational institutional torturer' in acts of torture for political and ideological advantages. The conclusions have, in accordance with the aim of the study, expanded the boundaries of the 'torture template' identifying crimes that were facilitated by France's role in the Argentine Dirty War (1976–1983).

Reiterating the aim

My research aimed at developing new and systematic evidence concerning France's involvement with the transformation of Argentine war professionals into official torturers. It sought to analyse this data within a transnational state crime framework, asking how and why France became involved. While Green and Ward (2004) provide the most coherent framework for understanding state crime, the transnational nature of state terror and torture is one of the few dimensions of their work that could be developed further. As Grewcock explains, 'State crime is often the by-product of complex political and socio-economic relationships and might be supported directly by other states' (2008: 155). If some states are to be routinely condemned and blamed for their use of torture on prisoners, the same condemnation should be extended to other states that not only use torture themselves but also export their techniques abroad.

Consequently, my research focused on examining three alleged manifestations of the torturer: *direct* perpetrator (the individual torturer), *institutional* perpetrator (the state that prescribes torture), and *transnational institutional* perpetrator (that which exports its *savoir-faire* in torture). Central to my argument was the view that an adequate explanation of torture perpetration required looking beyond the level of the torture chamber, or even of the states in which the torture is practised, and focusing attention on the larger policy context in which it is embedded. This monograph explored the utility of the concept of state crime for understanding and responding to the indirect use of torture by external nation states with a detailed examination of exportation of torture techniques and training expertise as complicity in torture.

The cooperation between France and Argentina provided a relevant case study in which to probe this transnational institutionalisation of torture. This enabled us to understand how the regime of torture came about in Argentina and the extent to which France played – paradoxically – a crucial role in it. From the literature review and the data analysis undertaken herein, it is evident that the Argentine officers were trained by the French military – whose skills were based on the experience they had acquired in the wars in Indochina and Algeria – for 'Revolutionary Warfare', a doctrine based on a furious anti-communist ideology that helped justifying the practice of torture, and led to its institutionalisation in Argentina during the Dirty War (1976–1983).

This was the central theme of this research, which was supported by documents and interviews proving the existence of a French military influence in the Argentine military from 1959 to 1981. Indeed, this interpretative and qualitative research involved analyses of government documents, public and private discourses, statements and reports from responsible government officials, autobiographies, army directives, documentary novels, newspaper articles, and letters. In addition to the primary sources – that is, the diplomatic archives – some interviews were also conducted. By utilising documentary evidence and interviews, this monograph attempted to provide a detailed insight into the extent of the role of the French government as a 'transnational institutional torturer' during the Argentine Dirty War. It explored the utility of the concepts of state crime and transnationalisation of state crime for understanding and responding to the indirect use of torture by external nation states, with a detailed examination of the exportation of torture techniques and training of foreign soldiers as proof of complicity in torture. In the current literature on the subject, *American* influence is well documented, but only rarely is French participation mentioned (Aguila 2010; Chomsky 1991; Fagen 1992; Gareau 2004; Hey 1995; McClintock 1992; Schirmer 1998). Research conducted for this book suggests that it would be more appropriate for us to refer to the French influence as being 'to a greater extent'.

The French transnational institutional torturer

Motivation

It has become received wisdom in criminology that all crimes require motivation and opportunity, an approach to crime that originated in the work of Cohen and Felson (1979). Hence the understanding of any crime calls for the exploration of both. Furthermore, building on Merton's (1961) theory of anomie as extended to organisational crime by Passas (1990) – and on earlier work by Kramer and Michalowski (1990) – Kauzlarich and Kramer (1998) established an integrated analytical framework designed to indicate the key factors that contribute to, or restrain, various forms of state crime, among which is state terror. Taking into consideration the fact that states to some extent behave as rational actors, the authors argue that states' criminal behaviours result from the coincidence of pressure for goal attainment (*motivation*), availability and perceived attractiveness of illegitimate means (*opportunity*), and an absence or weakness of social control mechanisms (*social control*) (1998: 148). These three interdependent concepts constituted the starting point of our own investigation into the role of the state.

Having analysed the data gathered for this monograph as discussed in Chapter 3 and Chapter 4, it became clear that the motivations driving the French government were historical, political and ideological factors that persisted from periods of colonisation. Such factors laid the foundations for the later crime of complicity in torture. Indeed, as this book has explained in Chapter 2, French sub-imperialist motives very obviously shaped patterns of criminal behavior, both before and during the Argentine Dirty War.

France's colonial history was marked by the self-perception and notion of France as transmitter of the 'essence of French civilization, presumed to be the noblest in existence' (Confer 1966: 3). Consequently, French initiatives abroad were justified on the basis of the understanding of its uniquely valuable contribution to the world: French culture (Maran 1989: 11). The peculiarly French inter-linkage of politics and culture led to development of the 'civilizing mission ideology' (Maran 1989: 12). The main assumption was that France – by virtue of its status as an enlightened civilization – had a duty to disseminate these concepts widely. The ideology of the civilizing mission covered the field, motivating soldiers and generals, providing the government with another patriotic banner to wave, and slowing criticism of the policy on, and practice of, torture. This ideology had 'the flavour of received wisdom; unquestioned, it prevailed so long as the conditions in which it flourished prevailed' (Maran 1989: 12).

Only with the end of colonialism did actions in the name of the civilizing mission dissipate, to be replaced by neo-imperialist and anti-communist ideologies in the discourse of 'development' (Maran 1989: 12). Indeed, just as French trainers professed to believe that losing the war in Algeria would be 'synonymous with the decline of Christian civilization' (Maran 1989: 16), the Argentine soldiers believed that if they were defeated within their own country 'world-wide communist domination would result' (Carlson 2000: 74).

In the postcolonial era, it remained a major concern that local forces should be equipped in order to help them defend and expand imperial interests, increasingly in the context of the Cold War and the bipolar imperial confrontation between the United States and the Soviet Union. The arming of the 'forward defense areas'[1] (the very notion shows the continued impact of imperial thinking) by the United States in the 1950s and the 1960s was aimed at the containment of the Soviet Union and China (Galtung 1994: 131). It was in this context that the French military started advising the Argentine army in the ways and means of dealing with a new type of 'enemy'. As explained in Chapter 3, those contacts appeared mainly in the form of a) training courses at the École Supérieure de Guerre, the Paris Higher School of War, and b) the establishment of a French military mission into its Argentine equivalent, the Escuela Superior de Guerra of Buenos Aires (Abramovici 2001; Carlson 2000: 71; Feierstein 2010: 45; Frontalini and Caiti 1984: 31; MacMaster 2004: 8; Potash 1980: 320; Rouquier 1978: 471–472).

From 1963, this institutional relationship between the two armies would have grafted onto the informal influence of a group of French military or paramilitary senior ranks who had been members of the bloodthirsty Organisation Armée Secrète (OAS), a secret French armed organisation formed of men who had fled justice in their home country and settled in Argentina with the blessing of Argentine senior military commanders. These exchanges allowed the French to 'pass their experience from Indochina and Algeria on to Argentine officers' (Oliveira-Cézar 2002: 27). French specialists in torture were able – 'with the authorisation of their superiors in the cabinet ministries and the military general staff' (Alleg 2006a: 101) – to pursue new careers well beyond the borders of Algeria. With natural fluctuations, this influence would continue well into the establishment and organisation of the 1976 dictatorship.

This monograph argues that the French training constituted a 'sub-imperial action of expansion' (Eide 1977: 100). Far from being used to protect Argentina from imperial onslaughts, the transfer of France's *savoir-faire* in Revolutionary War served the same main function as the colonial army of the past: the repression of its own population. Of course, it did this not by serving its former colonialist industrialised metropolis, but rather 'by serving the totality of the old international economic order' (Eide 1977: 100–101). It is therefore reasonable to suggest that the French training of the Argentine military was aimed at intensifying France's domination in the militarisation of the world.

Opportunity

For a long time, however, the French training of the Argentine military 'had no practical relevance for Argentina' (Heinz 1995: 75–76). In fact, the 'New War' described by the French assessors did not exist in Argentina at the beginning of the 1960s: 'It was an anticipated war that the Argentine military would actually fight less than twenty years later' (Carlson 2000: 73). Yet, because of Argentina's background, opportunities manifested themselves for French military advisers and veterans of Indochina and Algeria displaced by decolonisation.

Indeed, French nationals in Argentina found themselves in a

> society characterised by a state of tension over the social and financial advantages secured by the workers some years earlier, and by a state of agitation over what it thought were indicators of the presence of an internal enemy and the *expansion* of communist *subversion* within the social fabric.
>
> (Ranaletti 2005: 296)

This climate was familiar to them and they too believed in the same phantoms, interpreting colonial independence as the result of a manoeuvre orchestrated by 'international communism' to destroy 'Western Christian civilisation'. Those who moved to the great conurbations, such as Buenos Aires and Mendoza, were able quickly to recover old habits and practices:

> With a long tradition of welcoming the persecuted and displaced, [...] Argentina offered itself to those defeated representatives of late colonialism

as a promised land to forget the immediate past, to dream of new authoritarian utopias or to recommence a pathway interrupted by the atrocities of French colonialism.

(Ranaletti 2005: 298)

As the Argentine government was looking for an effective way to stop rebellious Peronists who were supposedly taking part in the communist 'conspiracy' against the established order, the counter-insurgency doctrine managed to find in Argentina a 'fertile ground' early on (Amaral 1998: 183; Feierstein 2010: 44; Ranalletti 2002; Robin 2004: 202). Indeed, even in the early 1960s, the French and Argentine militaries thought that 'Argentina and its people constituted an objective that was too important for international Marxism to overlook' (AMA/Nougués 1962: 30). Just as French trainers professed to believe that losing the war in Algeria would be 'synonymous with the decline of Christian civilisation' (Maran 1989: 16), the Argentine soldiers believed that if they were defeated within their own country 'world-wide communist domination would result' (Carlson 2000: 74). This might be due to the fact that the French doctrine of Revolutionary War had its foundations in a range of historical components of the Catholic-military way of thought, most especially in the idea of the 'enemy within' (Périès 1999: 838; Ranaletti 2005: 288). The main contribution of this 'French, Christian civilisation' ideology to Argentine military training was to strengthen the perception of political problems, especially growing violence and social inequalities (portrayed as the result of the Marxist penetration and subversion) (Ranaletti 2005: 303). This ideological support to terror was also largely responsible for intensive indoctrination and anti-communist training (García 1995).

Social control

A highly motivated state with easy access to illegal means of goal attainment may be blocked from exercising torture by the operation of social control mechanisms (Kauzlarich and Kramer 1998: 151). Thus, in order to be successful, the criminal state has to make its citizens feel uninformed, separate, fragmented, and powerless. Yet, as discussed in Chapter 4, the movement of the *Madres y Abuelas de la Plaza de Mayo* succeeded in mobilising opposition to the Argentine military regime in Argentina and in France: by bypassing their state and directly searching out an external ally allegedly respectful of human rights principles, the Mothers demonstrated that civil society is the most significant force in challenging national and transnational state criminality (Edwards 2009; Gramsci 1971; Risse *et al.* 1999). Although their marches and initiatives initially had a limited and very personal objective, they were the first demonstrations that denounced disappearances in Argentina and, eventually, helped to bring down the repressive military government (Aguila 2010; Bousquet 1983; De Bonafini 1985; Eckstein 2001; Navarro 2001; Stepan 2001: 88).

In 1982, the Argentine military, in an effort to restore its power and legitimacy, attempted to seize the Falkland Islands – *Islas Malvinas* – but was soundly defeated by Britain. Charged with cowardice, dishonesty and incompetence, the Junta further lost its grip on the country and the 'Dirty War' came to a close. On 30 October 1983, the state of siege was lifted and democratic elections took place, marking the return of civilian rule. President Raúl Alfonsín took office on 10 December 1983 and began trying to bring about truth and justice for the victims of the dictatorship. By the time the electoral campaign began, the women had successfully transformed the *desaparecidos* into a vital, paramount, and therefore not negotiable issue that no political party could ignore or afford to negotiate (Navarro 2001: 254–255). As a result, the *Comisión Nacional sobre la Desaparición de Personas (CONADEP)* – National Commission on the Disappearance of Persons – was set up to 'clarify the tragic events in which thousands of people disappeared' (CONADEP 2006: 8). The *CONADEP* report, *Nunca Más* – 'Never Again' – concluded that the human rights violations perpetrated by the military government were the result of 'state terrorism', since the Argentine armed forces had 'absolute control of the resources of the state' (CONADEP 2006: 479).

Consequently, in 1985, members of the military began to be brought to trial and sentenced to imprisonment. However, the need for accountability was frustrated when Alfonsín's government – under threat of a new military *coup d'état* – enacted the 1986 *Ley de Punto Final* ('Full Stop Law')[2] and the 1987 *Ley de Obediencia Debida* ('Due Obedience Law'),[3] both of which afforded immunity to members of the former regime. Furthermore, two years later, President Carlos Menem, who felt that the support of the military would benefit his party as well as the country, granted a pardon to already convicted or still indicted members of the Junta. But Argentine civil society refused to turn its back on the search for truth and justice. The *Madres y Abuelas de la Plaza de Mayo* continued, and still continue, to seek clarification of the fate and whereabouts of the disappeared, whereas other organisations like *Hijos e Hijas por la Identidad y la Justicia contra el Olvido y el Silencio (HIJOS)* – 'Sons and Daughters for Identity and Justice Against Oblivion and Silence' – have denounced former military officers by exposing them as torturers and killers to neighbours and community, using slogans such as *Si no hay Justicia, hay Escraches* – 'If there is no Justice, there is Outing'.

Following such movements, the then-governor of Santa Cruz province Nestor Kirchner garnered local and international support by promoting the annulment of the Full Stop and Due Obedience Laws, contributing to his presidential election victory in 2003. In 2005, Argentina's Supreme Court confirmed that these laws were unconstitutional and overturned amnesties for the military, paving the way for prosecutions to resume. In November 2011, an Argentine federal court sentenced 12 former military officers to life in prison for crimes against humanity carried out at one of Latin America's most notorious torture-centres, the *Escuela Superior de Mecánica de la Armada*

(ESMA) – Naval Superior School of Mechanics. While this number of convictions is small when more than 5,000 people were disappeared at the *ESMA*, such trials serve as a reminder to members of the military that impunity will not prevail, and to encourage people to speak out against state crimes.

The case of Argentina teaches us that for the institutionalisation of torture to come to come to an end and for the slogan *Nunca Más* to become a reality, civil society must be cognisant that even under democratic rule crimes of the state occur. Since it is the most significant force in challenging state criminality, civil society must keep on resisting and, undeniably, Argentinians make it their duty to do so.[4] As Broda claimed:

> We Latin Americans responded – and continue to respond – to military authoritarianism, to foreign intervention, to the indigence of the masses, and to the ill-conceived approach of the so-called 'economic and social development' policies imposed by the rich countries, abetted by local oligarchies

by protesting and demonstrating against them (1992: 303). Following this approach, the *Madres y Abuelas de la Plaza de Mayo*'s 'boomerang pattern' of influence and change – that is, the actions of the *Madres* who bypassed their own state, which had institutionalised torture, to seek help in the state that had contributed to its institutionalisation – clearly responded to both national and transnational institutional torturers (Risse *et al.* 1999: 18).

Liberty, equality, … complicity?

This Franco-Argentine case illustrates what Herman calls the 'institutional structure of domination built to violate human rights' (1991: 91). Torturers are not born: they are nurtured, trained and supported. In many countries 'they rely on the willingness of foreign governments to provide not only equipment but also personnel training and know-how' (Amnesty International 2001a: 41). It follows that the use of torture amidst human rights dialogue has to be discussed in its international structural context, and not merely as an issue about the infraction of human rights in the country where it is employed.

As discussed in Chapter 2, there is thus 'no room for doubt' that complicity in torture, if proven, would be a direct breach of the France's international human rights obligations, under the UN Convention Against Torture and Other Cruel, Inhuman or Degrading Treatment or Punishment, under customary international law, and according to the general principles of State Responsibility for internationally wrongful acts (House of Lords *et al.* 2009: 15). For the purposes of State responsibility for complicity in torture, it has been established that 'complicity' means simply 'one State giving assistance to another State in the commission of torture, or acquiescing in such torture, in the knowledge, including constructive knowledge, of the circumstances of the torture which is or has been taking place' (House of Lords *et al.* 2009: 16).

It is not alleged that the French government or its agents themselves engaged in torture, or directly authorised torture. In fact, the personnel who actually carried out torture in the Argentine military were not French. But these officers had been trained or influenced by France in their choice of weapons and strategies, as well as in the selection of targets. They were not tools of any outsiders in the direct sense of the word, but they responded to the domestic contradictions and tensions with means and methods not of their own making.

The essence of the allegations was that France has been complicit in the use of torture by the Argentine military. The research in Chapter 3 and Chapter 4 provides evidence that, by sharing their own *savoir-faire* in the art of turning ordinary soldiers into official torturers, the French prepared the ground for the institutionalisation of torture that would be implemented between 1976 and 1983 in Argentina. This monograph alleges that training in counter-insurgency strategies that relies heavily on anti-communist ideology that, in turn, justifies the use of torture, amounts to complicity in torture by the various French military agents concerned. This is in direct breach of the France's human rights obligations. Both recipient and donor states often go to great lengths to conceal the transfer of expertise which is used to facilitate serious human rights violations (Amnesty International 2001a: 41–42).

While it can be fully accepted that intelligence cooperation is both necessary and legitimate in countering terrorism, there must, however, be mechanisms for ensuring accountability for such cooperation (House of Lords *et al.* 2009: 23). It is undoubtedly true that the inadequate international control of transfer of French counter-insurgency expertise to Argentine military and security forces contributed to gross human rights violations in that country (Amnesty International 2001a: 40). Mechanisms ensuring that the training of military, security and police personnel of another country do not include the transfer of skills, knowledge or techniques likely to lend themselves to torture or ill-treatment in the recipient country are needed.

In order to achieve more transparency concerning transnational training of the military, Amnesty International has suggested the following strategies: (a) make public information on all government sponsored police, security and military training programs for foreign personnel, in particular the individuals and units trained, as well as the nature of the training, and the monitoring mechanisms put in place; and (b) establish mechanisms to rigorously monitor the human rights impact of the training provided (2001a: 52). A combination of constraints against training transfers inside the 'training' countries and efforts by concerned 'trained' governments to break out of the military dependency created by present pattern of import might eventually yield results (Eide 1977: 102).

Criminology and the transnational institutional torturer

It is undoubtedly true that the inadequate international control of transfer of French counter-insurgency expertise to Argentine military and security forces contributed to gross human rights violations in that country (Amnesty International 2001a: 40). Yet, the question as to whether states can be criminally responsible continues to be highly controversial, for example, with regard to the enactment of penal sanctions for states (Jorgensen 2000; Brownlie 1963). In the line of Cameron's (2009) research, however, this book argues that state responsibility and complicity can better be studied through criminology – rather than international law – and through a literal use of the concept of state crime, as applied to the use of state power for deviant purposes in ways that unambiguously violate human rights. It contends that criminology offers a varied and useful set of perspectives on the study of the 'transnational institutional torturer'.

It took more than 10 years after the return of democracy for the Argentine military to make its first ever apology for its 'excesses'. Indeed, on 25 April 1995, the Argentine Army Chief of Staff, General Martín Balza, admitted in a speech broadcast on a television news programme that the military persecuted and killed political opponents during the Dirty War from 1976 to 1983. He surprised many as he publicly declared with a firm voice, full of conviction:

> We must no longer deny the horror we lived through [...]. Without euphemisms, I say clearly: A criminal is whoever gives immoral orders. A criminal is whoever obeys immoral orders.[5]

These two last affirmations constituted the starting point of my investigation into the notion of torture as a process involving several sets of actors. Indeed, as I explain in Chapter 2 if it is true that most torturers were not born, it follows that they must have been made. As to the 'making ingredients', some pointed at obedience to authority or ideological persuasion – processes which, in turn, require authorisation, dehumanisation and routinisation. Others suggested bureaucratisation and its diffusion of responsibility. Others still thought that conformity to a violent group that promotes a culture marked by male domination assumes a more central role in the creation of official torturers. Sometimes, however, most agreed that would-be torturers must be taught to torture without question: training becomes necessary. Generally, this is a two-phase process: first, recruits must be made less sensitive to their own pain; and, second, they must be made less sensitive to the pain they inflict on others.

Yet, the 'training' we were dealing with in our case study was not only national, but also transnational. The main argument throughout this research has been that French military advisers transformed their Argentine peers into torturers. It has been argued that this transformation was made possible through the exportation and teaching of the French doctrine of so-called Revolutionary War – *doctrine de Guerre Révolutionnaire* – the direct outcome of which was the systematic use of torture (Branche 2001: 326; Lazreg 2008: 15). Indeed, this doctrine was based on a furious anti-communist ideology that helped to justify the practice of torture, and led to its institutionalisation in Argentina during the Dirty War (1976–1983).

Some years after his unexpected speech, General Martin Balza confirmed this argument when he was asked how Argentina could have gone that far in its exercise of repression. As we saw in Chapter 4, his answer was as follows:

> It is a question I haven't stopped asking myself. It was a political, ideological, military and religious cocktail that engendered the most criminal regime in our history. And for this cocktail to be mixed, the teaching provided by French military advisers from the end of the 1950s played a fundamental role. [...] the French took a harmful, pernicious concept to Argentina which literally poisoned the minds of officers of my generation: that of the 'enemy within' [...].
>
> (General Martín Antonio Balza, as interviewed by Robin 2004: 200–202)

Having analysed the data gathered for this monograph as discussed in Chapter 3 and Chapter 4, it has been shown how the French ideological persuasion and technical training contributed to the making of Argentine official torturers. This is not to argue that Argentine torture would not have been effective without 'French training'; however, institutionalised torture does not occur without ideological or logistical preparation and, from 1957 onwards, France performed an integral role in the architecture of the Argentine Dirty War. It became evident that the human rights tradition should not only condemn the torturing state, but also the structures enabling torture – thereby promoting a deeper human right 'to live in a social and world structure that does not produce torture' (Galtung 1994: 134).

Systematic torture appears to be impossible to sustain without a network of officials working towards a common aim (Herman 1982). Consequently, in line with General Martín Balza's speech, I would like to emphasise that the individual who works at the level of the torture chamber deserves the label of 'torturer'; the state that institutionalises torture within its own territory also deserves the label of 'torturer'. Additionally, the state that exports torture expertise and, in so doing, institutionalises torture beyond its own borders – even if it often verbally champions human rights values at home – deserves the label of 'torturer'. By training Argentine officers in an ideology that justifies torture, France contributed to the institutionalisation of torture in Argentina and, therefore, must be labelled as a 'transnational institutional torturer'.

There are important ethical–normative reasons for retaining the term 'torture' in describing some acts of the state. Accordingly, labelling certain states as '(transnational) institutional torturers' – a term with powerful connotations – could be a relevant means of advancing a progressive political project aimed at protecting marginalized and vulnerable populations from indiscriminate and oppressive forms of 'national', but also 'transnational', state violence.

Much has already been achieved in confronting the crimes of Argentina's military dictatorship, but many of the secret files and information held in military archives have yet to be released. For example, some 1,500 secret files, dating back to the years of military rule in Argentina, were discovered in Buenos Aires as recently as 5 November 2013.[6] They were found in an abandoned wing of the *ESMA* headquarters. The Argentine Minister of Defence, Agustin Rossi, claimed that these files contained the transcripts of all meetings held by the Junta, which ruled the country from 1976 to 1983. As official diplomatic archives are being opened and the dust is being blown away from history, this dark chapter in the Cold War is starting to come to light. In order for it to do so, it is necessary to navigate between Argentina's supposed willingness to confront its past and the proven desire of France to bury and deny its involvement. France's obfuscation constitutes another irony for a state that has so often, verbally at least, championed universal moral values and human rights. These documents are needed in order to understand the exact causes and scope of the horror that took place under the Junta during the Argentine Dirty War.

The case study of the cooperation between France and Argentina should highlight the role that criminologists could play in producing a better politics of crime (Loader and Sparks 2010; Bosworth and Hoyle 2011). If criminology has always, and often uncomfortably, found itself in close proximity to the state and its political needs, no discussion of its role is helpful that does not account for the historically specific conditions in which crime and crime policy operate today. From this perspective, the debate is not about whether criminologists should try to engage a broader non-academic audience, but whether and how criminological knowledge can make more 'effective' and 'intelligible' contributions in the public sphere in which it operates. By unearthing data that expose complicity in mass violence and murder and naming names of military attachés and politicians, I am hoping to be part of the globalised creation and transfer of knowledge that acts as some form of counterweight – alongside human right activists, forensic archaeologist, international criminal lawyers and others – to state crime.

Notes

1 None of the 'forward defense areas' ever used the weapons for the purpose for which they had been intended: defence against attack by the Soviet Union and China. All the areas made use of their military training, directly or indirectly, for internal control (Eide 1977: 102).

2 The Full Stop Law No 23,492 of 12 December 1986 stopped prosecution of such cases.

3 The Due Obedience Law No 23,521 of 4 June 1987 granted immunity in such cases to all members of the military except those in positions of command.

4 Today, strong from its experience, and despite deep psychological and social scars caused by repression, exile, and fear, civil society in Argentina still continues to make a difference. Indeed, many in Argentina are as concerned with contemporary crimes of the state as they are with dealing with the legacy of the 'Dirty War' and its social stigma: the death of 26 people during the 2001 riots following President Fernando de la Rúa's declaration of a state of siege; the extrajudicial killing by the police of social activist Darío Santillán in 2002; the forced disappearance of teen-ager Luciano Arruga following his arrest by police in 2009; or the assassination of 25-year-old farmer Cristian Ferreyra in 2011 following the violent displacement of small farmers (resulting from the expansion of the country's genetically modified soy production model that has spurred the nation's economic recovery), have all engendered significant protests. There is also some evidence to suggest that violent repercussions against survivors of the 'Dirty War' and witnesses participating in human rights trials may be taking place – such as the forced disappearance of Julio Lopez in 2006 and the murder of Silvia Suppo in 2010. See articles available on the *HIJOS*.'s (http://hijos-capital.org.ar/) and the *Centro de Estudios Legales y Sociales*' (www.cels.org.ar/home/index.php) websites.

5 See Canal 11 TV Programme 'Tiempo Nuevo', broadcast on Tuesday, 25 April 1995 at 2100AST on *Canal 11*.

6 See www.bbc.co.uk/news/world-latin-america-24814489.

Appendix I

French diplomatic archives by documents

- *First period: 1952–1963*

  - File #74 – America 1952–1963; Argentina: Military Matters, National Defence.

    1 Dossier 74 – Cote 18–6-1; No. 665/AM; A.s. Mission d'officiers argentins pour le compte du Commandement de la Défense anti-aérienne; Buenos Aires, le 1er Juin 1954; Le Chargé d'Affaires de France a.i. en Argentine, à Monsieur le Ministre des Affaires Etrangères, Direction d'Amérique. **(Doc.74/1)**

    2 Dossier 74 – Cote 18–6-1; No. 383/AM; A.s. Stage d'officiers argentins à l'Ecole Supérieure de Guerre; Buenos Aires, le 16 Mars 1956; L'Ambassadeur de France en Argentine, à son Excellence le Ministre des Affaires Etrangères, Direction d'Amérique. **(Doc.74/2)**

    3 Dossier 74 – Cote 18–6-1; No. 480/AM; A.s. Documents demandés par l'Armée argentine; Buenos Aires, le 6 Avril 1956, L'Ambassadeur de France en Argentine, à Son Excellence Monsieur le Ministre des Affaires Etrangères, Direction d'Amérique. **(Doc.74/3)**

    4 Dossier 74 – Cote 18–6-1; No. 404/AM; Buenos Aires le 29 Mars 1956; Le Colonel A. R. Bernard, Attaché Militaire Naval et de l'Air près de l'Ambassade de France en Argentine, à Monsieur le Ministre de la Défense Nationale et des Forces Armées, 2°Division, 51, Bd. Latour-Maubourg, Paris. **(Doc.74/4)**

    5 Dossier 74 – Cote 18–6-1; No. 926/AM; A.s. Relations entre l'Armée française et l'Armée argentine; Buenos Aires, le 5 Juillet 1956; L'Ambassadeur de France en Argentine, à Son Excellence Monsieur le Ministre des Affaires Etrangères, Direction d'Amérique. **(Doc.74/5)**

    6 Dossier 74 – Cote 18–6-1; No. 529/AM; Objet: Projet de voyage de fin d'étude de l'Ecole de Guerre argentine; Paris, le 3

Septembre 1958, Le Président du Conseil, à Monsieur le Ministre des Affaires Etrangères, Direction d'Amérique. **(Doc.74/6)**

7 Dossier 74 – Cote 18–6-1; No. 41/AM; A.s. Projet de voyage de fin d'études de l'Ecole de Guerre argentine; le 10 Septembre 1958, Le Ministre des Affaires Etrangères, à Monsieur le Président du Conseil, Etat Major de la Défense Nationale, Affaires Politiques. **(Doc.74/7)**

8 Dossier 74 – Cote 18–6-1; No. 614/AM; Objet: Projet de voyage en France de l'Ecole de Guerre argentine; Paris, le 11 Septembre 1958, Note pour le Général d'Armée Major Général des Armées E.M.G.A./2ème Division. **(Doc.74/8)**

9 Dossier 74 – Cote 18–6-1; No. 1092/AM; Objet: Project d'accord relatif aux assesseurs militaires français; Buenos Aires, le 9 Octobre 1959, Le Colonel François Serralta, Attaché Militaire Naval et de l'Air près de l'Ambassade de France en Argentine, à Monsieur le Ministre des Armées (TERRE), Etat Major de l'Armée, 2° Bureau. **(Doc.74/9)**

10 Dossier 74 – Cote 18–6-1; No. 1072/AM; A.s. Envoi du project d'accord relatif aux assesseurs militaires français; Buenos Aires, le 20 Novembre 1959; L'Ambassadeur de France en Argentine (Armand Blanquet Du Chayla), à Son Excellence Monsieur le Ministre des Affaires Etrangères, Direction d'Amérique. **(Doc.74/10)**

11 Dossier 74 – Cote 18–6-1; No. 2870/AM; Objet: Mission française auprès de l'Armée argentine; Paris, le 20 Novembre 1959, Le Premier Ministre (Michel Debré) à Monsieur le Ministre des Armées, Etat Major Général des Armées. **(Doc.74/11)**

12 Dossier 74 – Cote 18–6-1; Projet d'accord mettant à la disposition de l'Armée argentine une mission d'assesseurs militaires français (accord signé le 11 Février 1960). **(Doc.74/12)**

13 Dossier 74 – Cote 18–6-1; No. 07252/AM; Objet: Voyage en Argentine du Chef d'Etat-Major de l'Armée de Terre; Paris, le 2 Mai 1960, Le Ministre des Armées (Pierre Messmer), à Monsieur le Ministre des Affaires Etrangères. **(Doc.74/13)**

14 Dossier 74 – Cote 18–6-1; No. 07620/AM; Objet: Voyage en Argentine du Chef d'Etat-Major de l'Armée de Terre; Paris, le 6 Mai 1960, Le Ministre des Armées (Pierre Messmer), à Monsieur le Ministre des Affaires Etrangères. **(Doc.74/14)**

15 Dossier 74 – Cote 18–6-1; No. 3BIS/AM; Paris, le 7 mai 1960, J. Bayens. **(Doc.74/15)**

16 Dossier 74 – Cote 18–6-1; No. 523/AM; A.s. Visite du Général Demetz et Mission d'Assesseurs Militaires en Argentine; Buenos Aires, le 3 Juin 1960, L'Ambassadeur de France en Argentine (Armand Blanquet Du Chayla), à Son Excellence Monsieur le

Ministre des Affaires Etrangères, Direction d'Amérique. **(Doc.74/16)**

17 Dossier 74 – Cote 18–6-1; Assistance technique de l'Armée francaise à l'Armée argentine; 20 Juin 1960. **(Doc.74/17)**

18 Dossier 74 – Cote 18–6-1; Note à l'Attention de Monsieur l'Ambassadeur; Buenos Aires, le 4 Octobre 1961. **(Doc.74/18)**

19 Dossier 74 – Cote 18–6-1; No. 961/AM; A.s. Cours inter-américain de guerre contre-révolutionnaire; Buenos Aires, le 6 Octobre 1961, L'Ambassadeur de France en Argentine (Armand Blanquet Du Chayla), à Son Excellence Monsieur le Ministre des Affaires Etrangères, Direction d'Amérique. **(Doc.74/19)**

20 Dossier 74 – Cote 18–6-1; No. 516/AM; Buenos Aires, le 27 Août 1963, Ambassadeur de France en Argentine (Jean-Paul Boncour). **(Doc.74/20)**

- *Second period: 1964–1970*

  - File #141 – America 1964–1970; Argentina: National Defence.

    1 Dossier 141 – Cote 18–6-1; No. 115/AM; A.s. Personnalités militaires et leur repartition dans les principaux commandements des trois armes; Buenos Aires, le 28 Janvier 1964, Christian de Margerie, Ambassadeur de France en Argentine, à Son Excellence Monsieur le Ministre des Affaires Etrangères, Direction d'Amérique. **(Doc.141/1)**

    2 Dossier 141 – Cote 18–6-1; No. 5548/AM; Objet: Assesseurs français en Argentine; Paris, le 18 Juin 1965, Ministère des Armées, Division Organisation, à Monsieur le Ministre des Affaires Etrangères, Direction d'Amérique. **(Doc.141/2)**

    3 Dossier 141 – Cote 18–6-1; No. 159/AM; A.s. L'Armée Argentine; Buenos Aires, le 29 Janvier 1969, L'Ambassadeur de France en Argentine (Dimitri de Favitski), à Son Excellence Monsieur Michel Debré, Ministre des Affaires Etrangères, Direction d'Amérique. **(Doc.141/3)**

    4 Dossier 141 – Cote 18–6-1; No. 12150/AM; Special Report: The Economic Role of the Argentine Military; 22 August 1969. **(Doc.141/4)**

  - File #177 – America 1964–1970; Argentina: French Immigration and Colonies; Assistance to French Algerians who moved to Argentina.

    1 Dossier 177 – Cote 18–12–1; No. 378/AS; A.s. Reconduction en 1970 de la Mission du B.D.P.A. en Argentine; Buenos Aires, le 18 Août 1969, L'Ambassadeur de France en Argentine (Jean de La Chevardière de La Grandville), à Son Excellence Monsieur

Maurice Schumann, Ministre des Affaires Etrangères, Direction des Conventions Administratives et des Affaires Consulaires. **(Doc.177/1)**

2   Dossier 177 – Cote 18–12–1; No. 1410/AS; A.s. Reconduction en 1970 de la Mission du B.D.P.A. en Argentine; Buenos Aires, le 29 Octobre 1969, L'Ambassadeur de France en Argentine (Jean de La Chevardière de La Grandville), à Son Excellence Monsieur Maurice Schumann, Ministre des Affaires Etrangères, Direction des Conventions Administratives et des Affaires Consulaires. **(Doc.177/2)**

3   Dossier 177 – Cote 18–12–1; No. 403/AS; A.s. Communauté Francaise d'Argentine; Buenos Aires, le 28 Septembre 1970, L'Ambassadeur de France en Argentine (Jean de La Chevardière de La Grandville), à Son Excellence Monsieur Maurice Schumann, Ministre des Affaires Etrangères, Direction des Conventions Administratives et des Affaires Consulaires. **(Doc.177/3)**

4   Dossier 177 – Cote 18–12–1; No. 434/AS; A.s. Reconduction en 1971 de la Mission du B.D.P.A.; Buenos Aires, le 14 Octobre 1970, L'Ambassadeur de France en Argentine (Jean de La Chevardière de La Grandville), à Son Excellence Monsieur Maurice Schumann, Ministre des Affaires Etrangères, Direction des Conventions Administratives et des Affaires Consulaires. **(Doc.177/4)**

•   File #179 – America 1964–1970; Argentina: Military Assessors.

1   Dossier 179 – Cote 1–1-2; No. 3291/EMA; Objet: Rémunération des Assesseurs militaires francais en Argentine; Paris, le 23 Juin 1966, L'Ambassadeur de France en Argentine, à Monsieur le Ministre des Affaires Etrangères, Direction d'Amérique. **(Doc.179/1)**

2   Dossier 179 – Cote 1–1-2; No. 580/PAN; A.s. Assesseurs Militaires; Buenos Aires, le 6 Mai 1970, L'Ambassadeur de France en Argentine (Jean de La Chevardière de La Grandville), à Son Excellence Monsieur Maurice Schumann, Ministre des Affaires Etrangères, Service des Pactes et du Désarmement. **(Doc.179/2)**

3   Dossier 179 – Cote 1–1-2; No. 88/AM; A.s. Mission des trois assesseurs militaires en Argentine; Paris, le 25 Novemvre 1970, Le Ministre des Affaires Etrangères, à Monsieur le Ministre d'Etat Chargé de le Défense Nationale, Etat Major des Armées, Bureau 'Relations Internationales', 10 Rue St. Dominiquem Paris, 7ème. **(Doc.179/3)**

4   Dossier 179 – Cote 1–1-2; No. 29/AM; A.s. Assesseurs Militaires; Paris, le 25 Novembre 1970, La Direction des Affaires Politiques Amérique, à Son Excellence Monsieur l'Ambassadeur de France. **(Doc.179/4)**

5   Dossier 179 – Cote 1–1-2; Accord entre le Gouvernement de la République française et le Gouvernement de la République Argentine, modifiant l'accord du 11 Février 1960, concernant la mission d'assesseurs militaires français à la disposition de l'armée de terre argentine (accord signé le 29 Décembre 1970). **(Doc.179/5)**

- *Third period: 1971–1975*

  - File #188 – America 1971–1975; Argentina: Military Matters of the Country, and Connections with France.

    1   Dossier 188 – Cote 18–6-2; No. 555/AM; A.s. L'Armée en Argentine; Buenos Aires, le 11 Juin 1973, Jean-Claude Winckler, Ambassadeur de France en Argentine, à Son Excellence Monsieur Michel Jobert, Ministre des Affaires Etrangères, Direction d'Amérique. **(Doc.188/1)**
    2   Dossier 188 – Cote 18–6-1; No. 4/AM; A.s. Projet de Visite en France de l'Ecole Nationale de Guerre Argentine; Paris, le 15 Décembre 1973, Le Ministre des Affaires Etrangères, à Monsieur le Premier Ministre, Secrétariat Général de la Défense Nationale, Division des Affaires Civiles. **(Doc.188/2)**

  - File #201 – America 1971–1975; Argentina: French Military Mission in Argentina.

    1   Dossier 201 – Cote 18–6-1; No. 11092/EMA/RI/2; Objet: Compte Rendu Trimestriel du 2e Trimestre 1974, Activités de la Mission Militaire Française en Argentine; Le Lieutenant-Colonel Bernard Jozan, Attaché des Forces Armées près l'Ambassade de France en Argentine, à Monsieur le Ministre des Armées, Etat Major des Armées, Relations Internationales/2. **(Doc.201/1)**
    2   Dossier 201 – Cote 18–6-1; No. 11092/EMA/RI/2'; Objet: Compte Rendu Trimestriel du 3e Trimestre 1974, Activités de la Mission Militaire Française en Argentine; Le Lieutenant-Colonel Bernard Jozan, Attaché des Forces Armées près l'Ambassade de France en Argentine, à Monsieur le Ministre des Armées, Etat Major des Armées, Relations Internationales/2. **(Doc.201/2)**
    3   Dossier 201 – Cote 18–6-1; No. 11092/EMA/RI/2''; Objet: Compte Rendu Trimestriel du 4e Trimestre 1974, Activités de la Mission Militaire Française en Argentine; Le Lieutenant-Colonel Bernard Jozan, Attaché des Forces Armées près l'Ambassade de France en Argentine, à Monsieur le Ministre des Armées, Etat Major des Armées, Relations Internationales/2. **(Doc.201/3)**

- *Fourth period: 1976–1981*

  - File #229 – America 1976–1981; Argentina: National Defence, Military Matters.

    1 Dossier 229 – Cote 18–6-1; No. 358/AM; A.s. Aide Militaire à l'Argentine; Paris, le 10 Juin 1976, Note du Ministère des Affaires Etrangères, Direction des Affaires Politiques. **(Doc.229/1)**

    2 Dossier 229 – Cote 18–6-1; A.s. Relations franco-argentines; Le 19 Novembre 1976, Note Manuscrite de P.R. pour M. Césaire. **(Doc.229/2)**

    3 Dossier 229 – Cote 18–6-1; No. 84/AM; A.s. Visite en France d'élèves officiers de l'Armée de terre Argentine – Escale du navire-école argentin 'Libertad'; Le 25 Mai 1979, Note pour le Cabinet du Ministre. **(Doc.229/3)**

    4 Dossier 229 – Cote 18–6-1; No. 8/AM; A.s. Candidature de militaires argentins au titre de notre enseignement militaire supérieur, cycle 1980–1981; Le 24 Octobre 1979, Note pour le Service des Affaires Stratégiques et du Désarmement, Sous-Direction de l'Aide Militaire. **(Doc.229/4)**

    5 Dossier 229 – Cote 18–6-1; A.s. Coopération Technique Militaire avec l'Argentine; Paris, le 5 Juin 1981, Note du Ministère des Relations Extérieures, Direction des Affaires Politiques. **(Doc.229/5)**

- *Fifth period: 1982–1984*

  - File #2228c – America 1982–1984; Argentina: Stay of the Madres de la Plaza de Mayo in France.

    1 Dossier 2228c – Cote 4–2; No. 47/AM; A.s. Argentine: Visite en France d'une délégation des Mères de la Place de Mai; Le 28 Janvier 1983, Note pour le Cabinet du Ministre à l'intention de M. Dumont. **(Doc.2228c/1)**

    2 Dossier 2228c – Cote 4–2; No. 5446/AM; Objet: Séjour en France des Mères de la Place de Mai; Le 9 Février 1983, Télégramme du Ministère des Relations Extérieures. **(Doc.2228c/2)**

    3 Dossier 2228c – Cote 4–2; No. 60/AM; A.s. Audience du Président de la République à deux Mères de la Place de Mai (15 Février, à 17h30), Paris le 15 Février 1983, Note du Ministère des Relations Extérieures. **(Doc.2228c/3)**

    4 Dossier 2228c – Cote 4–2; No. 112/AM; Objet: Commentaires de presse sur l'audience accordée par le Président de la République aux Mères de la Place de Mai; Le 17 Février 1983, Télégramme de Jean Dominique Paolini, Ambassadeur de France en Argentine, au Ministère des Relations Extérieures. **(Doc.2228c/4)**

5   Dossier 2228c – Cote 4–2; No. 110/AM; Objet: Entretien avec M. Aguirre Lanari à propos des Mères de la Place de Mai; Le 17 Février 1983, Télégramme de Jean Dominique Paolini, Ambassadeur de France en Argentine, au Ministère des Relations Extérieures. (Doc.2228c/5)

6   Dossier 2228c – Cote 4–2; No. 202/AM; A.s.: Commentaire de la Revue 'Siete Dias' sur l'audience accordée par le Président Mittérand aux 'Mères de la Place de Mai' et à leur tournée en Europe; Buenos Aires, le 25 Février 1983, Jean Dominique Paolini, Ambassadeur de France en Argentine, à Son Excellence Monsieur Claude Cheysson, Ministre des Relations Extérieures, Direction d'Amérique. (Doc.2228c/6)

•   File #2233f – America 1982–1984; Argentina: Military Matters, Army and Defence of Argentina.

1   Dossier 2233f – Cote 8–1-1; No. 1053/DEF; Paris, le 20 Juin 1984; Objet: Compte Rendu de Mission en Argentine, Le Colonel Alain Baer du Bureau Etudes Générales de l'Etat-Major des Armées, à Monsieur le Général d'Armée, Chef d'Etat-Major des Armées. (Doc.2233f/1)

•   File #2234 – America 1982–1984; Argentina: Military Matters, Connections with France.

1   Dossier 2234 – Cote 8–2-1; No. 128/AM; Objet: Entretien avec le Général Torres, Chef d'Etat Major Conjoint. Buenos Aires, le 17 Février 1984, Télégramme de Jean Dominique Paolini, Ambassadeur de France en Argentine, au Ministère de la Défense. (Doc.2234/1)

2   Dossier 2234 – Cote 8–2-1; No. 303/ARG/AFA; Objet: Visite du Colonel Baer en Argentine. Buenos Aires, le 11 Juin 1984, Télégramme   au   Ministère   des   Affaires   Etrangères. (Doc.2234/2)

3   Dossier 2234 – Cote 8–2-3; No. 33/SAN; A.s. Demande de stages pour les forces armées argentines; Buenos Aires, le 7 Janvier 1982, Henri de Coignac, Chargé d'Affaires de France en Argentine, à Son Excellence Monsieur Claude Cheysson, Ministre des Relations Extérieures, Direction des Affaires Politiques, Service des Affaires Stratégiques et du Désarmement, sous Direction de l'Aide Militaire. (Doc.2234/3)

4   Dossier 2234 – Cote 8–2-3; No. 1/AM; A.s. Demande de stages pour les forces armées de l'Argentine; Le 26 Janvier 1982, Note pour la Direction des Affaires Politiques, Service des Affaires Stratégiques et du Désarmement, sous Direction de l'Aide Militaire. (Doc.2234/4)

5   Dossier 2234 – Cote 8–2-3; No. 1011/SAM; A.s. Opportunités des stages de militaires argentins en France (EMS); Buenos Aires, le 15 Juillet 1982, Jean Dominique Paolini, Ambassadeur de France en Argentine, à Son Excellence Monsieur Claude Cheysson, Minitre des Relations Extérieures, sous Direction de l'Aide Militaire. **(Doc.2234/5)**

6   Dossier 2234 – Cote 8–2-3; No. 624/ARG/AFA; Objet: Demande de stages au profit de l'Argentine pour le cycle continu 1983–1984; Buenos Aires, le 22 Septembre 1982, Le Colonel Michel Dudjari, Attaché des Forces Armées près l'Ambassade de France en Argentine, à Monsieur le Ministre des Relations Extérieures, sous Direction de l'Aide Militaire (Sous–couvert de Monsieur l'Ambassadeur de france en Argentine). **(Doc.2234/6)**

7   Dossier 2234 – Cote 8–2-3; No. 90/SAM; A.s. Demande de stages pour les forces armées argentines; Buenos Aires, le 20 Janvier 1983, Jean Dominique Paolini, Ambassadeur de France en Argentine, à Son Excellence Monsieur Claude Cheysson, Ministre des Relations Extérieures, Direction des Affaires Politiques, Service des Affaires Stratégiques et du Désarmement, sous Direction de l'Aide Militaire. **(Doc.2234/7)**

8   Dossier 2234 – Cote 8–2-3; No. 816/SAM; A.s. Demande d'admission de stagiaires argentins à l'enseignement militaire supérieur (EMS); Buenos Aires, le 20 Juillet 1983, Jean Dominique Paolini, Ambassadeur de France en Argentine, à Son Excellence Monsieur Claude Cheysson, Ministre des Relations Extérieures, Affaires Stratégiques et du Désarmement, sous Direction de l'Aide Militaire. **(Doc.2234/8)**

9   Dossier 2234 – Cote 8–2-3; No. 1171/SAM; A.s. Demande de stages de militaires argentins organisés par la Délégation Générale pour l'Armement; Buenos Aires, le 28 Septembre 1983, Jean Dominique Paolini, Ambassadeur de France en Argentine, à Son Excellence Monsieur Claude Cheysson, Ministre des Relations Extérieures, Direction des Affaires Politiques, Service des Affaires Stratégiques et du Désarmement, sous Direction de l'Aide Militaire. **(Doc.2234/9)**

Appendix 2
Argentine military archives by articles

I Chronological order

- *Year 1957:*

  - File #327: October–December 1957.

    - François Pierre Badie (Octubre–Diciembre 1957) 'La Resistencia Interior Francesa durante la Ocupación Alemana entre 1940–1945', *Revista de la Escuela Superior de Guerra*, No. 327, pp. 537–551.
    - Patrice de Naurois (Octubre–Diciembre 1957) 'Una Concepción Francesa: La División Mecanizada Rápida', *Revista de la Escuela Superior de Guerra*, No. 327, pp. 553–573.

- *Year 1958:*

  - File #328: January–March 1958.

    - François Pierre Badie (Enero–Marzo 1958) 'Las Operaciones Anglo-Francesas contra Port Said (Noviembre 1956)', *Revista de la Escuela Superior de Guerra*, No. 328, pp. 76–95.
    - Patrice de Naurois (Enero–Marzo 1958) 'Algunos Aspectos de la Estrategia y Táctica Aplicados por el Viet Minh durante la Campaña de Indochina', *Revista de la Escuela Superior de Guerra*, No. 328, pp. 97–128.
    - Carlos Jorge Rosas (Enero–Marzo 1958) 'Estrategia y Táctica', *Revista de la Escuela Superior de Guerra*, No. 328, pp. 129–149.

  - File #329: April–June 1958.

    - Patrice de Naurois (Abril–Junio 1958) 'Una Teoría para la Guerra Subversiva', *Revista de la Escuela Superior de Guerra*, No. 329, pp. 226–240.
    - François Pierre Badie (Abril–Junio 1958) 'Operaciones Anfibias Conjuntas. Operación "Mosquetero" Revisada', *Revista de la Escuela Superior de Guerra*, No. 329, pp. 282–305.

- File #330: July–September 1958.

  - François Pierre Badie (Julio–Septiembre 1958) 'Protección de Fronteras', *Revista de la Escuela Superior de Guerra*, No. 330, pp. 503–518.
  - Patrice de Naurois (Julio–Septiembre 1958) 'La Nato: Origenes y Contenido del Tratado del Atlantico Norte Organización de la Nato', *Revista de la Escuela Superior de Guerra*, No. 330, pp. 519–540.
  - Robert Weibel Richard (Julio–Septiembre 1958) 'Francia y la Union Francesa', *Revista de la Escuela Superior de Guerra*, No. 330, pp. 552–568.

- File #331: October–December 1958.

  - Manrique Miguel Mom (Octubre–Diciembre 1958) 'Guerra Revolucionaria: El Conflicto Mundial en Desarrollo' *Revista de la Escuela Superior de Guerra*, No. 331, pp. 641–664.
  - François Pierre Badie (Octubre–Diciembre 1958) 'La Guerra Psicológica', *Revista de la Escuela Superior de Guerra*, No. 331, pp. 665–686.
  - Patrice de Naurois (Octubre–Diciembre 1958) 'Guerra Subversiva y Guerra Revolucionaria', *Revista de la Escuela Superior de Guerra*, No. 331, pp. 687–702.
  - Patrice de Naurois (Octubre–Diciembre 1958) 'Un Metodo de Razonamiento para un Problema Tactico', *Revista de la Escuela Superior de Guerra*, No. 331, pp. 703–719.

- *Year 1959:*

  - File #334: July–September 1959.

    - Manrique Miguel Mom (Julio–Septiembre 1959) 'Guerra Revolucionaria: Causas-Proceso-Desarrollo', *Revista de la Escuela Superior de Guerra*, No. 334, pp. 489–515.
    - François Pierre Badie (Julio–Septiembre 1959) 'La Guerra Revolucionaria en China', *Revista de la Escuela Superior de Guerra*, No. 334, pp. 516–549.
    - Ricardo R. Caillet-Bois (Julio–Septiembre 1959) 'La Revolucion Francesa', *Revista de la Escuela Superior de Guerra*, No. 334, pp. 601–606.

  - File #335: October–December 1959.

    - Alcides López Aufranc (Octubre–Diciembre 1959) 'Guerra Revolucionaria en Argelia', *Revista de la Escuela Superior de Guerra*, No. 335, pp. 611–648.
    - Robert Louis Bentresque (Octubre–Diciembre 1959) 'Un Método de Razonamiento en Guerra Subversiva', *Revista de la Escuela Superior de Guerra*, No. 335, pp. 733–754.

- *Year 1960:*
  - File #337: April–June 1960.
    - Jean Nougués (Abril–Junio 1960) 'Características Generales de las Operaciones en Argelia', *Revista de la Escuela Superior de Guerra*, No. 337, pp. 174–204.
  - File #338: July–September 1960.
    - Henri Grand d'Esnon (Julio–Septiembre 1960) 'Guerra Subversiva', *Revista de la Escuela Superior de Guerra*, No. 338, pp. 339–363.
  - File #339: October–December 1960.
    - Tomás A. Sánchez de Bustamante (Octubre–Diciembre 1960) 'La Guerra Revolucionaria', *Revista de la Escuela Superior de Guerra*, No. 339, pp. 602–614.
    - Robert Louis Bentresque (Octubre–Diciembre 1960) 'Los Acontecimientos de Laos', *Revista de la Escuela Superior de Guerra*, No. 339, pp. 615–629.
- *Year 1961:*
  - File #343: October–December 1961.
    - Tomás A. Sánchez de Bustamante (Octubre–Diciembre 1961) 'La Guerra Revolucionaria Comunista. La Guerra de China', *Revista de la Escuela Superior de Guerra*, No. 343, pp. 589–635.
- *Year 1962:*
  - File #344: January–March 1962.
    - Tomás A. Sánchez de Bustamante (Enero–Marzo 1962) 'La Situación Mundial. El Cerco Estratégico', *Revista de la Escuela Superior de Guerra*, No. 344, pp. 5–23.
    - Jean Nougués (Enero–Marzo 1962) 'Radioscopia Subversiva en la Argentina', *Revista de la Escuela Superior de Guerra*, No. 344, pp. 24–43.
  - Files #345–346: April–September 1962.
    - Jorge Raúl Orfila (Abril–Septiembre 1962) 'Del Proceso Salán, ¿Surgen Experiencias asimilables al Mando Militar Actual?', *Revista de la Escuela Superior de Guerra*, Nos. 345–346, pp. 174–199.
- *Year 1963:*
  - File #349: April–June 1963.
    - Prefacio de la Dirección (Abril–Junio 1963) "La Guerra de Indochina", *Revista de la Escuela Superior de Guerra*, No. 349.

- *Year 1996:*

  - File #523: October–December 1996.

    - José Luis Picciuolo (Octubre–Diciembre 1996) 'La Escuela Superior de Guerra después de la Revolución de 1930 y hasta Mediados del Siglo XX', *Revista de la Escuela Superior de Guerra*, No. 523, pp. 9–35.

2 Alphabetical order

Badie, F. P. (1957) 'La Resistencia Interior Francesa durante la Ocupación Alemana entre 1940–1945', *Revista de la Escuela Superior de Guerra*, No. 327, pp. 537–551.

Badie, F. P. (1958a) 'Las Operaciones Anglo-Francesas contra Port Said (Noviembre 1956)', *Revista de la Escuela Superior de Guerra*, No. 328, pp. 76–95.

Badie, F. P. (1958b) 'Operaciones Anfibias Conjuntas. Operación "Mosquetero" Revisada', *Revista de la Escuela Superior de Guerra*, No. 329, pp. 282–305.

Badie, F. P. (1958c) 'Protección de Fronteras', *Revista de la Escuela Superior de Guerra*, No. 330, pp. 503–518.

Badie, F. P. (1958d) 'La Guerra Psicológica', *Revista de la Escuela Superior de Guerra*, No. 331, pp. 665–686.

Badie, F. P. (1959) 'La Guerra Revolucionaria en China', *Revista de la Escuela Superior de Guerra*, No. 334, pp. 516–549.

Bentresque, R. L. (1959) 'Un Método de Razonamiento en Guerra Subversiva', *Revista de la Escuela Superior de Guerra*, No. 335, pp. 733–754.

Bentresque, R. L. (1960) 'Los Acontecimientos de Laos', *Revista de la Escuela Superior de Guerra*, No. 339, pp. 615–629.

de Naurois, P. (1957) 'Una Concepción Francesa: La División Mecanizada Rápida', *Revista de la Escuela Superior de Guerra*, No. 327, pp. 553–573.

de Naurois, P. (1958a) 'Algunos Aspectos de la Estrategia y Táctica Aplicados por el Viet Minh durante la Campaña de Indochina', *Revista de la Escuela Superior de Guerra*, No. 328, pp. 97–128.

de Naurois, P. (1958b) 'Una Teoría para la Guerra Subversiva', *Revista de la Escuela Superior de Guerra*, No. 329, pp. 226–240.

de Naurois, P. (1958c) 'La Nato: Origenes y Contenido del Tratado del Atlantico Norte Organización de la Nato', *Revista de la Escuela Superior de Guerra*, No. 330, pp. 519–540.

de Naurois, P. (1958d) 'Guerra Subversiva y Guerra Revolucionaria', *Revista de la Escuela Superior de Guerra*, No. 331, pp. 687–702.

de Naurois, P. (1958e) 'Un Metodo de Razonamiento para un Problema Tactico', *Revista de la Escuela Superior de Guerra*, No. 331, pp. 703–719.

Grand d'Esnon, H. (1960) 'Guerra Subversiva', *Revista de la Escuela Superior de Guerra*, No. 338, pp. 339–363.

López Aufranc, A. (1959) 'Guerra Revolucionaria en Argelia', *Revista de la Escuela Superior de Guerra*, No. 335, pp. 611–648.

Mom, M. M. (1958) 'Guerra Revolucionaria: El Conflicto Mundial en Desarrollo' *Revista de la Escuela Superior de Guerra*, No. 331, pp. 641–664.

Mom, M. M. (1959) 'Guerra Revolucionaria: Causas-Proceso-Desarrollo', *Revista de la Escuela Superior de Guerra*, No. 334, pp. 489–515.

Nougués, J. (1960) 'Características Generales de las Operaciones en Argelia', *Revista de la Escuela Superior de Guerra*, No. 337, pp. 174–204.

Nougués, J. (1962) 'Radioscopia Subversiva en la Argentina', *Revista de la Escuela Superior de Guerra*, No. 344, pp. 24–43.

Orfila, J. R. (1962) 'Del Proceso Salán, ¿Surgen Experiencias asimilables al Mando Militar Actual?', *Revista de la Escuela Superior de Guerra*, Nos. 345–346, pp. 174–199.

Picciuolo, J. L. (1996) 'La Escuela Superior de Guerra después de la Revolución de 1930 y hasta Mediados del Siglo XX', *Revista de la Escuela Superior de Guerra*, No. 523, pp. 9–35.

Prefacio de la Dirección (1963) 'La Guerra de Indochina', *Revista de la Escuela Superior de Guerra*, No. 349.

Rosas, C. J. (1958) 'Estrategia y Táctica', *Revista de la Escuela Superior de Guerra*, No. 328, pp. 129–149.

Sánchez de Bustamante, T. A. (1960) 'La Guerra Revolucionaria', *Revista de la Escuela Superior de Guerra*, No. 339, pp. 602–614.

Sánchez de Bustamante, T. A. (1961) 'La Guerra Revolucionaria Comunista. La Guerra de China', *Revista de la Escuela Superior de Guerra*, No. 343, pp. 589–635.

Sánchez de Bustamante, T. A. (1962) 'La Situación Mundial. El Cerco Estratégico', *Revista de la Escuela Superior de Guerra*, No. 344, pp. 5–23.

Appendix 3
Interview schedule

- *Interview #1:*
  Marie Orensanz. Friday 12 November 2010. Paris. Major Argentine artist, who left Buenos Aires during the military regime to go to Paris. She won several prizes, notably in 1999 with the sculpture *'Pensar es un hecho revolucionario'* ('Thinking is a revolutionary phenomenon'), a memorial to the victims of State Terror, and in 2009 with *'Las raíces son femeninas'* ('The roots are feminine'), a tribute to the mothers of the Playa de Mayo.

- *Interview #2:*
  Martine Billard. Wednesday 20 July 2011. Email conversation. Member of the Green Party who in 2003 tabled the ultimately rejected[1] request for a French parliamentary commission of inquiry concerning the role played by France in support of Latin American military regimes between 1973 and 1984.[2]

- *Interview #3:*
  Horacio Verbitsky. Tuesday 6 September 2011. Buenos Aires, Lavalle 1282 1° 14 (esquina Talcahuano). Argentine Journalist.

- *Interview #4:*
  Colonel Sergio. Wednesday 25 April 2012. Buenos Aires. Former Argentine Officer of the *Escuela Superior de Mecánica de la Armada*, Naval Higher School of Mechanics.

- *Interview #5:*
  Lieutenant-Colonel Federico. Monday 30 April 2012. Rosario. Former Argentine Officer of the *Jefatura de Policía de Rosario*, Police Headquarter of Rosario.

- *Interview #6:*
  General Matias. Tuesday 8 May 2012. Buenos Aires. Former Argentine Officer of the Ejercito Argentino, Argentine Army.

- *Interview #7:*
  María. Wednesday 16 May 2012. Victim of Argentine state terror. Law student at the begininning of the Dirty War, she was abducted from outside the university of Buenos Aires, on 4 November 1976. She 'disappeared' for three months and was tortured in the *Escuela Superior de Mecánica de la Armada (ESMA)*, Superior School of Mechanics of the Navy.

- *Interview #8:*
  Lieutenant-Colonel Juan. Monday 23 September 2013. Flight BA0244 Buenos Aires to London. Former Argentine Officer of the *Escuela Superior de Mecánica de la Armada*, Superior School of Mechanics of the Navy.

Notes

1 Assemblée Nationale, Constitution du 4 Octobre 1958, Douzième Législature, Rapport n° 1295, Fait au Nom de la Commission des Affaires Etrangères sur la Proposition de Résolution n° 1060, *Tendant à la Création d'une Commission d'Enquête sur le Rôle de la France dans le Soutien aux Régimes Militaires d'Amérique Latine entre 1973 et 1984*, Enregistré à la Présidence de l'Assemblée nationale le 16 décembre 2003.

2 Assemblée Nationale, Constitution du 4 Octobre 1958, Douzième Législature, Proposition de Résolution n° 1060, *Tendant à la Création d'une Commission d'Enquête sur le Rôle de la France dans le Soutien aux Régimes Militaires d'Amérique Latine entre 1973 et 1984*, Enregistré à la Présidence de l'Assemblée Nationale le 10 Septembre 2003.

Appendix 4

Claims for exemption (French diplomatic archives)

RÉPUBLIQUE FRANÇAISE

**MINISTÈRE DES AFFAIRES ÉTRANGÈRES
ET EUROPÉENNES**

DIRECTION DES ARCHIVES

N° 1773AR/ARCH/FW/fw
Dossier suivi par : Françoise WATEL
Tél. : 01 43 17 42 84
Mél : francoise.watel@diplomatie.gouv.fr

Paris, le 19 septembre 2011

Mademoiselle,

J'ai le regret de vous faire savoir qu'il ne m'est pas possible de donner une suite favorable à votre demande du 12 août dernier concernant l'article suivant :

- série Amérique, sous-série Argentine, 1964-1970, article 179.

Il a été en effet jugé préférable de maintenir la réserve sur les documents contenus dans cet article, qui portent atteinte à la vie privée de personnes nommément désignées, ainsi qu'au secret de la défense nationale et aux intérêts fondamentaux de l'Etat dans la conduite de la politique extérieure.

En revanche, l'article suivant est consultable et peut vous être communiqué en salle de lecture des archives diplomatiques à La Courneuve dans les conditions habituelles :

- série Amérique, sous-série Argentine, 1964-1970, article 188;

En application de l'article 5 de la loi n°78-753 du 17 juillet 1978, modifiée par la loi n° 2000-321 du 12 avril 2000 relative aux droits des citoyens dans leurs relations avec les administrations, je vous informe qu'il vous est possible de saisir de cette décision, pour avis, dans un délai de deux mois, la Commission d'accès aux documents administratifs (35, rue Saint-Dominique, 75700 Paris).

Veuillez agréer, Mademoiselle, l'expression de ma considération distinguée.

Monique CONSTANT
Adjoint au Directeur

Mademoiselle Mélanie COLLARD
Rue Zabay 10
4000 LIEGE
BELGIQUE

Direction des Archives – 3 rue Suzanne Masson – 92126 La Courneuve - Tél. 01 43 17 42 42 – Fax 01 43 17 48 44

Liberté • Égalité • Fraternité
RÉPUBLIQUE FRANÇAISE

COMMISSION D'ACCÈS
AUX DOCUMENTS ADMINISTRATIFS

Cada

La Secrétaire générale

Mademoiselle Mélanie COLLARD
18 Pembridge Gardens Flat 4
W2 4DU LONDON
UNITED KINGDOM

Paris, le 19 octobre 2011

Références à rappeler : 20114377-MFL

Mademoiselle,

J'ai l'honneur d'accuser réception de la demande d'avis que vous avez présentée à la commission d'accès aux documents administratifs par lettre parvenue à son secrétariat le 14 octobre 2011.[*]

L'examen de votre demande est prévu pour la séance du 17 novembre 2011. L'avis de la commission vous sera ensuite transmis par courrier dans les meilleurs délais.

Je vous prie de croire, Mademoiselle, à l'assurance de ma considération distinguée.

Anne JOSSO

[*] Conformément aux dispositions de la loi du 6 janvier 1978, je vous informe que vos nom, adresse et qualité sont enregistrés sur le système automatisé de gestion des affaires de la CADA. Les membres de la CADA, ses rapporteurs et collaborateurs sont seuls destinataires de ces informations. Vous pouvez exercer votre droit d'accès et de rectification en vous adressant au secrétariat de la commission.

35, rue Saint-Dominique 75700 PARIS 07 SP ☎ 01 42 75 79 90 • Télécopie : 01 42 75 80 70 • www.cada.fr • cada@cada.fr

Liberté • Égalité • Fraternité
RÉPUBLIQUE FRANÇAISE

COMMISSION D'ACCÈS
AUX DOCUMENTS ADMINISTRATIFS

Cada

La Secrétaire générale

Mademoiselle Mélanie COLLARD
18 Pembridge Gardens Flat 4
W2 4DU LONDON
UNITED KINGDOM

Paris, le 15 novembre 2011

Références à rappeler : 20114377-MFL

Mademoiselle,

L'étude de l'affaire que vous avez soumise à la commission d'accès aux documents administratifs a nécessité un complément d'instruction. Aussi l'examen de votre affaire a-t-il été reporté à la séance du 1er décembre 2011.

Je vous prie de croire, Mademoiselle, à l'assurance de ma considération distinguée.

Anne JOSSO

Liberté · Égalité · Fraternité
RÉPUBLIQUE FRANÇAISE

COMMISSION D'ACCÈS
AUX DOCUMENTS ADMINISTRATIFS

Cada

Mademoiselle Mélanie COLLARD
18 Pembridge Gardens Flat 4
W2 4DU LONDON
UNITED KINGDOM

Le Président

Paris, le   0 5 DEC. 2011

Références à rappeler : 20114377-MFL

Mademoiselle,

Je vous prie de trouver ci-dessous l'avis rendu par la commission d'accès aux documents administratifs dans sa séance du 1er décembre 2011 sur votre demande. Cet avis est également adressé à l'autorité administrative que vous aviez saisie.

———————— Avis n° 20114377-MFL du 1er décembre 2011 ————————

Mademoiselle Mélanie COLLARD a saisi la commission d'accès aux documents administratifs, par courrier enregistré à son secrétariat le 14 octobre 2011, à la suite du refus opposé par le ministre des affaires étrangères et européennes (direction des archives) à sa demande de communication, dans le cadre de sa thèse de doctorat, et par dérogation aux délais fixés par l'article L. 213-2 du code du patrimoine, du dossier de la série Amérique, sous-série Argentine, 1964-1970, n°179.

La commission note que ces documents, datés de 1964 à 1970, ne deviendront, conformément au 3° du I de l'article L. 212-2 du code du patrimoine, librement communicables qu'en 2020. Cependant, ayant été informée par le ministre des Affaires étrangères que le carton était composé de plusieurs sous-dossiers de natures différentes, dont un seul porte sur le renouvellement d'un accord portant mise à disposition d'assesseurs Français en Argentine en 1970, qui intéresse tout particulièrement Mademoiselle Collard et dont le contenu ne recèle aucune information dont la communication porterait atteinte au secret de la défense nationale, la commission donne, eu égard à l'intérêt et au sérieux des recherches effectuées par Mademoiselle COLLARD, un avis favorable à l'accès, par dérogation, de la demanderesse à ce sous-dossier, et un avis défavorable pour le reste du dossier.

Je vous prie de croire, Mademoiselle, à l'assurance de ma considération distinguée.

Pour le Président,
Le Rapporteur général adjoint

Emilie BOKDAM-TOGNETTI
Auditeur au Conseil d'Etat

35, rue Saint-Dominique 75700 PARIS 07 SP ☎ 01 42 75 79 99 • Télécopie : 01 42 75 80 70 • www.cada.fr • cada@cada.fr

Liberté • Égalité • Fraternité
RÉPUBLIQUE FRANÇAISE

MINISTÈRE DES AFFAIRES ÉTRANGÈRES

DIRECTION DES ARCHIVES

Paris, le 14 août 2012

N° 115 AR/ARCH/FW/fw
Dossier suivi par : Françoise WATEL
Tél. : 01 43 17 42 84
Mél : francoise.watel@diplomatie.gouv.fr

Mademoiselle,

En réponse à votre demande du 16 janvier dernier, j'ai le plaisir de vous faire savoir que je vous autorise par dérogation à consulter les articles suivants :

- série Amérique, sous-série Argentine, 1976-1981, article 229,
- série Amérique, sous-série Argentine, 1982-1984, article 2234.

Vous pourrez obtenir communication de ces dossiers à la salle de lecture des Archives diplomatiques à La Courneuve, sur présentation de la présente lettre au conservateur de permanence.

Les reproductions ne sont pas autorisées.

Veuillez agréer, Mademoiselle, l'expression de ma considération distinguée.

Isabelle RICHEFORT
Chef du département des Archives

Mademoiselle Mélanie COLLARD
18 Pembridge Gardens
Flat 4
W2 4DU
LONDON
ROYAUME-UNI

RÉPUBLIQUE FRANÇAISE

MINISTÈRE DES AFFAIRES ÉTRANGÈRES

DIRECTION DES ARCHIVES   Paris, le 14 janvier 2014

N° 74 AR/ARCH/FW/fw

Dossier suivi par : Françoise WATEL
Tél. : 01 43 17 42 84
Mél : francoise.watel@diplomatie.gouv.fr

Mademoiselle,

En réponse à votre demande du 6 décembre dernier, j'ai le plaisir de vous faire savoir que je vous autorise par dérogation à consulter le dossier suivant, par extrait de l'article 80QO/201 :

- série Amérique, sous-série Argentine, 1971-1975, article 80QO/201, dossier 18-6-1 : mission militaire française en Argentine, 1974-1975.

Vous pourrez obtenir communication de ce dossier à la salle de lecture des Archives diplomatiques à La Courneuve, sur présentation de la présente lettre au conservateur de permanence.

Les reproductions ne sont pas autorisées.

Veuillez agréer, Mademoiselle, l'expression de ma considération distinguée.

Isabelle RICHEFORT
Adjoint au directeur des Archives

Mademoiselle Mélanie COLLARD
Rue Zabay 10
4000 LIEGE
BELGIQUE

Bibliography

Abramovici, P. (15 June 2001) 'Comment la France a exporté la Torture en Argentine: L'Autre Sale Guerre d'Aussaresses', *Le Point*, No. 1500, pp. 26–34.

Ackroyd, C., Margolis, K., Rosenhead, J. and Shallice, T. (1980) *The Technology of Political Control*, Second Edition, London: Pluto Press.

Acuña, C. H. and Smulovitz, C. (1997) 'Guarding the Guardians in Argentina: Some Lessons about the Risks and Benefits of Empowering the Courts', in A. J. McAdams (ed.) *Transitional Justice and the Rule of Law in New Democracies*, Notre Dame, IN: University of Notre Dame Press, pp. 93–122.

Adamson, W. L. (1987/1988) 'Gramsci and the Politics of Civil Society', *Praxis International*, Vol. 7, No. 3/4, pp. 320–329.

Aguila, G. (2006) 'Dictatorship, Society, and Genocide in Argentina: Repression in Rosario, 1976–1983', *Journal of Genocide Research*, Vol. 8, No. 2, pp. 169–180.

Aguila, G. (2010) 'State Violence and Repression in Rosario during the Argentine Dictatorship, 1976–83', in M. Esparza, H. R. Huttenbach and D. Feierstein (eds) *State Violence and Genocide in Latin America: The Cold War Years*, London and New York: Routledge, pp. 137–151.

Aguilera Peralta, G. and Beverly, J. (1980) 'Terror and Violence as Weapons of Counterinsurgency in Guatemala', *Latin American Perspectives*, Vol. 7, No. 2/3, pp. 91–113.

Alba, R. and Silberman, R. (2002) 'Decolonization Immigration and the Social Origins of the Second Generation: The Case of North Africans in France', *International Migration Review*, Vol. 6, No. 4, pp. 1169–1193.

Alexander, J. (2006) *The Civil Sphere*, Oxford: Oxford University Press.

Alleg, H. (1958) *La Question*, Paris: Editions de Minuits.

Alleg, H. [1961] (2006a) *The Question*, translated by J. Calder, Lincoln, NE: University of Nebraska Press Bison Books.

Alleg, H. [1958] (2006b) 'Afterword to Henri Alleg, The Question', translated by D. L. Schalk, in H. Alleg, *The Question*, translated by J. Calder, Lincoln, NE: University of Nebraska Press Bison Books, pp. 97–102.

Almirón, F. (1999) *Campo Santo. Los Asesinatos Del Ejército en Campo de Mayo*, Buenos Aires: Editorial 21.

Alves, M. H. M. (1992) 'Cultures of Fear, Cultures of Resistance: The New Labor Movement in Brazil', in J. E. Corradi, P. W. Fagen and M. A. Garreton (eds) *Fear at the Edge: State Terror and Resistance in Latin America*, Berkeley: University of California Press, pp. 184–211.

Alvesalo, A. and Virta, E. (2003) 'Researching Regulators and the Paradoxes of Access', in S. Tombs and D. Whyte (eds) *Unmasking the Crimes of the Powerful: Scrutinizing States and Corporations*, New York: Peter Lang, pp. 181–198.

Amaral, S. (1998) 'Guerra Revolucionaria: de Argelia a la Argentina, 1957–1962', *Academia Nacional de la Historia, Investigaciones y Ensayos*, Vol. 48, pp. 105–137.

Ambler, J. S. (1966) *The French Army in Politics 1945–1962*, Ohio: Ohio State University Press.

Amery, J. [1966] (1995) *Par-delà le Crime et le Châtiment: Essai pour Surmonter l'Insurmontable*, Translated by F. Wuilmart, Arles: Actes Sud.

Amnesty International (1977) *Report of an Amnesty International Mission to Argentina, 6–13 November 1976*, New York: Author.

Amnesty International (1984) *Torture in the Eighties*, London: Author.

Amnesty International (2000a) 'United States of America: A Briefing for the UN Committee Against Torture', AI Index: AMR 51/56/00.

Amnesty International (2000b) *Take a Step to Stamp out Torture*, London: Author.

Amnesty International (2001a) *Stopping the Torture Trade*, London: Author.

Amnesty International (2001b) *Broken Bodies, Shattered Minds: Torture and Ill-Treatment of Women*, London: Author.

Anderson, M. and López Crespo, A. (31 January 1986) 'Un Libro Inédito del General Acdel Vilas: la Guerra Sucia Empezó en 1975', *El Periodista*.

Arcel, L. T. (2002) 'Torture, Cruel, Inhuman, and Degrading Treatment of Women: Psychological Consequences', *Torture*, Vol. 12, No. 1, pp. 5–16.

Archer, D. and Gartner, R. (1984) *Violence and Crime in Cross-National Perspective*, New Haven, CT: Yale University Press.

Arendt, H. [1951] (1985) *The Origins of Totalitarianism*, New York: Harcourt Brace Jovanovich.

Arendt, H. (1958) *The Human Condition*, Chicago: University of Chicago Press.

Arendt, H. [1963] (1965) *Eichmann in Jerusalem: A Report on the Banality of Evil*, New York: Viking.

Atkinson, R. and Flint, J. (2004) 'Snowball Sampling', in M. S. Lewis-Beck, A. Bryman and T. Futing Liao (eds) *The Sage Encyclopedia of Social Science Research Methods*, London: Sage, pp. 1043–1044.

Atkinson, P. and Silverman, D. (1997) 'Kundera's Immortality: The Interview Society and the Invention of the Self', *Qualitative Inquiry*, Vol. 3, No. 3, pp. 304–325.

Aussaresses, P. (2001) *Services Spéciaux, Algérie 1955–1957*, Paris: Editions Perrin.

Aussaresses, P. (2004) *Pour la France, Services Spéciaux, 1942–1954*, Paris: Editions du Rocher.

Aussaresses, P. (2007) 'The Battle of the Casbah', in W. F. Schulz (ed.) *The Phenomenon of Torture: Readings and Commentary*, Philadelphia: University of Pennsylvania Press, pp. 137–138.

Aussaresses, P. (2008) *Je n'ai pas tout dit*, Paris: Editions du Rocher.

Aust, H. P. (2011) *Complicity and the Law of State Responsibility*, Cambridge: Cambridge University Press.

Banuazizi, A and Movahedi, S. (1975) 'Interpersonal Dynamics in a Simulated Prison: A Methodological Analysis', *American Psychologist*, Vol. 30, pp. 152–160.

Barak, G. (ed.) (1991) *Crimes by the Capitalist State: An Introduction to State Criminality*, New York: State University of New York Press.

Barron, A. (2002) 'Foucault and Law', in J. E. Penner, D. Schiff and R. Nobles (eds) *Introduction to Jurisprudence and Legal Theory: Commentary and Materials*, Oxford: Oxford University Press, pp. 955–1034.

Bauman, Z. (1989) *Modernity and the Holocaust*, Cambridge: Polity Press.

Baumrind, D. (1964) 'Some Thoughts on Ethics after Reading Milgram's "Behavioral Study of Obedience"', *American Psychologist*, Vol. 19, pp. 421–423.

BBC Documentary (2005) 'We Have Ways of Making You Talk', broadcast on Tuesday, 5 April 2005 at 2100BST on *BBC Two*.

Beaugé, F. (20 June 2000) 'Le Général Massu Exprime ses Regrets pour la Torture en Algérie', *Le Monde*.

Beccaria, C. (1963) *On Crimes and Punishments*, New York: Bobbs-Merrill.

Becker, H. (1963) *Outsiders: Studies in the Sociology of Deviance*, New York: The Free Press.

Becker, H. (1967) 'Whose side are we on?', *Social Problems*, Vol. 14, No. 3, pp. 239–247.

Bell, J. B. (1975) *Transnational Terror*, Washington D.C.: American Enterprise Institute for Public Policy.

Berg, B. (1998) *Qualitative Research Methods for the Social Sciences*, Third Edition, Boston: Allyn and Bacon.

Bernard, P. (22 June 2000) 'La «Gangrène» au Coeur de la République', *Le Monde*.

Bertaux, D. (1988) 'El Enfoque Biográfico: Su Validez Metodológica, Sus Potencialidades', in *Historia Oral e Historias de Vida*, Vol. 18, pp. 63–65.

Blaikie, N. (2000) *Designing Social Research: The Logic of Anticipation*, Cambridge: Polity.

Blaikie, N. (2004) 'Research Question', in M. S. Lewis-Beck, A. Bryman and T. Futing Liao (eds) *The Sage Encyclopedia of Social Science Research Methods*, London: Sage, pp. 966–967.

Blakeley, R. J. (2006) *Repression, Human Rights, and US Training of Military Forces from the South*, PhD Thesis, University of Bristol.

Blanquer, J. M. (1992) *Michel Baroin, les Secrets d'une Influence*, Paris: Plon.

Boniface, X. (2001) *L'Aumônerie Militaire Française (1914–1962)*, Paris: Cerf.

Bosworth, M. and Hoyle, C. (eds) (2011) *What is Criminology?*, Oxford: Oxford University Press.

Bourke, J. (1999) *An Intimate History of Killing: Face-to-Face Killing in 20th Century Warfare*, New York: Basic Books.

Bousquet, J. P. (1983) *Las Locas de Plaza de Mayo*, Buenos Aires: El Cid Editor.

Branche, R. (2001) *La Torture et l'Armée Pendant la Guerre d'Algérie: 1954–1962*, Paris: Gallimard.

Brockett, C. D. (1991a) 'Sources of State Terrorism in Rural Central America', in P. T. Bushnell, V. Shlapenthokh, C. K. Vanderpool, and J. Sundram (eds) *State Organized Terror*, Boulder, CO: Westview, pp. 59–76.

Brockett, C. D. (1991b) 'The Structure of Political Opportunities and Peasant Mobilization in Central America', *Comparative Politics*, Vol. 23, No. 3, pp. 253–274.

Browning, C. R. (1998) *Ordinary Men: Reserve Police Battalion 101 and the Final Solution in Poland*, London: Penguin Books.

Brownlie, I. (1963) *International Law and the Use of Force by States*, Oxford: Oxford University Press.

Bryman, A. (2001) *Social Research Methods*, Oxford: Oxford University Press.

Bryman, A. (2004) 'Multimethod Research', in M. S. Lewis-Beck, A. Bryman and T. Futing Liao (eds) *The Sage Encyclopedia of Social Science Research Methods*, London: Sage, pp. 677–681.

Bryman, A. (2008) *Social Research Methods*, Third Edition, Oxford: Oxford University Press.

Brysk, A. (2000) 'Democratizing Civil Society in Latin America', *Journal of Democracy*, Vol. 11, No. 3, pp. 151–165.

Burgers, J. H. and Danelius, H. (1988) *The United Nations Convention against Torture: A Handbook on the Convention against Torture and Other Cruel, Inhuman or Degrading Treatment or Punishment*, Dordrecht, Netherlands: Martinus Nijhoff.

Burnett, J. and Whyte, D. (2005) 'Embedded Expertise and the New Terrorism', *Journal for Crime, Conflict and the Media*, Vol. 1, No. 4, pp. 1–18.

Burnham, P., Gilland, K., Grant, W. and Layton-Henry, Z. (2004) *Research Methods in Politics*, Basingstoke, Palgrave Macmillan.

Calderon, F., Piscitelli, A. and Reyna, J. L. (1992) 'Social Movements: Actors, Theories, Expectations', in A. Escobar and S. E. Alvarez (eds) *The Making of Social Movements in Latin America: Identity, Strategy, and Democracy*, Boulder, CO: Westview Press, pp. 19–36.

Cameron, H. M. (2009) *Illuminating External Institutional Bystander Complicity in Genocide: Case Study Rwanda*, University of Liverpool: PhD Thesis.

Campbell, B. B. (2000) 'Death Squads: Definition, Problems and Historical Concept', in B. B. Campbell and A. D. Brenner (eds) *Death Squads in Global Perspective*, London: Palgrave Macmillan, pp. 1–26.

Camps, R. J. (4 January 1981) 'Derrota de la Subversión. Apogeo y Declinación de la Guerrilla en la Argentina', *La Prensa*.

Canal 11 TV Programme 'Tiempo Nuevo', broadcast on Tuesday, 25 April 1995 at 2100AST on *Canal 11*.

Carlson, E. S. (2000) 'The Influence of French "Revolutionary War" Ideology on the Use of Torture in the Argentine "Dirty War"', *Human Rights Review*, Vol. 1, No. 4, pp. 71–84.

Chambers, S. (2002) 'A Critical Theory of Civil Society', in S. Chambers and W. Kymlicka (eds) *Alternative Conceptions of Civil Society*, Princeton, NJ: Princeton University Press.

Chambers, S. and Kymlicka, W. (2002) *Alternative Conceptions of Civil Society*, Princeton, NJ: Princeton University Press.

Chambliss, W. (1989) 'State Organized Crime', *Criminology*, Vol. 27, pp. 183–208.

Chan, J., Devery, C. and Doran, S. (2003) *Fair Cop: Learning the Art of Policing*, Toronto: University of Toronto Press.

Chandler, D. (1999) *Voices from S-21: Terror and History in Pol Pot's Secret Prison*, Berkeley: University of California Press.

Chelala, C. (22 June 2001) 'The French Connection in the Export of Torture', *The International Herald Tribune*.

Chomsky, N. (1991) 'International Terrorism: Image and Reality', in A. George (ed.) *Western State Terrorism*, Oxford: Polity Press, pp. 12–38.

Chomsky, N. and Herman, E. S. (1979) *The Political Economy of Human Rights*, Nottingham: Spokesman Books for the Bertrand Russell Peace Foundation Ltd.

Christie, N. (1997) 'Four Blocks Against Insight: Notes on the Oversocialisation of Criminologists, *Theoretical Criminology*, Vol, 1, No. 1, pp. 13–23.

Claridge, D. (1996) 'State Terrorism: Applying a Definitional Model', *Terrorism and Political Violence*, Vol. 8, No. 3, pp. 47–63.

Clarke, A. (2008) 'Creating a Torture Culture', *Suffolk Transnational Law Review*, Vol. 32, No. 1, pp. 1–50.

Coffey, A. and Atkinson, P. (1996) *Making Sense of Qualitative Data*, London: Sage.

Cohen, J. (1999) 'American Civil Society Talk', in R. Fullwinder (ed.) *Civil Society, Democracy and Civic Renewal*, Lanham, MD: Rowman & Littlefield.

Cohen, L. and Felson, M. (1979) 'Social Change and Crime Rate Trends: A Routine Activity Approach', *American Sociological Review*, Vol. 44, No. 4, pp. 588–608.

Cohen, S. (1993) 'Human Rights and Crimes of the State: The Culture of Denial', in J. Muncie, E. McLaughlin and M. Langan (eds) *Criminological Perspectives: A Reader*, London: Sage, pp. 489–507.

Cohen, S. (2001) *States of Denial: Knowing about Atrocities and Suffering*, Cambridge: Polity Press.

Cohen, S. (2003) 'Human Rights and Crimes of the State: The Culture of Denial', in E. McLaughlin, J. Muncie, and G. Hughes (eds) *Criminological Perspectives: Essential Readings*, London: Sage.

Cohen, S. and Golan, D. (1991) *The Interrogation of Palestinians During the Intifada: Ill-treatment, 'Moderate Physical Pressure' or Torture?*, Jerusalem: B'tselem – The Israeli Information Center for Human Rights in the Occupied Territories.

Coleman, J. S. (1958) 'Relational Analysis: The Study of Social Organization with Survey Methods', *Human Organization*, Vol. 17, pp. 28–36.

Coleman, R. (2003) 'Researching the Emergent City-States: Articulating the Proper Objects of Power and CCTV', in S. Tombs and D. Whyte (eds) *Unmasking the Crimes of the Powerful: Scrutinizing States and Corporations*, New York: Peter Lang, pp. 88–104.

Comblin, J. (1977) *Le Pouvoir Militaire en Amérique Latine. L'idéologie de la Sécurité Nationale*, Paris: Jean-Pierre Delarge/Editions Universitaires.

Comisión Argentina por los Derechos Humanos (CADHU) (1977) *Argentina: Proceso al Genocidio*, Madrid: Elías Querejeta Ediciones.

Comisión Nacional sobre la Desaparición de Personas (CONADEP) [1985] (2006) *Nunca Mas: Informe de la Comision Nacional sobre la Desaparicion de Personas*, 8th Edition, Buenos Aires: Eudeba.

Commission on Human Rights (1995) *Military Aid to Governments Practising Torture: Written Statement Submitted by Human Rights Watch*, UN. Doc. E/CN.4/1995/NGO/6 of 31 January 1995.

Commission on Human Rights (1997) *Report of the Special Rapporteur, Mr. Nigel S. Rodley: Torture and other Cruel, Inhuman or Degrading Treatment or Punishment*, UN. Doc. E/CN.4/ 1997/7 of 10 January 1997.

Confer, V. (1966) *France and Algeria: The Problem of Civil and Political Reform 1870–1920*, Syracuse: Syracuse University Press.

Corradi, J. E. (1992) 'Toward Societies without Fear', in J. E. Corradi, P. W. Fagen and M. A. Garreton (eds) *Fear at the Edge: State Terror and Resistance in Latin America*, Berkeley: University of California Press, pp. 267–292.

Corradi, J. E., Fagen, P. W. and Garreton, M. A. (1992) 'Fear: A Cultural and Political Construct', in J. E. Corradi, P. W. Fagen and M. A. Garreton (eds) *Fear at the Edge: State Terror and Resistance in Latin America*, Berkeley: University of California Press, pp. 1–10.

Corti, L. (2004) 'Archival Research', in M. S. Lewis-Beck, A. Bryman and T. Futing Liao (eds) *The Sage Encyclopedia of Social Science Research Methods*, London: Sage, pp. 20–21.

Cox, R. W. (1993) 'Gramsci, Hegemony and International Relations', in S. Gill (ed.) *Gramsci, Historical Materialism and International Relations*, Cambridge: Cambridge University Press, pp. 21–48.

Crelinsten, R. D. (1995) 'In Their Own Words: The World of the Torturer' in R. D. Crelinsten and A. P. Schmid (eds) *The Politics of Pain: Torturers and their Masters*, Boulder: Westview Press, pp. 35–64.

Crelinsten, R. D. (2003) 'The World of Torture: A Constructed Reality', *Theoretical Criminology*, Vol. 7, No. 3, pp. 293–318.

Crelinsten, R. D. (2007a) 'In Their Own Words', in W. F. Schulz (ed.) *The Phenomenon of Torture: Readings and Commentary*, Philadelphia: University of Pennsylvania Press, pp. 141–152.

Crelinsten, R. D. (2007b) 'How to Make a Torturer', in W. F. Schulz (ed.) *The Phenomenon of Torture: Readings and Commentary*, Philadelphia: University of Pennsylvania Press, pp. 210–214.

Crelinsten, R. D. and Schmid, A. P. (eds) (1995) *The Politics of Pain: Torturers and their Masters*, Boulder: Westview Press.

Dassin, J. (1992) 'Testimonial Literature and the Armed Struggle in Brazil', in J. E. Corradi, P. W. Fagen and M. A. Garreton (eds) *Fear at the Edge: State Terror and Resistance in Latin America*, Berkeley: University of California Press, pp. 161–183.

De Bonafini, H. (1985) *Historias de Vida*, Buenos Aires: Fraterna.

De Swaan, A. (2001) 'Dyscivilization, Mass Extermination and the State', *Theory, Culture & Society*, Vol. 18, pp. 265–276.

Delmas, J. (2007) *La Bataille d'Alger*, Paris: Larousse.

Dershowitz, A. (2002) *Why Terrorism Works: Understanding the Threat, Responding to the Challenge*, New Haven: Yale University Press.

Dhombres, D. (September 3, 2003) 'D'Etranges Instructeurs', *Le Monde*.

Diamond, L. (1996) 'Democracy in Latin America: Degrees, Illusions, and Directions for Consolidation', in T. Farer (ed.) *Beyond Sovereignty: Collectively Defending Democracy in the Americas*, Baltimore: Johns Hopkins University Press, pp. 52–104.

Droz, B. and Lever, E. (1982) *Historie de la Guerre d'Algérie*, Paris: Editions du Seuil.

DuBois, L. (1990) 'Torture and the Construction of an Enemy: The Example of Argentina 1976–1983', *Dialectical Anthropology*, Vol. 15, No. 4, pp. 317–328.

Eckstein, S. [1989] (2001) *Power and Popular Protest: Latin America Social Movements*, Updated and Expanded Edition, Berkeley and Los Angeles: University of California Press.

Edwards, M. (2009) *Civil Society*, Second Edition, Cambridge: Polity Press.

Ehrenberg, J. (1999) *Civil Society: The Critical History of an Idea*, New York: New York University Press.

Eide, A. (1977) 'Arms Transfer and Third World Militarization', *Security Dialogue*, Vol. 8, pp. 99–102.

Einaudi, J. L. (1991) *La Bataille de Paris*, Paris: Plon.

Elias, N. (1982–1983) 'Civilisation and Violence: On the State Monopoly of Physical Violence and Its Infringements', *Telos*, No. 54, Vol. 16, pp. 133–154.

Elias, N. (2000) *The Civilizing Process: Sociogenetic and Psychogenetic Investigations*, Revised Edition, Translated by E. Jephcott, Oxford: Blackwell.

Enloe, C. (2004) *The Curious Feminist*, Berkeley: University of California Press.

Epley, N. and Huff, C. (1998) 'Suspicion, Affective Response, and Educational Benefit of Deception in Psychology Research', *Personality and Social Psychology Bulletin*, Vol. 24, pp. 759–768.

Evans, M. and Morgan, R. (1998) *Preventing Torture: A Study of the European Convention for the Prevention of Torture and Inhuman or Degrading Treatment or Punishment*, Oxford: Clarendon Press.

Fagen, P. W. (1992) 'Repression and State Security', in J. E. Corradi, P. W. Fagen, and M. A. Garreton (eds) *Fear at the Edge: State Terror and Resistance in Latin America*, Berkeley: University of California Press, pp. 39–71.

Falk, R. (1981) *Human Rights and State Sovereignty*, New York: Holmes & Meier Publishers.

Fanon, F. (1963) *The Wretched of the Earth*, Translation C. Farrington, London: Penguin Books.

Fanon, F. (1965) 'Algeria Unveiled', *The New Left Reader*, New York: Monthly Review Press, pp. 161–185.

Fanon, F. [1952] (1986) *Black Skin, White Masks*, translation by C. L. Markmann, London: Pluto Press.

Farmer, P. (2003) *Pathologies of Power: Health, Human Rights and the New War on the Poor*, Berkeley: University of California Press.

Fattah, E. (1997) *Criminology: Past, Present and Future*, London: Palgrave.

Faugier, J. and Sargeant, M. (1997) 'Sampling Hard to Reach Populations', *Journal of Advanced Nursing*, Vol. 26, pp. 790–797.

Feagin, J. Orum, A. and Sjoberg, G. (eds) (1991) *A Case for Case Study*, Chapel Hill: University of North Carolina Press.

Feierstein, D. (2010) 'Political Violence in Argentina and its Genocidal Characteristics', in M. Esparza, H. R. Huttenbach, and D. Feierstein (eds) *State Violence and Genocide in Latin America: The Cold War Years*, London and New York: Routledge, pp. 44–63.

Fein, H. (1990) 'Genocide: A Sociological Perspective', *Current Sociology*, Vol. 38, pp. 1–111.

Feitlowitz, M. (1998) *A Lexicon of Terror: Argentina and the Legacies of Terror*, Oxford: Oxford University Press.

Fielding, N. and Lee, R. M. (1998) *Computer Analysis and Qualitative Research*, London: Sage.

Foley, M. and Hodgkinson, V. (2002) *The Civil Society Reader*, Hanover, NH: University Press of New England.

Foucault, M. [1969] (2002) *The Archaeology of Knowledge*, London: Routledge.

Foucault, M. [1977] (1991) *Discipline and Punish: The Birth of the Prison*, translated by A. Sheridan, London: Penguin Books.

Foucault, M. (19/04/1983) *Replies to Questions from the Audience at Berkeley's History Department*, transcribed from audiofiles that can be downloaded at www.lib.berkeley.edu/MRC/audiofiles.html#foucault, UC Berkeley: History Department, Reel 64.

Franco, J. (1992) 'Gender, Death, and Resistance: Facing the Ethical Vacuum', in J. E. Corradi, P. W. Fagen and M. A. Garreton (eds) *Fear at the Edge: State Terror and Resistance in Latin America*, Berkeley: University of California Press, pp. 104–118.

Freud, S. [1930] (1961) *Civilization and its Discontents*, New York: Norton.

Frontalini, D. and Caiti, M. C. (1984) *El Mito de la Guerra Sucia*, Buenos Aires: Centro de Estudios Legales y Sociales.

Gadd, D. and Jefferson, T. (2007) *Psychosocial Criminology*, London: Sage.

Galtung, J. (1994) *Human Rights in Another Key*, Cambridge: Polity Press.

Ganser, D. (2005) *NATO's Secret Armies: Operation GLADIO and Terrorism in Western Europe*, London: Routledge.

García, P. (1995) *El Drama de la Autonomía Militar: Argentina Bajo las Juntas Militares*, Madrid: Alianza, D. L.

Gareau, F. H. (2004) *State Terrorism and the United States*, London: Zed Books.

Garreton, M. A. (1992) 'Fear in Military Regimes: An Overview', in J. E. Corradi, P. W. Fagen and M. A. Garreton (eds) *Fear at the Edge: State Terror and Resistance in Latin America*, Berkeley: University of California Press, pp. 13–25.

Garrigou-Lagrange, M. (1959) 'Intégrisme et National-Catholicisme', *Esprit*, November 1959, pp. 515–542.

Gibbs, G. R. (2004) 'CAQDAS (Computer-Assisted Qualitative Data Analysis Software)', in M. S. Lewis-Beck, A. Bryman and T. Futing Liao (eds) *The Sage Encyclopedia of Social Science Research Methods*, London: Sage, pp. 87–89.

Gibson, J. T. (1990) 'Factors Contributing to the Creation of a Torturer', in P. Suedfeld (ed.) *Psychology and Torture*, New York: Hemisphere, pp. 77–88.

Gibson, J. T. and Haritos-Fatouros, M. (1986) 'The Education of a Torturer', *Psychology Today*, Vol. 20, No. 11, pp. 50–58.

Goldhagen, D. J. (1997) *Hitler's Willing Executioners: Ordinary Germans and the Holocaust*, London: Abacus.

Golston, J. C. (2007) 'Ritual Abuse', in W. F. Schulz (ed.) *The Phenomenon of Torture: Readings and Commentary*, Philadelphia: University of Pennsylvania Press, pp. 124–126.

Goyret, J. T. (1980) *Geopolitica y Subversion*, Buenos Aires: De Palma.

Gramsci, A. (1971) *Selections from the Prison Notebooks*, London: Lawrence & Wishart.

Graziano, F. (1992) *Divine Violence. Spectacle, Psychosexuality and Radical Christianity in the Argentine 'Dirty War'*, Boulder: CO: Westview Press.

Green, P. (1993) 'Taking Sides: Partisan Research on the 1984–1985 Miners' Strike', in D. Hobbs and T. May (eds) *Interpreting the Field: Account of Ethnography*, Oxford: Clarendon Press, pp. 99–119.

Green, P. (2003) 'Researching the Turkish State', in S. Tombs and D. Whyte (eds) *Unmasking the Crimes of the Powerful: Scrutinizing States and Corporations*, New York: Peter Lang, pp. 166–180.

Green, P. and Ward, T. (2000a) 'Legitimacy, Civil Society and State Crime', *Social Justice*, Vol. 27, No. 1, pp. 76–93.

Green, P. and Ward, T. (2000b) 'State Crime, Human Rights and the Limits of Criminology', *Social Justice*, Vol. 27, No. 1, pp. 101–115.

Green, P. and Ward, T. (2004) *State Crime: Governments, Violence and Corruption*, London: Pluto Press.

Green, P. and Ward, T. (2005) 'State Crime: Introduction', *British Journal of Criminology*, Vol. 45, pp. 431–433.

Green, P. and Ward, T. (2009a) 'Violence and the State', in R. Coleman, J. Sim, S. Tombs and D. Whyte (eds) *State, Power, Crime*, London: Sage Publishing, pp. 116–128.

Green, P. and Ward, T. (2009b) 'Torture and the Paradox of State Violence', in B. Clucas, G. Johnstone and T. Ward (eds) *Torture: Moral Absolutes and Ambiguities*, Baden-Baden: Nomos, pp. 163–175.

Green, P. and Ward, T. (2012) 'State Crime: A Dialectical View', in M. Maguire, R. Morgan and R. Reiner (eds) *The Oxford Handbook of Criminology*, Fifth Edition, Oxford: Oxford University Press, pp. 717–740.

Grewcock, M. (2008) 'State Crime: Some Conceptual Issues', in T. Anthony and C. Cunnen (eds) *The Critical Criminology Companion*, Sydney: Hawkins Press, pp. 146–157.

Grey, S. (2007) *Ghost Plane: The Untold Story of the CIA's Torture Program*, Melbourne: Scribe.

Grimal, H. [1965] (1985) *La Décolonisation*, Bruxelles: Editions Complexe.

Gubrium, J. and Holstein, J. (2002) 'From Individual Interview to Interview Society', in J. Gubrium and J. Holstein (eds) *Handbook of Interview Research: Context and Method*, Thousand Oaks, CA: Sage Publications.

Gurr, T. R. (1986) 'The Political Origins of State Violence and Terror: A Theoretical Analysis', in M. Stohl and G. A. Lopez (eds) *Government Violence and Repression: An Agenda for Research*, Westport, CT: Greenwood Press, pp. 45–71.

Gutting, G. (2011) '*Michel Foucault*', *The Stanford Encyclopedia of Philosophy*, E. N. Zalta (ed.), available at http://plato.stanford.edu/archives/fall2011/entries/foucault/.

Habermas, J. (1976) *Legitimation and Crisis*, London: Heinemann.

Hall, J. and Trentmann, F. (2005) *Civil Society: A Reader in History, Theory and Global Politics*, Basingstoke: Palgrave Macmillan.

Hammersley, M. (2000) *Taking Sides in Social Research: Essays on Partisanship and Bias*, London: Routledge.

Hammersley, M. (2004) 'Case Study', in M. S. Lewis-Beck, A. Bryman and T. Futing Liao (eds) *The Sage Encyclopedia of Social Science Research Methods*, London: Sage, pp. 92–94.

Haney, C., Banks, C. and Zimbardo, P. G. (1973) 'Interpersonal Dynamics in a Simulated Prison', *International Journal of Criminology and Penology*, Vol. 1, pp. 69–97.

Haritos-Fatouros, M. (1988) 'The Official Torturer: A Learning Model for Obedience to the Authority of Violence', *Journal of Applied Social Psychology*, Vol. 18, pp. 1107–1120.

Haritos-Fatouros, M. (2003) *The Psychological Origins of Institutionalized Torture*, London: Routledge.

Heaton, J. (1998) 'Secondary Analysis of Qualitative Data', *Social Research Update*, Vol. 22, available at http://sru.soc.surrey.ac.uk/SRU22.html.

Heinz, W. S. (1995) 'The Military, Torture and Human Rights: Experiences from Argentina, Brazil, Chile and Uruguay', in R. D. Crelinsten and A. P. Schmid (eds) *The Politics of Pain: Torturers and their Masters*, Oxford: Westview Press, pp. 65–97.

Herman, E. S. (1982) *The Real Terror Network*, Boston: South End Press.

Herman, E. S. (1991) 'The United States versus Human Rights in the Third World', *Harvard Human Rights Journal*, vol. 4, pp. 85–105.

Herman, E. S. and Peterson, D. (2002) 'The Threat of Global State Terrorism: Retail versus Wholesale Terror', *Z Magazine*, available at: www.thirdworldtraveler.com/Herman%20/Threat_Global_Terrorism.html.

Hey, H. (1995) *Gross Human Rights Violations: A Search for Causes. A Study of Guatemala and Costa Rica*, The Hague: Nijhoff.

Hill, M. (1993) 'Archival Strategies and Techniques', *Qualitative Research Methods*, Vol. 31, Thousand Oaks, CA: Sage.

Hillyard, P. (2003) 'The Secret State: Researching Alleged Conspiracies', in S. Tombs and D. Whyte (eds) *Unmasking the Crimes of the Powerful: Scrutinizing States and Corporations*, New York: Peter Lang, pp. 201–218.

Hinds, P. S., Vogel, R. J. and Clarke-Steffen, L. (1997) 'The Possibilities and Pitfalls of Doing a Secondary Analysis of a Qualitative Data Set', *Qualitative Health Research*, Vol. 7, pp. 408–424.

Hobsbawm, E. (1998) *On History*, London: Abacus.

Hochschild, A. (2007) 'The Torturers' Notebooks', in W. F. Schulz (ed.) *The Phenomenon of Torture: Readings and Commentary*, Philadelphia: University of Pennsylvania Press, p. 136.

Hodges, D. (1991) *Argentina's "Dirty War". An Intellectual Biography*, Austin: University of Texas Press.

Hollway, W. and Jefferson, T. (2000) *Doing Qualitative Research Differently: A Free Association, Narrative and the Interview Method*, London: Sage.

Horne, A. (2006) *A Savage War for Peace*, New York: Review Books Classics.

House of Lords, House of Commons, and Joint Committee on Human Rights (2009) *Allegations of UK Complicity in Torture: Twenty-third Report of Session 2008–09*, London: The Stationery Office Limited.

Huggins, M. K. (2003) 'Moral Universes of Brazilian Torturers', *Albany Law Review*, Vol. 67, pp. 527–535.

Huggins, M. K. (2005) 'Torture 101: Lessons from the Brazilian Case', *Journal of Third World Studies*, Vol. 22, No. 2, pp. 161–173.

Huggins, M. K. and Haritos-Fatouros, M. (1998) 'Bureaucratic Masculinities among Brazilian Torturers and Murderers', in L. H. Bowker (ed.) *Masculinities and Violence*, London: Sage.

Huggins, M. K., Haritos-Fatouros, M. and Zimbardo, P. G. (2002) *Violence Workers: Police Torturers and Murderers Reconstruct Brazilian Atrocities*, Berkeley: University of California Press.

Hughes, G. (1996) 'The Politics of Criminological Research', in R. Sapsford (ed.) *Researching Crime and Criminal Justice*, Milton Keynes: Open University Press.

Human Rights Council (2010) *Report of the Special Rapporteur, Mr. Manfred Nowak: Torture and other Cruel, Inhuman or Degrading Treatment or Punishment*, UN. Doc. A/HRC/13/39 of 9 February 2010.

Human Rights Council (2013) *Report of the Special Rapporteur, Mr. Juan E. Méndez: Torture and other Cruel, Inhuman or Degrading Treatment or Punishment*, UN. Doc. A/HRC/22/53 of 1 February 2013.

Human Rights Watch (2005) *Getting Away with Torture? Command Responsibility for the US Abuse of Detainees*, New York: Author.

Humphrey, M. (2002) *The Politics of Atrocity and Reconciliation: From Terror to Trauma*, London: Routledge.

Ighilahriz, L. (2001) *L'Algérienne*, Récit recueilli par Anne Nivat, Paris: Fayard.

Ignatieff, M. (1988) *The Warrior's Honor: Ethnic War and the Modern Conscience*, London: Chatto and Windus.

Ignatieff, M. (2004) *The Lesser Evil: Political Ethics in an Age of Terror*, Princeton: Princeton University Press.

International Court of Justice (1986) *Military and Paramilitary Activities against Nicaragua: Nicaragua versus USA*, Judgement of 27 June 1986.

International Law Commission (1957) Yearbook of the International Law Commission 1950, Vol. 11, New York: United Nations, available online at: http://untreaty.un.org/ilc/publications/yearbooks/Ybkvolumes(e)/ilc_1950_v2_e.pdf

International Law Commission (2001) 'Draft Articles on Responsibility of States for Internationally Wrongful Acts', report of its 53rd Session (23 April-1 June and 2 July-10 August 2001), available online at: http://untreaty.un.org/ilc/texts/instruments/english/draft%20articles/9_6_2001.pdf

Jackson, R., Murphy, E. and Poynting, S. (2010) 'Introduction: Terrorism, the State and the Study of Political Terror', in R. Jackson, E. Murphy and S. Poynting (eds) *Contemporary State Terrorism: Theory and Practice*, London and New York: Routledge, pp. 1–11.

James, D. (1990) *Resistencia e Integración. El Peronismo y la Clase Trabajadora Argentina 1946–1976*, Buenos Aires: SudAmericana.

Jauffret, J. C. (2005) *Ces Officiers Qui Ont Dit Non à la Torture: Algérie 1954–1962*, Paris: Autrement.

Jenkins, R. (2004a) 'Field Relations', in M. S. Lewis-Beck, A. Bryman and T. Futing Liao (eds) *The Sage Encyclopedia of Social Science Research Methods*, London: Sage, pp. 384–385.

Jenkins, R. (2004b) 'Field Research', in M. S. Lewis-Beck, A. Bryman and T. Futing Liao (eds) *The Sage Encyclopedia of Social Science Research Methods*, London: Sage, pp. 385–386.

Jordi, J. J. (1993) *De l'Exode à l'Exil. Rapatriés et Pieds-Noirs en France. L'Exemple Marseillais, 1954–1992*, Paris: L'Harmattan.

Jorgensen, N. H. B. (2000) *The Responsibility of States for International Crimes*, Oxford: Oxford University Press.

Jupp, V. (1996) 'Documents and Critical Research' in R. Sapsford and V. Jupp (eds) *Data Collection and Analysis*, London: Sage.

Kaiser, S. (2005) 'To Punish or to Forgive? Young Citizens' Attitudes on Impunity and Accountability in Contemporary Argentina', *Journal of Human Rights*, Vol. 4, No. 2, pp. 171–196.

Kalyvas, S. (2004) 'The Paradox of Terrorism in Civil War', *Journal of Ethics*, Vol. 8, No. 1, pp. 97–138.

Kappeler, S. (1986) *The Pornography of Representation*, Cambridge: Polity Press.

Kassimeris, G. (ed.) (2006) *Warrior's Dishonour: Barbarity, Morality and Torture in Modern Warfare*, Aldershot: Ashgate Publishing.

Katz, J. (1988) *Seductions of Crime: Moral and Sensual Attractions in Doing Evil*, New York: Basic Books.

Kauffer, R. (2002) *OAS. Histoire d'une Guerre Franco-Française*, Paris: Editions du Seuil.

Kaufman, M. T. (31 October 2002) 'Jacques Massu, 94, General Who Led Battle of Algiers', *New York Times*.

Kauzlarich, D. and Kramer, R. C. (1998) *Crimes of the American Nuclear State: At Home and Abroad*, Boston: Northeastern University Press.

Keane, J. (1996) *Reflections on Violence*, London: Verso.

Keane, J. (1998) *Civil Society: Old Images, New Visions*, Stanford, CA: Stanford University Press.

Keenan, J. H. (2003) 'The Lesser Gods of the Sahara', *The Journal of North African Studies*, Vol. 8, Nos. 3–4, pp. 193–225.

Keenan, J. H. (2009) *The Dark Sahara*, London: Pluto Press.

Keenan, J. H. (2013) *The Dying Sahara*, London: Pluto Press.

Kelman, H. C. (1995) 'The Social Context of Torture: Policy Process and Authority Structure', in R. D. Crelinsten and A. P. Schmid (eds) *The Politics of Pain: Torturers and their Masters*, Oxford: Westview Press, pp. 19–34.

Kelman, H. C. (2005) 'The Policy Context of Torture: A Social-Psychological Analysis', *International Review of the Red Cross*, Vol. 87, No. 857, pp. 123–134.

Kelman, H. C. (2006) 'The Policy Context of International Crimes', *Paper prepared for the Conference on System Criminality in International Law, Amsterdam Center for International Law*, 20–21 October, pp. 1–28.

Kelman, H. C. and Hamilton, V. L. (1989) *Crimes of Obedience: Toward a Social Psychology of Authority and Responsibilities*, New Haven: Yale University Press.

Kendall, G. and Wickham, G. (1999) *Using Foucault's Methods*, London: Sage.

Kendall, G. and Wickham, G. (2007) 'The Foucaultian Framework', in C. Seale, G. Gobo, J. F. Gubrium and D. Silverman (eds) *Qualitative Research Practice*, Second Edition, London: Sage Publication, pp. 129–138.

Kepner, T. (2001) 'Torture 101: The Case Against the United States for Atrocities Committed by School of the Americas Alumni', *Dickinson International Law Journal*, Vol. 19, pp. 475–487.

Koonings, K. and Kruijt, D. (1999) *Societies of Fear: The Legacy of Civil War and Terror in Latin America*, New York: Zed Books.

Korczynski, M. (2004) 'Access', in M. S. Lewis-Beck, A. Bryman and T. Futing Liao (eds) *The Sage Encyclopedia of Social Science Research Methods*, London: Sage, pp. 2–3.

Kramer, R. C. (2009) 'Foreword to Dawn L. Rothe, State Criminality: The Crime of All Crimes', in D. L. Rothe, *State Criminality: The Crime of All Crimes*, Plymouth: Lexington Books, pp. ix–xii.

Kramer, R. C. and Michalowski, R. (1990) *Toward an Integrated Theory of State Corporate Crime*, Presented at the American Society of Criminology, Baltimore, MD.

Kvale, S. (1996) *InterViews: An Introduction to Qualitative Research Interviewing*, Thousand Oaks, CA: Sage.

Kvale, S. (2004) 'Interviewing in Qualitative Research', in M. S. Lewis-Beck, A. Bryman and T. Futing Liao (eds) *The Sage Encyclopedia of Social Science Research Methods*, London: Sage, pp. 521–524.

La Cité Catholique (1959) *Pour qu'Il Règne*, Paris: Cité Catholique.

Lacheroy, C. (1958) 'La Guerre Révolutionnaire', *Bibliothéque des Centres d'Etudes Supérieures Spécialisés, Extrait de la Défense Nationale*, Paris: P.U.F., pp. 307–330.

Lacheroy, C. (2003) *De Saint-Cyr à l'Action Psychologique. Mémoires d'un Siècle*, Paris: Editions Lavauzelle.

Lankford, A. (2009) 'Promoting Aggression and Violence at Abu Ghraib: The U.S. Military's Transformation of Ordinary People into Torturers', *Aggression and Violent Behavior*, Vol. 14, No. 5, pp. 388–395.

Larraquy, M. (2003) *López Rega. La Biografía*, Buenos Aires: Editorial SudAmericana.

Lazreg, M. (2008) *Torture and the Twilight of Empire: From Algiers to Baghdad*, Princeton: Princeton University Press.

Lea, H. C. (1878) *Superstition and Force*, Third Edition, Philadelphia: Author.

Le Cour Grandmaison, O. (2005) *Coloniser, Exterminer. Sur la Guerre et l'Etat Colonial*, Paris: Arthème Fayard.

Lee, R. M. (1993) *Doing Research on Sensitive Topics*, London: Sage.

Lee, R. M. (1995) *Dangerous Fieldwork*, London: Sage.

Lee, R. M. (2004a) 'Danger in Research', in M. S. Lewis-Beck, A. Bryman and T. Futing Liao (eds) *The Sage Encyclopedia of Social Science Research Methods*, London: Sage, pp. 233–234.

Lee, R. M. (2004b) 'Sensitive Topics, Researching', in M. S. Lewis-Beck, A. Bryman and T. Futing Liao (eds) *The Sage Encyclopedia of Social Science Research Methods*, London: Sage, pp. 1021–1022.

Lefebvre, D. (2001) *Guy Mollet face à le Torture*, Paris: Editions Bruno Leprince.

Le Sueur, J. D. [1958] (2006) 'Introduction to Henri Alleg, The Question', in H. Alleg, *The Question*, translated by J. Calder, Lincoln, NE: University of Nebraska Press Bison Books, pp. xiii–xxv.

Lewis-Beck, M. S., Bryman, A. and Futing Liao, T. (eds) (2004) *The Sage Encyclopedia of Social Science Research Methods*, London: Sage.

Lhote, H. (1958) *À la Decouverte des Fresques du Tassili*, Paris: Arthaud.

Liauzu, C. (April 28, 2005) 'Une Loi Contre l'Histoire', *Le Monde Diplomatique*.

Lichtman, A. and French, V. (1978) *Historians and the Living Past*, Wheeling Illinois: Harlan Davidson.

Lifton, R. J. (1986) *The Nazi Doctors: Medical Killing and the Psychology of Genocide*, London: Macmillan.

Llumá, D. (2002a) 'La Influencia Francesa en los Militares Argentinos: Los Maestros de la Tortura', *Todo Es Historia*, No. 422, pp. 6–16.

Llumá, D. (2002b) 'Entrevista a Pierre Abramovici: El Derrotero de la Contrarrevolución en América Latina', *Todo Es Historia*, No. 422, pp. 20–23.

Loader, I. and Sparks, R. (2010) *A Review of Public Criminology?*, London: Routledge.

Lofland, J. and Lofland, L. (1984) *Analyzing Social Settings: A Guide to Qualitative Observation and Analysis*, Belmont: Wadsworth.

Lopez, E. (1987) *Seguridad Nacional y Sedición Militar*, Buenos Aires: Legasa.

Loveman, B. and Davies, T. M. (eds) (1989) *The Politics of Antipolitics: The Military in Latin America*, London: Lincoln.

Luban, D. J. (2000) 'The Ethics of Wrongful Obedience', in D. L. Rhode (ed.) *Ethics in Practice: Lawyers' Roles, Responsibilities, and Regulations*, Oxford: Oxford University Press, pp. 94–120.

MacDonald, K. (2001) 'Using Documents', in N. Gilber (ed.) *Researching Social Life*, London: Sage.

MacMaster, N. (2004) 'Torture: From Algiers to Abu Ghraib', *Race & Class*, Vol. 46, No. 2, pp. 1–21.

Mahmood, C. K. (2000) 'Trials by Fire: Dynamics of Terror in Punjab and Kashmir', in J. A. Sluka (ed.) *Death Squads*, Philadelphia: University of Pennsylvania Press, pp. 70–90.

Maillard de la Morandais, A. (1990) *L'Honneur est Sauf*, Paris: Editions du Seuil.

Mann, M. (2005) *The Dark Side of Democracy: Explaining Ethnic Cleansing*, Cambridge: Cambridge University Press.

Maran, R. (1989) *Torture: The Role of Ideology in the French-Algerian War*, New York: Praeger.

Marchak, P. (1999) *God's Assassins: State Terrorism in Argentina in the 1970s*, Montreal: McGill-Queen's University Press.

Marton, R. (1995) 'Introduction', in N. Gordon and R. Marton (eds) *Torture: Human Rights, Medical Ethics and the Case of Israel*, London: Zed Books.

Mason, J. [1996] (2002) *Qualitative Researching*, London: Sage.

Mason, J. (2004) 'Semistructured Interview', in M. S. Lewis-Beck, A. Bryman and T. Futing Liao (eds) *The Sage Encyclopedia of Social Science Research Methods*, London: Sage, pp. 1020–1021.

Maxfield, M. G. and Babbie, E. (2009) *Basics of Research Methods for Criminal Justice and Criminology*, Second Edition, Wadsworth: Cengage Learning.

May, W. F. (1974) 'Terrorism as Strategy of Ecstasy', *Social Research*, Vol. 41, No. 2, pp. 277–298.

Mazzei, D. H. (2002) 'La Misión Militar Francesa en la Escuela Superior de Guerra y los Orígenes de la Guerra Sucia, 1957–1962', *Revista de Ciencias Sociales*, No. 13, pp. 105–137.

McClintock, M. (1992) *Instruments of Statecraft. U.S. Guerrilla Warfare, Counterinsurgency, and Counter-Terrorism, 1940–1990*, New-York: Pantheon.

McCoy, A. W. (2006) *A Question of Torture: CIA Interrogation, From the Cold War to the War on Terror*, New York: Metropolitan Books.

McSherry, J. P. (2005) *Predatory States: Operation Condor and Covert War in Latin America*, New York: Rowman & Littlefield Publishers.

Mellor, A (1961) *La Torture: son Histoire, son Évolution, sa Réapparition au XXe Siècle*, Tours: Mame.

Mercier, J. (Mai/Octobre 1958) 'Rebellion en Algérie et Guerre Revolutionaire', DOC.O.I. No. 501/505, *Revue Militaire d'Information*, Paris: Bibliothèque de l'Ecole Supérieure de Guerre, available at: http://guerrealautre.hypotheses.org/196.

Merton, R. (1961) *Social Theory and Social Structure*, New York: Basic Books.

Messner, S. F. and Rosenfeld, R. (1997) 'Political Restraint of the Market and Levels of Criminal Homicide: A Crossnational Application of Institutional-Anomie Theory', *Social Forces*, Vol. 75, pp. 1393–1416

Michalowski, R. (2009) 'Power, Crime and Criminology in the New Imperial Age', *Law and Social Change*, Vol. 51, pp. 303–325.

Michalowski, R. and Kramer, R. (2006) *State-Corporate Crime: Wrongdoing at the Intersection of Business and Government*, New Brunswick, NJ: Rutgers University Press.

Milgram, S. (1963) 'Behavioural Study of Obedience to Authority', *Journal of Abnormal Social Psychology*, Vol. 67, No. 4, pp. 277–285.

Milgram, S. (1974) *Obedience to Authority*, New York: Harper and Row.

Miller, A. G. (1986) *The Obedience Experiments: A Case Study of Controversy in Social Science*, New York: Praeger.

Miller, A. G. (1995) 'Constructions of the Obedience Experiments: A Focus upon Domains of Relevance', *Journal of Social Issues*, Vol. 51, pp. 33–53.

Miller, A. G. (2004) 'The Milgram Experiments', in M. S. Lewis-Beck, A. Bryman and T. Futing Liao (eds) *The Sage Encyclopedia of Social Science Research Methods*, London: Sage, pp. 644–645.

Molas, R. R. (1984) *Historia de la Tortura y el Orden Represivo en la Argentina*, Buenos Aires: Editorial Universitaria de Buenos Aires.

Moore, B. (1966) *Social Origins of Dictatorship and Democracy: Lord and Peasant in the Making of the Modern World*, Boston, MA: Beacon Press Books.

Morgan, R. (2000) 'The Utilitarian Justification of Torture: Denial, Desert and Disinformation', *Punishment and Society*, Vol. 2, No. 2, pp. 181–196.

Muir, W. K., Jr (1977) *Police: Streetcorner Politicians*, Chicago: University of Chicago Press.

Navarro, M. [1989] (2001) 'The Personal is Political: Las Madres de Plaza de Mayo', in S. Eckstein (ed.) *Power and Popular Protest: Latin America Social Movements*, Updated and Expanded Edition, Berkeley and Los Angeles: University of California Press, pp. 241–258.

Noaks, L. and Windcup, E. (2004) *Criminological Research: Understanding Qualitative Methods*, London: Sage Publications.

O'Donnell, G. and Schmitter, P. (1986) *Transitions from Authoritarian Rule: Tentative Conclusions about Uncertain Democracies*, Baltimore, MD: Johns Hopkins University Press.

O'Kane, R. T. (1996) *Terror, Force and States*, Cheltenham: Edward Elgar.

Oliveira-Cézar, M. (2002) 'Indonesia, Argelia, Argentina: Las Raices Francesas de la Guerra Antisubversiva', *Todo Es Historia*, No. 422, pp. 24–34.

Oliveira-Cézar, M. (2003) 'De los Militares Franceses de Indochina y Argelia a los Militares Argentinos de los Años 50 y 60: El Aprendizaje de la Guerra Contrarrevolucionaria', *Todo Es Historia*, No. 435, pp. 70–80.

Orne, M. T. and Holland, C. H. (1968) 'On the Ecological Validity of Laboratory Deceptions', *International Journal of Psychiatry*, Vol. 6, No. 4, pp. 282–293.

Orsolini, M. (1964) *La Crisis del Ejército*, Buenos Aires: Ediciones Arayú.

Osiel, M. (2004) 'The Mental State of Torturers: Argentina's Dirty War', in S. Levinson (ed.) *Torture: A Collection*, Oxford: Oxford University Press, pp. 129–141.

Otero, H. (2012) *Historia de los Franceses en Argentine*, Buenos Aires: Editorial Biblos Colección La Argentina Plural.

Palacio, L. (1968) *Les Pieds-Noirs dans le Monde*, Paris: Editions J. Didier.

Paret, P. (1964) *French Revolutionary Warfare from Indochina to Algeria*, New York: Frederick A. Praeger.

Passas, N. (1990) 'Anomie and Corporate Deviance', *Contemporary Crises*, Vol. 14, pp. 157–178.

Pearce, F. (2003) 'Holy Wars and Spiritual Revitalisation', in S. Tombs and D. Whyte (eds) *Unmasking the Crimes of the Powerful: Scrutinizing States and Corporations*, New York: Peter Lang, pp. ix–xiv.

Perelli, C. (1990) 'The Military's Perception of Threat in the Southern Cone of South America' in L. W. Goodman, J. S. R. Mendelson and J. Rial (eds) *The Military and Democracy: The Future of Civil-Military Relations in Latin America*, Lexington: Lexington Books, pp. 99–106.

Périès, G. G. (1999) *De l'Action Militaire à l'Action Politique. Impulsion, Codification et Application de la Doctrine de la «Guerre Révolutionnaire» au Sein de l'Armée Française (1944–1960)*, Université de Paris I-Sorbonne: Thèse de Doctorat.

Perry, G. (2012) *Behind the Shock Machine: The Untold Story of the Notorious Milgram Psychology Experiments*, Brunswick: Scribe Publications.

Peters, E. (1985) *Torture*, Philadelphia: University of Pennsylvania Press.

Pickering, S. (2005) *Refugees and State Crime*, Sydney: The Federation Press.

Pion-Berlin, D. (1989) *The Ideology of State Terror. Economic Doctrine and Political Repression in Argentina and Peru*, London: Lynne Rienner.

Pion-Berlin, D. (1997) *Through Corridors of Power: Institutions and Civil-Military Relations in Argentina*, University Park: The Pennsylvania State University Press.

Pole, S. and Lampard, R. (2002) *Practical Social Investigation: Qualitative and Quantitative Methods in Social Research*, New York: Harlow.

Potash, R. A. (1980) *The Army and Politics in Argentina, 1945–1963*, Stanford, CA: Stanford University Press.

Power, C. (2003). 'Telling It Like It Is: Cultural Prejudice, Power and the Qualitative Process', in S. Tombs and D. Whyte (eds) *Unmasking the Crimes of the Powerful: Scrutinizing States and Corporations*, New York: Peter Lang, pp. 146–165.

Prescott, C. (2005) 'The lie of the Stanford Prison Experiment', *Stanford Daily*, News section.

Presdee, M. and Walters, R. (1998) 'The Perils and Politics of Criminological Research and the Threat to Academic Freedom', *Current Issues in Criminal Justice*, Vol. 10, No. 2, pp. 156–167.

Prevost, J. P. (1960) 'L'Épreuve Algerienne', *Recherches et Débats*.

Ranalletti, M. (2002) 'Une Présence Française Fonctionnelle: Les Militaires Français en Argentine Après 1955', *Matériaux pour l'Histoire de Notre Temps*, Vol. 67, No. 67, pp. 104–106.

Ranalletti, M. (2005) 'La Guerra de Argelia y la Argentina. Influencia e Inmigración Francesa desde 1945', *Anuario de Estudio Americanos*, Vol. 62, No. 2, pp. 285–308.

Ranalletti, M. (2010a) 'Aux Origines du Terrorisme d'État en Argentine: Les Influences Françaises dans la Formation des Militaires Argentins (1955–1976)', *Vingtième Siècle Revue d'Histoire*, Vol. 1, No. 105, pp. 45–56.

Ranalletti, M. (2010b) 'Denial of the Reality of State Terrorism in Argentina as Narrative of the Recent Past: A New Case of "Negationism"?', *Genocide Studies and Prevention*, Vol. 5, No. 2, pp. 160–173.

Rapley, T. (2007) 'Interviews', in C. Seale, G. Gobo, J. F. Gubrium, and D. Silverman (eds) *Qualitative Research Practice*, Second Edition, London: Sage Publication, pp. 15–33.

Rasmussen, O. V., Amris, S., Blaauw, M. and Danielsen, L. (2005) 'Medical Physical Examination in Connection with Torture', *Torture*, Vol. 15, No. 1, pp. 37–45.

Ray, E. [1958] (2006) 'Foreword to Henri Alleg, The Question', in H. Alleg, *The Question*, translated by J. Calder, Lincoln, NE: University of Nebraska Press Bison Books, pp. vii–xii.

Rejali, D. (1994) *Torture and Modernity: Self, Society, and State in Modern Iran*, Boulder, CO: Westview Press.

Rejali, D. (2003) 'Torture as a Civic Marker: Solving a Global Anxiety with a New Political Technology', *Journal of Human Rights*, Vol. 2, No. 2, pp. 153–171.

Rejali, D. (2007a) *Torture and Democracy*, Princeton: Princeton University Press.

Rejali, D. (2007b) 'Does Torture Work?', in W. F. Schulz (ed.) *The Phenomenon of Torture: Readings and Commentary*, Philadelphia: University of Pennsylvania Press, pp. 255–259.

Risse, T., Ropp, S. C. and Sikkink, K. (1999) *The Power of Human Rights: International Norms and Domestic Change*, First Edition, Cambridge: Cambridge University Press.

Roberts, K. M. (1998) *Deepening Democracy? The Modern Left and Social Movements in Chile and Peru*, Stanford: Stanford University Press.

Robin, M. M. (2003) *Escadrons de la Mort: l'Ecole Française*, TV documentary broadcast in September 2003 on *Canal Plus*.

Robin, M. M. [2004] (2008) *Escadrons de la Mort, l'Ecole Française*, Paris: Editions La Découverte.

Rock, D. (1993) *Authoritarian Argentina*, Berkeley, CA: University of California Press.

Rodley, N. S. (1999) *The Treatment of Prisoners Under International Law*, Oxford: Clarendon.

Ross, J. (ed.) (1995) *Controlling State Crime: An Introduction*, New York: Garland Publishing.

Rothe, D. L. (2009) *State Criminality: The Crime of All Crimes*, Plymouth: Lexington Books.

Rothe, D. L. and Friedrichs, D. (2006) 'The State of the Criminology of Crimes of the State', *Social Justice*, Vol. 33, No. 1, pp. 147–161.

Rouquier, A. (1978) *Pouvoir Militaire et Société Politique en République Argentine*, Paris: Presses de la Fondation Nationale des Sciences Politiques.

Rubin, H. J. and Rubin, I. S. (1995) *Qualitative Interviewing; The Art of Hearing Data*, Thousand Oaks, CA: Sage.

Rudestam, K. E. and Newton, R. R. (2001) *Surviving Your Dissertation*, London: Sage Publications.

Salimovich, S., Lira, E. and Weinstein, E. (1992) 'Victims of Fear: The Social Psychology of Repression', in J. E. Corradi, P. W. Fagen and M. A. Garreton (eds) *Fear at the Edge: State Terror and Resistance in Latin America*, Berkeley: University of California Press, pp. 72–89.

Sandelowski, M. (2004) 'Qualitative Research', in M. S. Lewis-Beck, A. Bryman and T. Futing Liao (eds) *The Sage Encyclopedia of Social Science Research Methods*, London: Sage, pp. 893–894.

Sartre, J. P. [1958] (2006) 'Preface to Henri Alleg, The Question', in H. Alleg, *The Question*, translated by J. Calder, Lincoln, NE: University of Nebraska Press Bison Books, pp. xxvii–xliv.

Scarry, E. (1985) *The Body in Pain: The Making and Unmaking of the World*, Oxford: Oxford University Press.

Scarry, E. (2004) 'Five Errors in the Reasoning of Alan Dershowitz', in S. Levinson (ed.) *Torture: A Collection*, Oxford: Oxford University Press, pp. 281–290.

Scheper-Hughes, N. (1992) *Death Without Weeping: The Violence of Everyday Life in Brazil*, Berkeley: University of California Press.

Schirmer, J. (1998) *The Guatemalan Military Project: A Violence Called Democracy*, Philadelphia: University of Pennsylvania Press.

Schwendinger, H. and Schwendinger, J. (1975) 'Defenders of Order or Guardians of Human Rights?' in I. Taylor, P. Walton, and J. Young (eds) *Critical Criminology*, London: Routledge & Kegan Paul, pp. 113–146.

Scott, J. (1990) *A Matter of Record*, Cambridge: Polity Press.

Scraton, P. (2002) 'Introduction: Witnessing 'Terror', Anticipating 'War'', in P. Scraton (ed.) *Beyond September 11: An Anthology of Dissent*, London: Pluto Press, pp. 1–10.

Seale, C. and Filmer, P. (1998) 'Doing Social Surveys', in C. Seale (ed.) *Researching Society and Culture*, London: Sage, pp. 125–145.

Segura Valero, G. (2004) *A la Sombra de Franco. El Refugio Español de los Activistas Franceses de la OAS*, Barcelona: Ediciones B.

Seligman, A. (1992) *The Idea of Civil Society*, Princeton, NJ: Princeton University Press.

Seri, G. S. (2010) 'Vicious Legacies? State Violence(s) in Argentina', in M. Esparza, H. R. Huttenbach and D. Feierstein (eds) *State Violence and Genocide in Latin America: The Cold War Years*, London and New York: Routledge, pp. 182–195.

Shanab, M. E. and Yahya, K. A. (1978) 'A Cross-Cultural Study of Obedience', *Bulletin of the Psychonomic Society*, Vol. 11, pp. 267–269.

Shaffir, W. (2004) 'Fieldnotes', in M. S. Lewis-Beck, A. Bryman and T. Futing Liao (eds) *The Sage Encyclopedia of Social Science Research Methods*, London: Sage, pp. 386–388.

Sharkansky, I. (1995) 'A State Action May Be Nasty But Is Not Likely To Be A Crime', in J. Ross (ed.) *Controlling State Crime: An Introduction*, New York: Garland Publishing, pp. 35–52.

Shute, J. (2012) 'Towards a Criminology of Mass Violence and the Body', in E. Anstett and J. M. Dreyfus (eds) *Corpses of Mass Violence: The Unthought and the Unsaid*, Paris: Petra, pp. 43–55.

Sim, J. (2003) 'Whose Side Are We Not On? Researching Medical Power in Prisons', in S. Tombs and D. Whyte (eds) *Unmasking the Crimes of the Powerful. Scrutinizing States and Corporations*, Berne: Peter Lang, pp. 239–257.

Sironi, F. and Branche, R. (2002) 'Torture and the Borders of Humanity', *International Social Science Journal*, Vol. 174, pp. 539–548.

Sivananda, A. (2001) 'Poverty is the New Black', *Race and Class*, Vol. 43, No. 2, pp. 1–5.

Skocpol, T. (1984) 'Emerging Agendas and Recurrent Strategies in Historical Sociology', in T. Skocpol (ed.) *Vision and Method in Historical Sociology*, New York: Cambridge University Press, pp. 356–391.

Smith, B. (1982) 'U.S. Latin American Military Relations Since The Second World War: Implications for Human Rights', in M. E. Crahan (ed.) *Human Rights and Basic Needs in the Americas*, Washington, D.C.: Georgetown University Press.

Smith, P. B. and Bond, M. H. (1998) *Social Psychology Across Cultures*, London: Prentice Hall.

Sottas, E. (1998) 'Perpetrators of Torture', in B. Dunér (ed.) *An End to Torture: Strategies for its Eradication*, London and New York: Zed Books, pp. 63–84.

Spierenburg, P. C. (1984) *The Spectacle of Suffering*, Cambridge: Cambridge University Press.

Stanley, E. E. (2004) 'Torture, Silence and Recognition', *Current Issues in Criminal Justice*, Vol. 16, No. 1, pp. 5–25.

Stanley, E. E. (2007) *Torture and Transitional Justice in Timor-Leste*, Victoria University of Wellington: PhD Thesis.

Stanley, E. E. (2008) 'Torture and Terror', in T. Anthony and C. Cunnen (eds) *The Critical Criminology Companion*, Sydney: Hawkins Press, pp. 158–159.

Stanley, E. E. (2009) *Torture, Truth and Justice: The Case of Timor-Leste*, London: Routledge.

Staub, E. (1989) *The Roots of Evil: The Origins of Genocide and Other Group Violence*, Cambridge: Cambridge University Press.

Staub, E. (1995) 'Torture: Psychological and Cultural Origins', in R. D. Crelinsten and A. P. Schmid (eds) *The Politics of Pain: Torturers and their Masters*, Boulder: Westview Press, pp. 99–111.

Staub, E. (2007) 'The Psychology and Culture of Torture and Torturers', in W. F. Schulz (ed.) *The Phenomenon of Torture: Readings and Commentary*, Philadelphia: University of Pennsylvania Press, pp. 204–209.

Stepan, A. (1985) 'State Power and the Strength of Civil Society in the Southern Cone of Latin America', in P. B. Evans, D. Rueschmeyer and T. Skocpol (eds) *Bringing the State Back in*, Cambridge: Cambridge University Press, pp. 317–345.

Stepan, A. (2001) *Arguing Comparative Politics*, Oxford: Oxford University Press.

Stover, E. and Nightingale, E. O. (1985) *The Breaking of Bodies and Minds: Torture, Psychiatric Abuse and the Health Professions*, New York: Freeman.

Sykes, G. and Matza, D. (1957) 'Techniques of Neutralisation: A Theory of Delinquency', *American Sociological Review*, Vol. 22, pp. 664–670.

Tallandier, J. (1972) 'La Guerre d'Algérie: Le Terrorisme et la Torture en Algérie', *Historia Magazine*, No. 226, pp. 991–1022.

Taussig, M. (2002) 'Culture of Terror – Space of Death: Roger Casement's Putumayo Report and the Explanation of Torture', in A. L. Hinto (ed.) *Genocide: An Anthropological Reader*, Oxford: Blackwell, pp. 172–186.

Thénault, S. (2001) *Une Drôle de Justice: Les Magistrats dans la Guerre d'Algérie*, Paris: Éditions La Découverte.

Thompson, A. C. and Paglen, T. (2006) *Torture Taxi: On the Trail of the CIA's Rendition Flights*, Melbourne: Hardie Grant Books.

Thorne, S. E. (1994) 'Secondary Analysis in Qualitative Research: Issues and Implications', in J. Morse (ed.) *Critical Issues in Qualitative Research Methods*, Thousand Oaks, CA: Sage, pp. 263–279.

Thorne, S. E. (2004) 'Secondary Analysis of Qualitative Data', in M. S. Lewis-Beck, A. Bryman and T. Futing Liao (eds) *The Sage Encyclopedia of Social Science Research Methods*, London: Sage, p. 1006.

Thornton, T. P. (1964) 'Terror as a Weapon of Political Agitation', in H. Eckstein (ed.) *Internal War*, New York: Free Press, pp. 71–99.

Tilly, C. (1985) 'War Making and State Making as Organized Crime', in P. B. Evans, D. Rueschmeyer and T. Skocpol (eds) *Bringing the State Back in*, Cambridge: Cambridge University Press, pp. 169–191.

Timerman, J. (1981) *Prisoner Without a Name, Cell Without a Number*, New York: Knopf.

Tomasevski, K. (1998) 'Foreign Policy and Torture', in B. Dunér (ed.) *An End to Torture: Strategies for its Eradication*, London and New York: Zed Books, pp. 183–202.

Tombs, S. and Whyte, D. (2002) 'Unmasking the Crimes of the Powerful', *Critical Criminology*, Vol. 11, pp. 217–236.

Tombs, S. and Whyte, D. (2003a) 'Scrutinising the Powerful: Crime, Contemporary Political Economy and Critical Social Research', in S. Tombs and D. Whyte (eds) *Unmasking the Crimes of the Powerful: Scrutinizing States and Corporations*, New York: Peter Lang, pp. 3–45.

Tombs, S. and Whyte, D. (2003b) 'Unmasking the Crimes of the Powerful: Establishing Some Rules of Engagement', in S. Tombs and D. Whyte (eds) *Unmasking the Crimes of the Powerful: Scrutinizing States and Corporations*, New York: Peter Lang, pp. 261–272.

Trinquier, R. (1964) *Modern Warfare: A French View of Counterinsurgency*, Translated by D. Lee, New York: Frederick A. Praeger Publisher.

Trinquier, R. (1980) *La Guerre*, Paris: Albin Michel.

Tweedale, G. (2000) *Magic Mineral to Killer Dust. Turner & Newall and the Asbestos Hazard*, Oxford: Oxford University Press.

Van Der Vyver, J. D. (1988) 'State Sponsored Terror Violence', *South African Journal on Human Rights*, Vol. 4, pp. 55–75.

Vaughan, D. (1996) *The Challenger Launch Decision: Risky Technology, Culture, and Deviance at NASA*, Chicago: University of Chicago Press.

Vaughan, D. (2007) 'Beyond Macro- and Micro-Levels of Analysis, Organizations, and the Cultural Fix', in H. Pontell and G. Geis (eds) *International Handbook of White-Collar and Corporate Crime*, New York: Springer, pp. 3–24.

Vaujour, J. (1985) *De la Révolte à la Révolution*, Paris: Albin Michel.

Verbitsky, H. (1988) *Medio Siglo de Proclamas Militares*, Buenos Aires: Editora/12.

Verbitsky, H. (1995) *El Vuelo: Arrojados al Atlántico desde Aviones en Vuelo*, Barcelona: Seix Barral.

Verbitsky, H. (1996) *Confessions of an Argentine Dirty Warrior The Flight/El Vuelo*, translated from Spanish by E. Allen, New York: The New Press.

Verbitsky, H. [2006] (2007a) *Doble Juego: La Argentina Católica y Militar*, Buenos Aires: Debolsillo.

Verbitsky, H. (2007b) *Cristo Vence: La Iglesia en la Argentina. Un Siglo de Historia Política*, Buenos Aires: SudAmericana.

Verbitsky, H. (2008) *La Violencia Evangélica: Historia Política de la Iglesia Católica*, Buenos Aires: SudAmericana.

Verbitsky, H. (2009) *Vigilia de Armas: Historia Política de la Iglesia Católica*, Buenos Aires: SudAmericana.

Verbitsky, H. (2010) *La Mano Izquierda de Dios: Historia Política de la Iglesia Católica*, Buenos Aires: SudAmericana.

Verdo, G. (1989) *Les Français d'Afrique du Nord en Argentine: Bilan Provisoire d'une Migration (1964–1988)*, Paris Université de Paris I-Sorbonne: Thèse de Doctorat.

Vidal-Naquet, P. (1963) *Torture: Cancer of Democracy. France and Algeria 1954–62*, Harmondsworth: Penguin Books.

Vidal-Naquet, P. (2001) *Les Crimes de l'Armée Française. Algérie 1954–1962*, Paris: La Découverte.

Villatoux, M. C. and Villatoux, P. (2012) Aux Origines de la «Guerre Révolution-naire»: le Colonel Lacheroy Parle, pp. 45–53.

Villegas, O. G. (1962) *Guerra Revolucionaria Comunista*, Buenos Aires: Circulo Militar.

Vittori, J. P. (2000) *On a torturé en Algérie. Témoignages recueillis par Jean-Pierre Vittori*, Paris: Editions Ramsay.

Wall, I. M. (2001) *France, the United States and the Algerian War*, Berkeley, CA: University of California Press.

Walter, E. V. (1969) *Terror and Resistance: A Study of political Violence*, New York: Oxford University Press.

Walters, R. (2003) *Deviant Knowledge*, Devon: Willan Publishing.

Ward, T. (2005) 'State Crime in the Heart of Darkness', *British Journal of Criminology*, Vol. 45, pp. 434–445.

Webb, S. and Webb, B. (1932) *Methods of Social Study*, London: Longmans.

Weber, M. (1948) *Essays in Sociology*, London: Routledge & Kegan Paul.

Weffort, F. (1984) *Por Que Democracia?*, São Paulo: Brasiliense.

Weffort, F. (1998) 'Why Democracy?', in A. Stepan (ed.) *Democratizing Brazil: Problems Of Transition And Consolidation*, New York: Oxford University Press.

Weschler, L. (1998) *A Miracle, A Universe: Settling Accounts with Torturers*, Chicago: University of Chicago Press.

Wilkinson, P. (1974) *Political Terrorism*, London: Macmillan.

Wilson, K. (1993) 'Thinking about the Ethics of Fieldwork', in S. Devereux and J. Hoddinott (eds) *Fieldwork in Developing Countries*, Colorado: Lynne Rienner Publisher, Inc.

Wolfendale, J. (2006) 'Training Torturers: A Critique of the Ticking Bomb Argument', *Social Theory and Practice*, Vol. 32, No. 2, pp. 269–287.

Yin, R. K. [1984] [2003] (2009) *Case Study Research: Design and Methods*, Fourth Edition, London: Sage Publications.

Zimbardo, P. (2007) *The Lucifer Effect: How Good People Turn Evil*, London: Rider.

Index

Page numbers in *italics* denote figures.

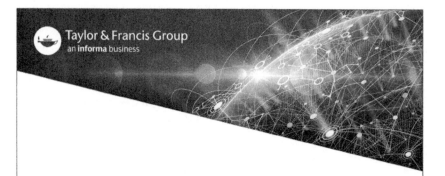

Printed in Great Britain
by Amazon